IMAGES
of America

HILLSBOROUGH

I0805877

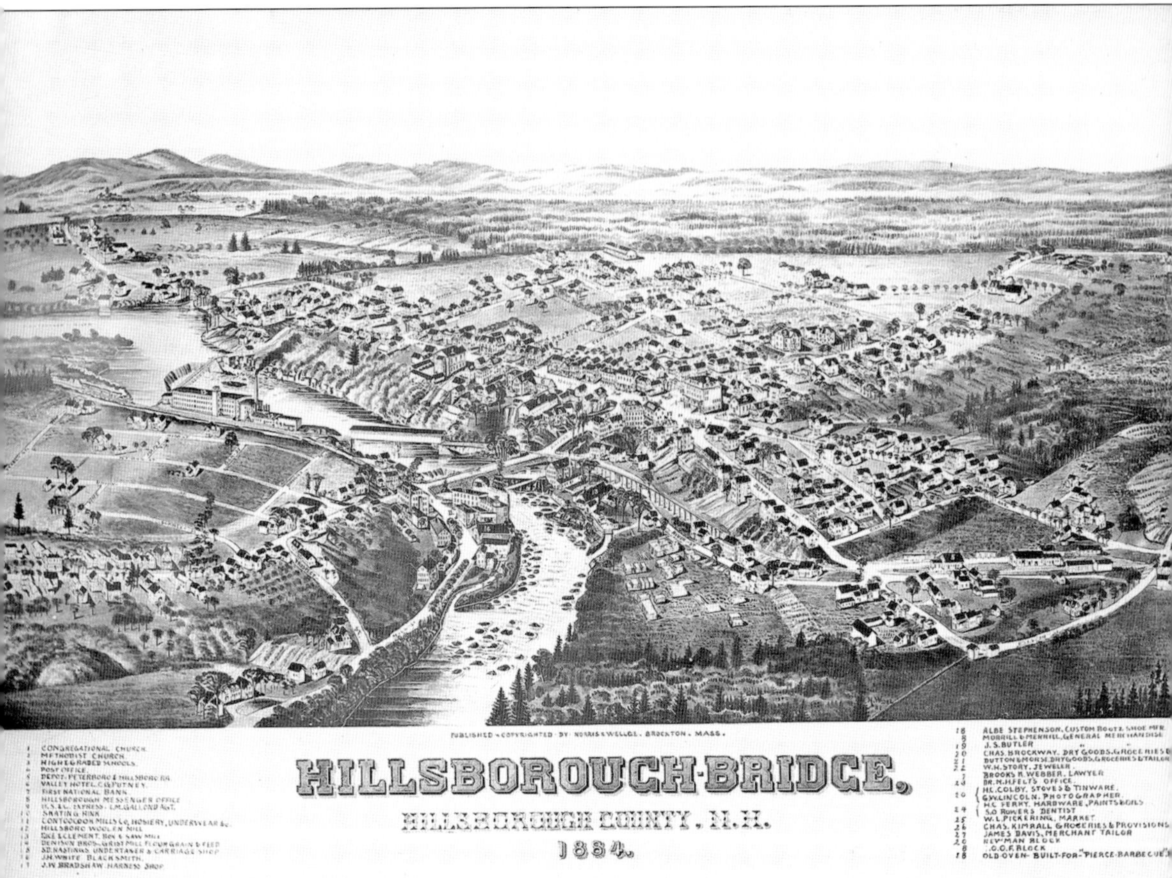

This aerial bird's-eye view of the town of Hillsborough was drawn in 1884. (Courtesy of Hillsborough Historical Society.)

ON THE COVER: Small steamboats were a real attraction for early Hillsborough tourists. They traveled in the Contoocook River between the Hillsborough and Bennington mills, as well as in the larger lakes. The steamboat on the cover was operating on Loon Pond, a popular summer retreat in the late 1890s. The townspeople on the steamboat are mill employees and their families enjoying their annual summer outing. Note the logs being preserved on the lake, waiting to be sent to a local sawmill. (Courtesy of Hillsborough Historical Society).

IMAGES
of America

HILLSBOROUGH

Hillsborough Historical Society

ARCADIA
PUBLISHING

ISBN 978-0-7385-7672-5

Published by Arcadia Publishing
Charleston, South Carolina

Printed in the United States of America

Library of Congress Control Number: 2011933822

For all general information, please contact Arcadia Publishing:
Telephone 843-853-2070
Fax 843-853-0044
E-mail sales@arcadiapublishing.com
For customer service and orders:
Toll-Free 1-888-313-2665

Visit us on the Internet at www.arcadiapublishing.com

*This book is dedicated to all the past, present,
and future citizens of Hillsborough.*

Contents

Acknowledgments

We would like to thank the board of directors of the Hillsborough Historical Society for their support in making this pictorial history possible. We would also like to give special thanks to the contributing authors of each chapter and to the Manahan-Phelps-McCulloch Collection team. The contributing authors include Christina Chadwick, Jean Gannon, Jeff Rand, Gil Shattuck, Gary Sparks, and Cynthia van Hazinga. They were responsible for selecting the photographs and researching the historical material. The Manahan-Phelps-McCulloch Collection committee included Gil Shattuck, Tom Talpey, Ennio Gerini, and Bea Jillette. Also part of this team was the late David Feather and Arthur Jillette. The team has spent countless hours scanning, organizing, and labeling the rich portfolio of negatives ranging from early glass plate technology through conventional film.

The material came from three primary sources: the Manahan-Phelps-McCulloch Collection of Photographs, Waldo Brown's *Hillsborough Town History* and its later updates by Harrison Baldwin and Cynthia van Hazinga, and from several long-time residents of Hillsborough, who generously provided their insights and commentary to the project.

The Manahan-Phelps-McCulloch Collection is a collection of more than 100,000 negatives from a photographic studio in continuous operation in Hillsborough from as early as 1866. The studio originally opened under the ownership of Solon Newman, and has changed ownership many times over the years. Starting in 1899, William H. Manahan Jr. ran the studio for 54 years until Cyrus Phelps took over in 1953. In 2002, Donald McCulloch and Catherine Phelps McCulloch donated the collection to the Hillsborough Historical Society. The society has been preserving and documenting the collection ever since. There is no other collection in New Hampshire comparable in its time extent and collection breadth. Most of the photographs used in this book are Manahan's work. Manahan was a close friend and colleague of Boston's John Garo and Canadian Yousuf Karsh, all highly acclaimed photographers.

All the images in this text are the property of the Hillsborough Historical Society. The society remains the driving force in preserving Hillsborough's history as the caretaker of not only the Manahan-Phelps-McCulloch Collection, but also the President Franklin Pierce Homestead and the Heritage Museum, and as primary sponsor of the Annual Living History Event each August.

—Allison Reopel, lead author, and Mike Reopel, coauthor and president of the Hillsborough Historical Society

INTRODUCTION

The Massachusetts Bay Company in 1735 granted Col. John Hill of Boston land approximately 36 miles square in the heart of unsurveyed wilderness, being "number 7" of 10 towns laid out as a barrier to incursions from French Canada. This was the frontier for northern New Hampshire, at the time governed by Massachusetts. Common belief is that Hillsborough, which was initially spelled without the "s" got its name from Colonel Hill. It is also possible that Hillsborough gets its name from the Earl of Hillsborough, secretary for North America and advisor to King George III.

Acquiring the land was relatively easy for Colonel Hill and his associate Maj. Francis Keyes, but finding people to populate the wilderness from Boston was an entirely different matter. In 1737, Samuel Gibson, a recent immigrant from Scotland, built a cabin on a path leading to the current village of Hillsborough Center. Other early settlers came from the Scotch-Irish community in Londonderry, New Hampshire. Shortly thereafter, Robert McClure and James Lyon settled in the center, while James McColley built a house on the site that is now the Marcy Block in Hillsborough Bridge along the Contoocook River. Within a short amount of time, the population grew to around 40. Unfortunately, war was being waged between England and France, and in April 1746, when French-allied Indians attacked the next nearest settlement, Hopkinton, the early settlers panicked, packed their goods hurriedly, and returned to the Londonderry area. Fifteen years passed until Philip Riley and his wife returned. By 1764, around a dozen families resettled in Hillsborough, and in that year, the first child was born in town to married couple John McColley and Elizabeth Gibson, siblings of the earliest settlers. In 1772, Hillsborough was incorporated as a town. Five years later, Colonel Hill granted 200 acres of land in the center to Rev. Jonathan Barnes, the first pastor. Fifteen acres of this grant were held back for "town purposes," which eventually provided for a meetinghouse, town pound, and militia training field, most of which survives today.

Hillsborough, although a small town that barely exceeded 2,000 citizens in 1920, has had many historical incidents, legends, and several famous citizens. Chief Passaconway of the local Penacook tribe had a vision that whites would conquer his race. He was around the woods of Hillsborough when he died and legend has it that his body was taken away by a wagon pulled by wolves. Bible Hill was named after the first Bible in town. Tradition has it that it was kept in Deacon Simon's house and that he allowed anyone to read it, but no one was allowed to remove it from the premises. The Bible was kept separated from the center meeting house for fear if the Indians attacked, both would be lost if co-located. Several men of Hillsborough played important roles in the Revolutionary War, with one of its most famous citizens, Gov. Benjamin Pierce, earning fame. Leaving his farm to join at Lexington, he served throughout the duration of the war, mustering out in 1784 at West Point. Capt. Isaac Baldwin was one of the first New Hampshire citizens mortally wounded at Bunker Hill. Lieutenant Andrews, Baldwin's neighbor, removed the bullet and sent it to Baldwin's wife, Eunice. She kept it on the fireplace mantel until taking it with her to her final resting place. Captain Carr, a militia leader, earned his fame later not in the armed service but by running a ring of counterfeiters who funded several homes and stone bridges in the area.

Some of Hillsborough's most famous citizens include Benjamin Pierce, governor of New Hampshire, general of the New Hampshire Militia, and father of Franklin Pierce; Gen. John McNeil, hero of the Battle of Chippewa in the War of 1812; Gen. Franklin Pierce, our 14th president and friend of Nathaniel Hawthorne, who visited often; Benjamin Pierce Cheney, the founder of American Express; Benjamin Frank Dutton, who established the second department store concept under the name of Houghton and Dutton and builder of the Dutton Twins, a centerpiece structure on Main Street; Benjamin Franklin Keith, a founder of vaudeville, entertainer, and friend of Houdini; Rear Admiral James Grimes Walker, a hero of Vicksburg in the Civil War; Gen. Christopher Columbus Andrews, liberator of Arkansas in the Civil War; Gov. John Smith, a well respected businessman, mill owner, benefactor, and politician; and Amy Cheney Beach, a child prodigy who wrote music when she was four years old and became the foremost woman composer in North America at the turn of the 20th century.

Hillsborough is located in the valley of the Contoocook River. Wooded hills, 35 lakes and ponds, and a series of eight in-service, stone arch bridges surround it. The business center has always been known as Hillsborough Bridge, and was, in fact, the first area settled and has been the commercial center of the town ever since. It had two mills operating, the Contoocook Mills, which manufactured men's knit half-hose and underwear, and the Hillsborough Woolen Mills, which produced overcoats, cloaking, and suits from woven woolen fabric. In 1841, there were 56 dwellings, two churches, two gristmills and sawmills, and several merchants and professional services. Except for a few more dwellings and the historic Dutton Twins buildings and Governor Smith House, nothing has really changed.

Radiating from Hillsborough Bridge are three historic villages. Hillsborough Center, a quaint village of early homes of the late 1700s and early 1800s, is truly one of the most picturesque communities in New Hampshire. It retains its common training ground, one-room schoolhouse, town pound, club center, and two churches. Its cemetery is the final resting place of several French and Indian War and Revolutionary War veterans. Lower Village to the southwest was the early industrial center, with multiple sawmills, furniture makers, tanneries, blacksmiths, and other woodworking shops. The Franklin Pierce Homestead in the Lower Village remains one of New Hampshire's historic jewels. The Lower Village is also home to the Union Chapel, built with the aid of the Ladies Aid Society, whose annual membership dues are still 25¢. The Upper Village, just north of the Pierce Homestead, was home to a carriage maker, furniture maker, and the first telephone exchange. The Upper Village leads to the vacation towns of Washington and Windsor. All four villages, unique in their own way, add their own historical significance and beauty to the town.

> Come to New Hampshire For Nestled in her lovely foothills' Rarest jewel in her crown, Clothed in colors like the morning, Proud of all this wide renown, Is Hillsborough.
>
> —1911 board of trade pamphlet

One

Around Main Street

Hillsborough is divided into four villages: Upper, Lower, and Bridge Villages and Hillsborough Center. Each has its own distinct features that make it unique and add great value to the town as a whole. Of all Hillsborough's villages, Bridge Village is the largest. It is located on the banks of the Contoocook River in the southeast corner of town, approximately three miles southeast of the Hillsborough Center and two miles east of the Lower Village.

The greatest numbers of residents have lived in Bridge Village and the largest percentage of businesses and industries have been located here. The success of the mills on the Contoocook River was the driving force behind the growth of Bridge Village and the increasing number of homes and business blocks being built. The coming of the railroad gave a further incentive to the growth of the town. By the 1840s, some of the notable residents of Bridge Village included Colonel Kimball, John Eaton, George Little, and Samuel Taggard. As the population steadily grew, so too did the number of small businesses along Main Street. Some of these early businesses included the Hillsborough Dairy Company, Boynton's Grocery Store, Moxley's Drug Store, Halladay's Sporting Goods Store, and Bruce & Rumrill's Millinery Store. The offices of lawyers, doctors, and dentists were scattered among the businesses along Main Street. A bank and a post office provided their services to the village. To accommodate the increasing number and diversity of parishioners, Congregational, Methodist, and Catholic churches were established.

Today, even though many of the old businesses are now long gone, you are still able to see the historic buildings that once housed them along Main Street and the textile mills along the river banks that once made Hillsborough a booming manufacturing town.

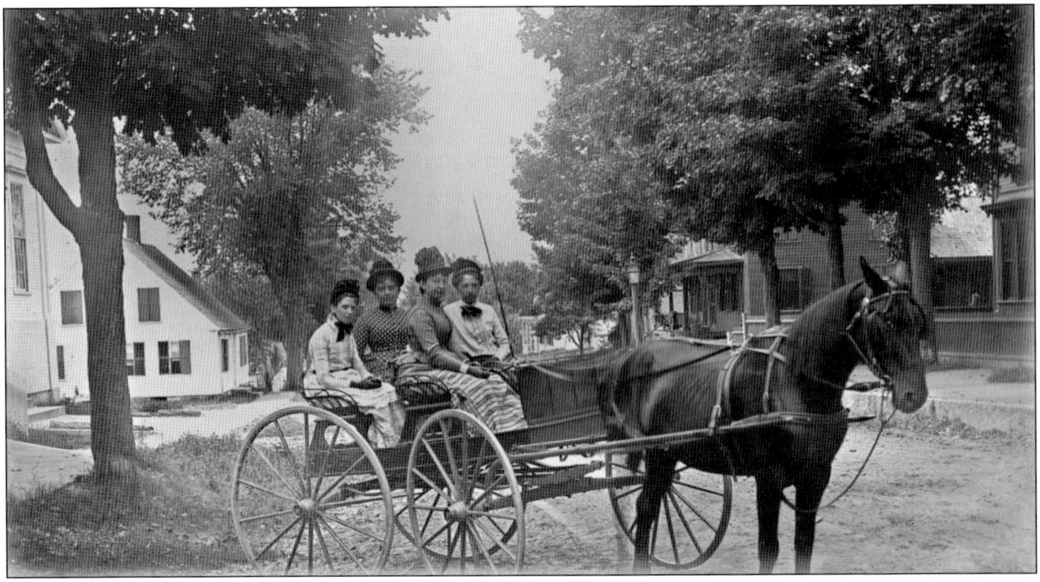

This c. 1890 photograph of four Hillsborough ladies in their Sunday dresses was taken on West Main Street looking west in front of the Smith Memorial Church. The horse-drawn four-passenger carriage was the typical mode of transportation, and may have been built in the carriage shop in the Lower Village.

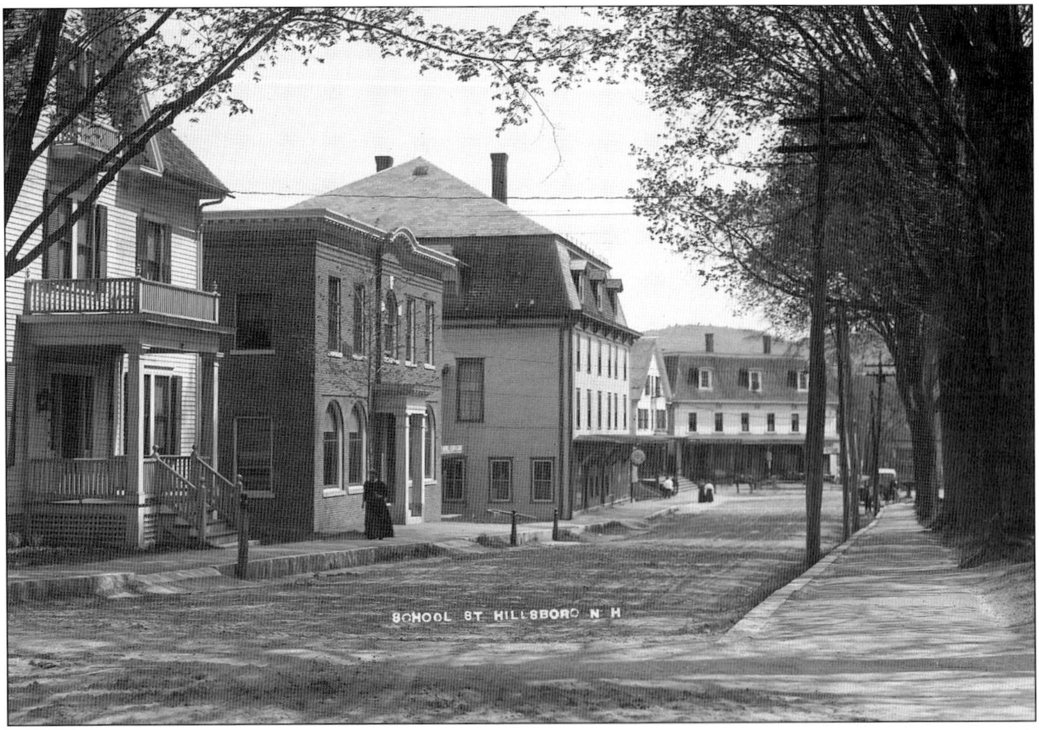

This image is of School Street looking south toward Central Square at the turn of the 20th century. The large building in the center is Child's Opera House, and the building at the end is the Whittemore Block. The brick building originally housed the Hillsborough National Bank and now is the home of TD Bank. Note the horse drinking fountain at the end of the sidewalk.

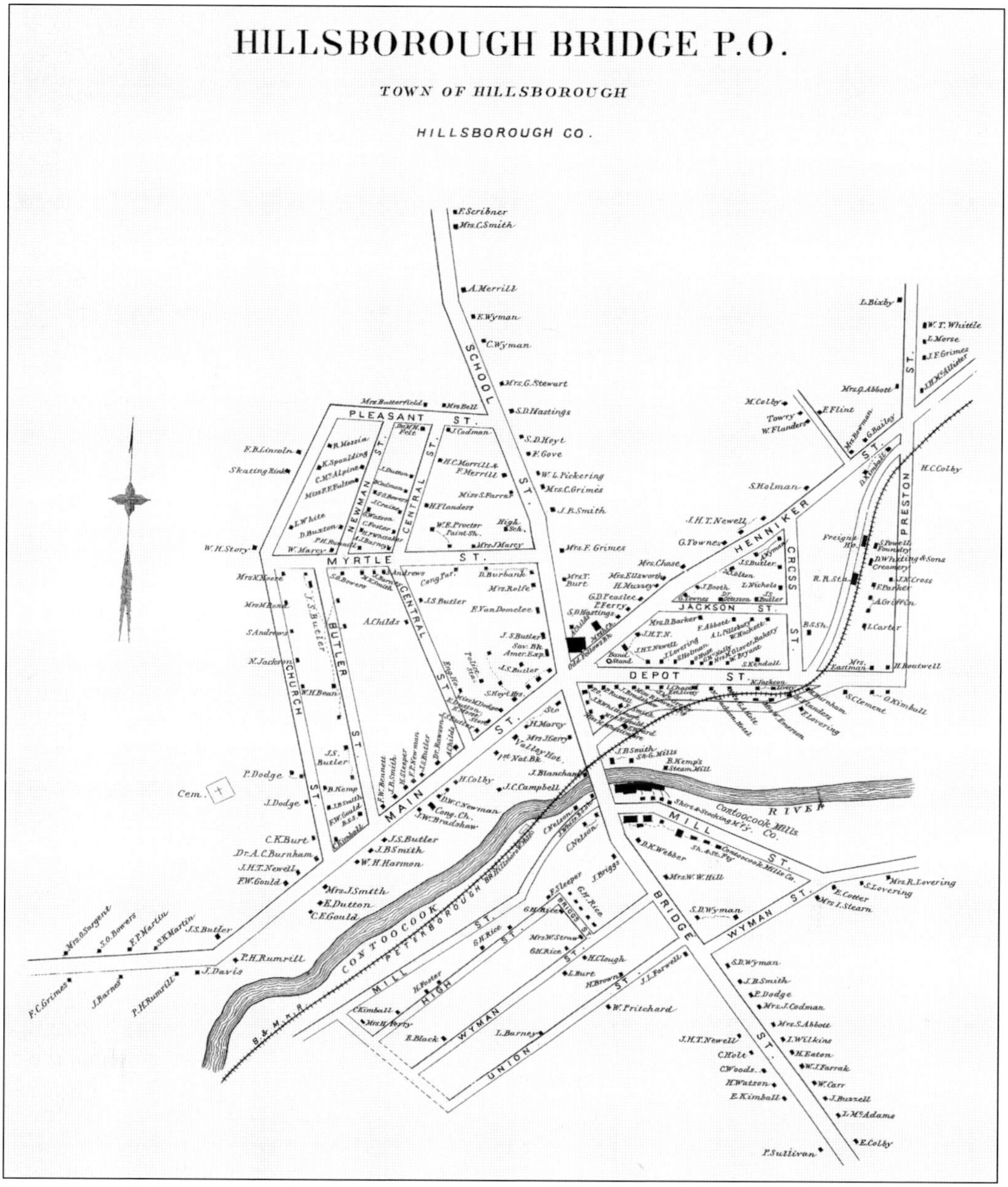

This map of Hillsborough Bridge and its associated historic buildings provides a good general orientation. Central Square is the intersection of five streets: Main, Henniker, Depot, School, and Bridge Streets. The mills are located on the south bank of the Contoocook River. The map, from the *1892 Town and City Atlas of the State of New Hampshire*, identifies all property owners. Along Main Street, the Butler Block, Marcy Building, Valley Hotel, Smith Church, and Dutton Twins are clearly marked. The bandstand is located at the intersection of Henniker Street and Depot Street. Also in Central Square, one can clearly see the Alba Childs Opera House, the post office, and the Whittemore Block. North on School Street is the Governor Smith House. From the map, one can see the significant number of properties owned by J.S. Butler. Along the Contoocook River one can also identify the smaller mills such as S&G Mills and Kemp's steam mill, which no longer exist.

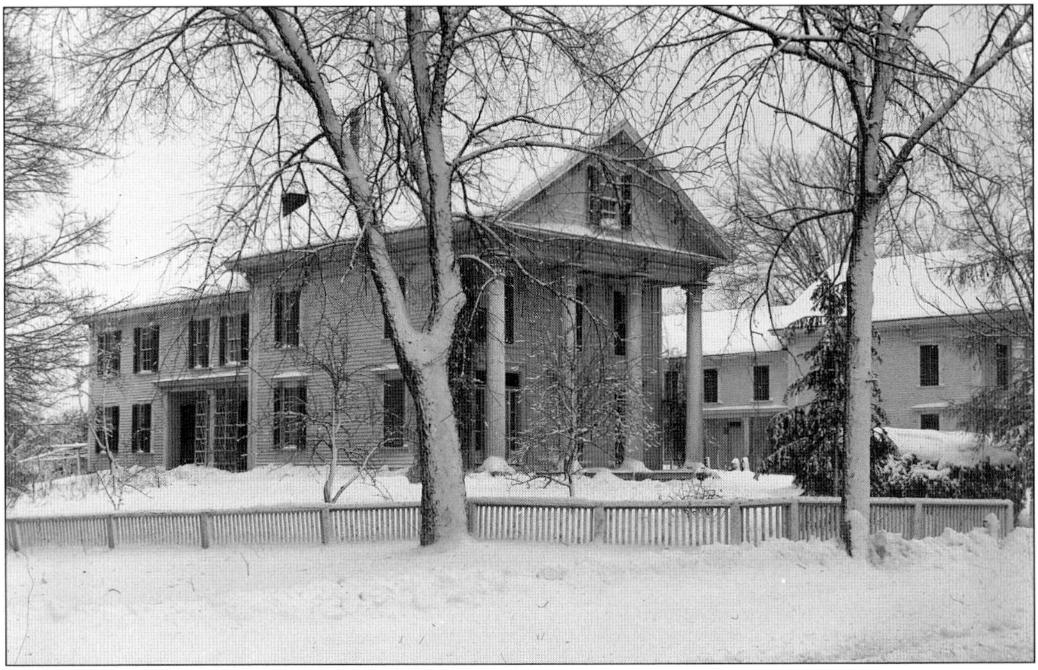

The "twin" houses above the river on West Main Street were built in the mid-19th century by life-long Hillsborough resident Ephraim Dutton and his son Deacon Benjamin Franklin Dutton. Ephraim was a senior partner in the store Dutton & Morse, served as postmaster, and played French horn in the town band. The identical houses pay homage to the Greek revival style, popular from 1800 to 1850, with their low, pitched roofs, cornices, wide friezes, fluted Corinthian columns, and gable ends facing the street like a Greek temple.

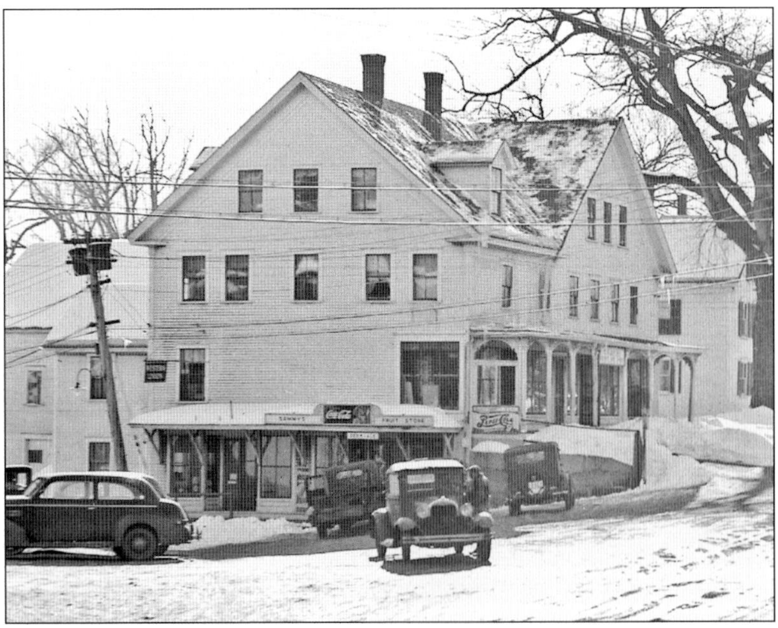

This 1946 photograph was taken from Central Square looking west down Main Street. The center building is Marcy Block. It was a thriving business corner and housed Judge Marshall Derby's office, whose qualification consisted of running the five and dime store, and landscape artist Alice Knight who painted well into her 90s. This was also the site of the first log cabin, built by James McColley in 1741.

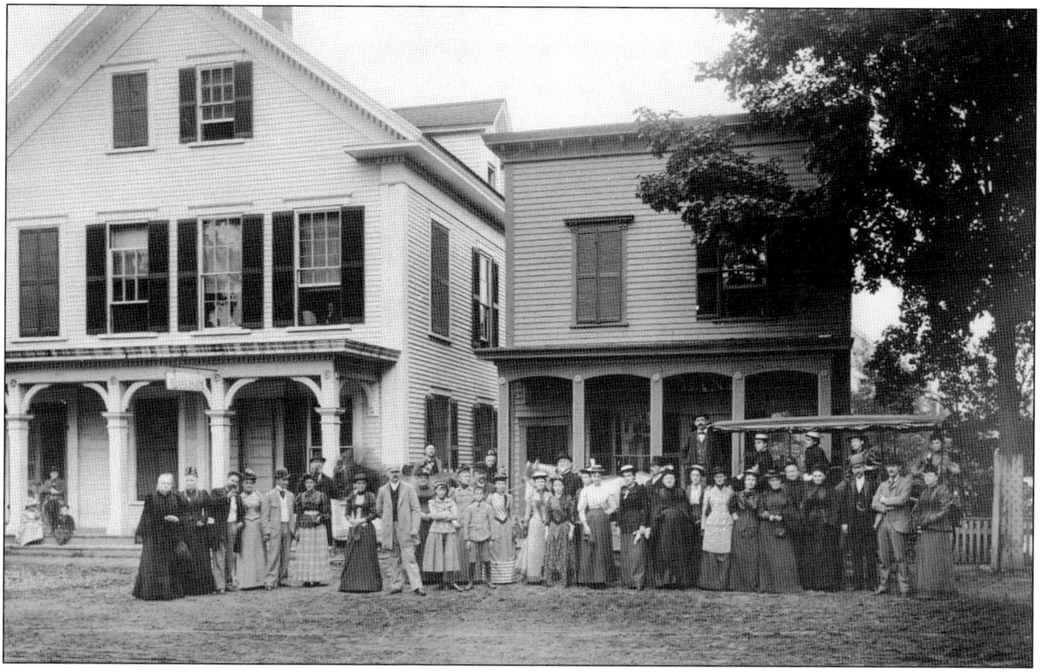

The First National Bank of Hillsborough was originally adjacent to the Valley Hotel and is shown here with the annual gathering of the Old School Society. When the bank moved to School Street, the old bank vault was too heavy to move and now lies buried in the parking lot.

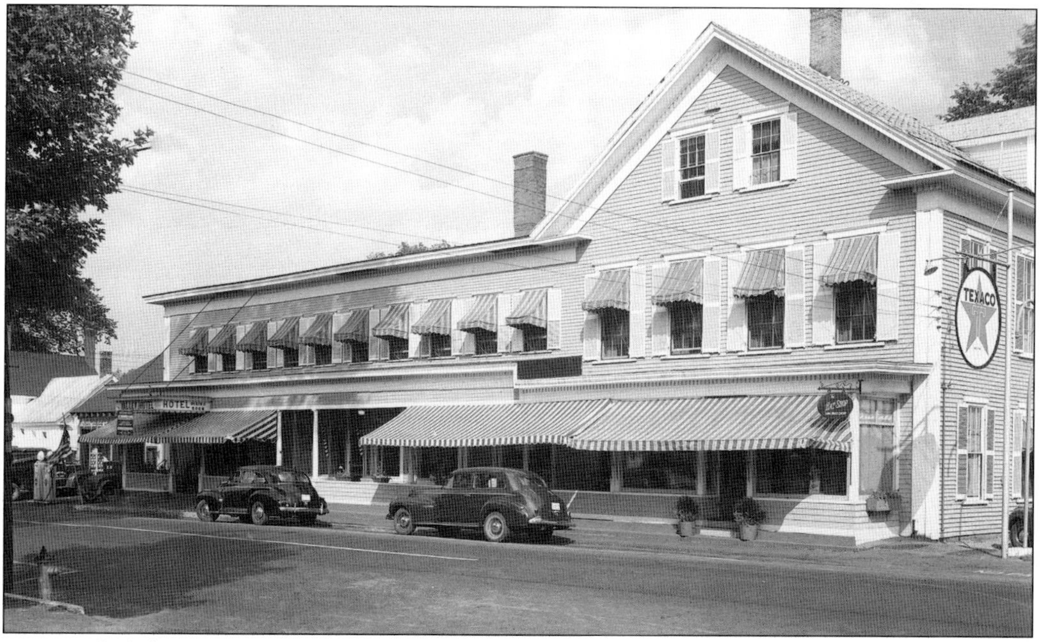

Once called the Railroad House, the Valley Hotel was opened in response to the coming of the railroad. Built in 1850, the two-and-a-half-story building was used as a hotel until the late 1970s, although its decline began with the end of railroad service. During the first half of the 20th century, most local celebrations and meetings were held in the large dining room. Anna Bruce Crosby's hat shop and a lounge occupied the ground floor.

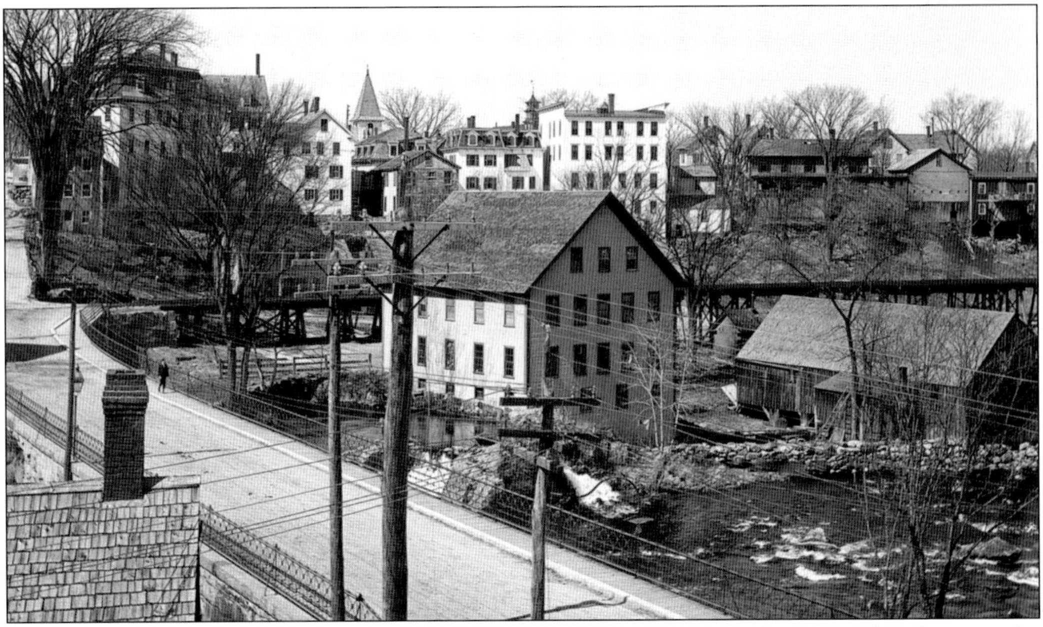

Hillsborough Bridge got its name from this bridge over the Contoocook River. The photograph, oriented to the northeast, provides a good view of the sawmill/box shop area, the railroad trestle, and the downtown area. The steeple in the background is that of the Methodist church. This view of downtown reveals the multiple bottom floors of some of the commercial buildings, largely hidden from the Central Square perspective.

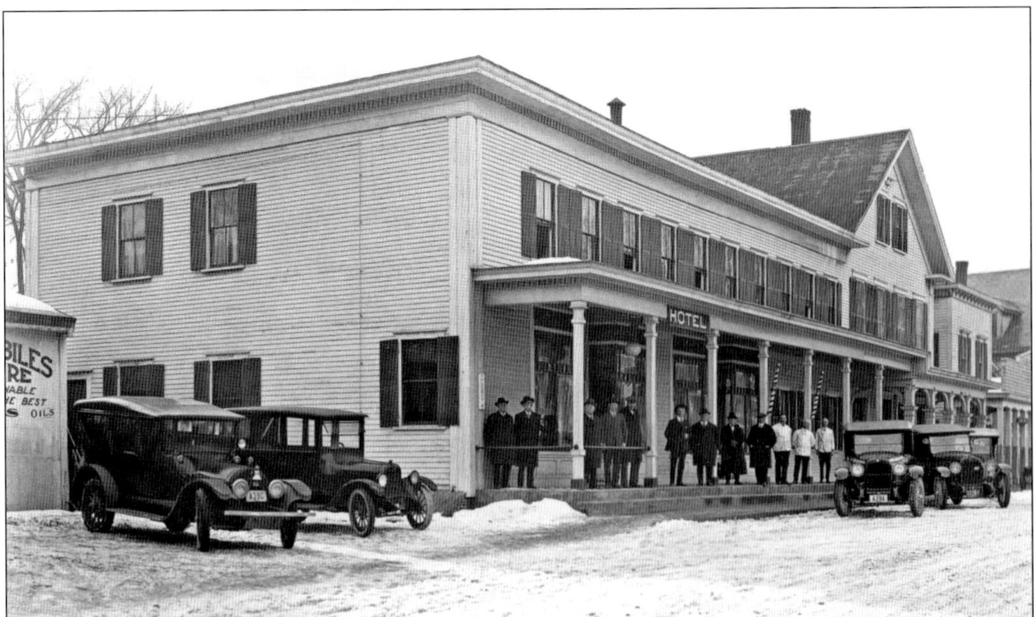

This winter picture of the Valley Hotel was taken from the east side, adjacent to the town's first service station. The 1920s cars date the picture and most likely belong to the guests lined up on the porch with three hotel staff members. The barber poles identify Frank Rumrill's barbershop.

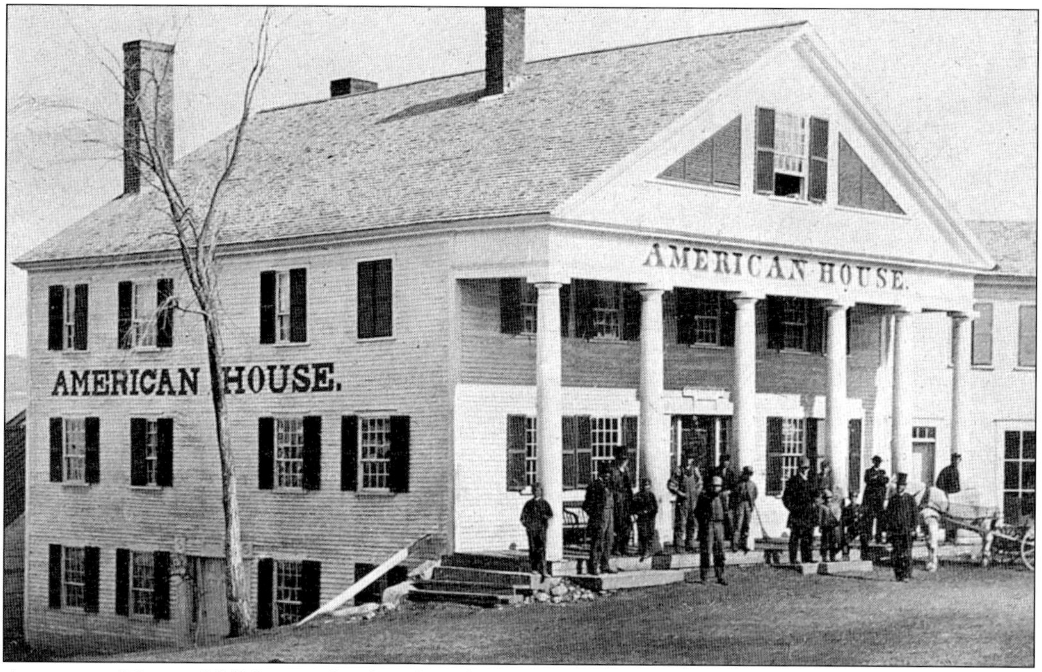

American House, Hillsborough's first hotel, stood at the eastern end of Central Square. It was opened around 1810 by Cyrus and Jonathan Sargent, and was noted for its public meetings, balls, and suppers. The building, last owned by Eli Sargent, burned to the ground on March 10, 1869, ignited by a fire in a stable on Depot Street. Solon Newman, the first town photographer, took this photograph in 1868.

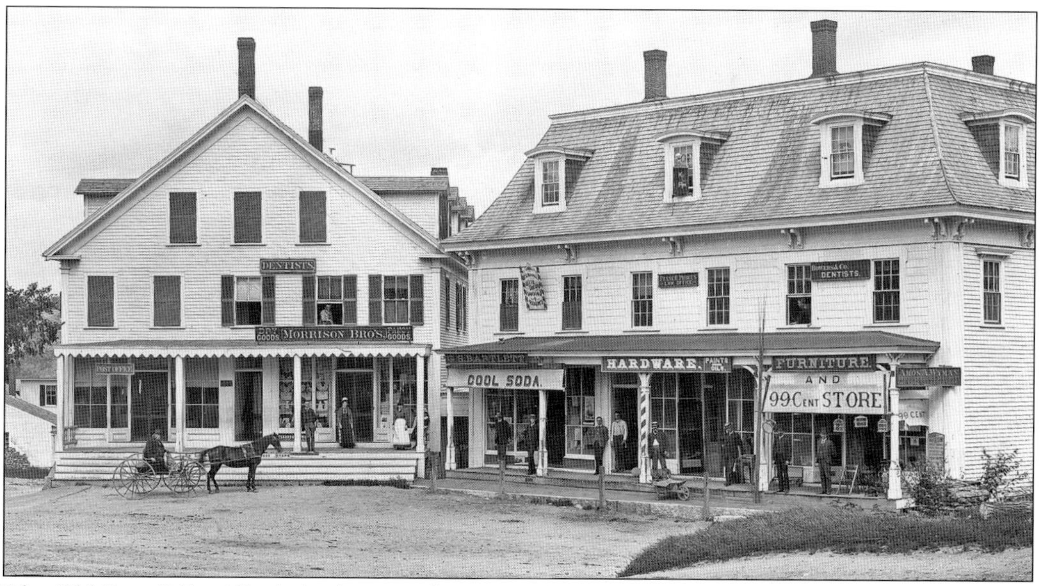

The Old Post Office Block, built upon the ruins of the American House by Reuben Lovering, is on the left. His wife, Martha Lovering, was the first postmistress. The block was better known for its restaurant on the Depot Street side, having the town's first liquor license. The Whittemore Block is on the right, erected in 1871 following the American House fire. The block housed several stores and services.

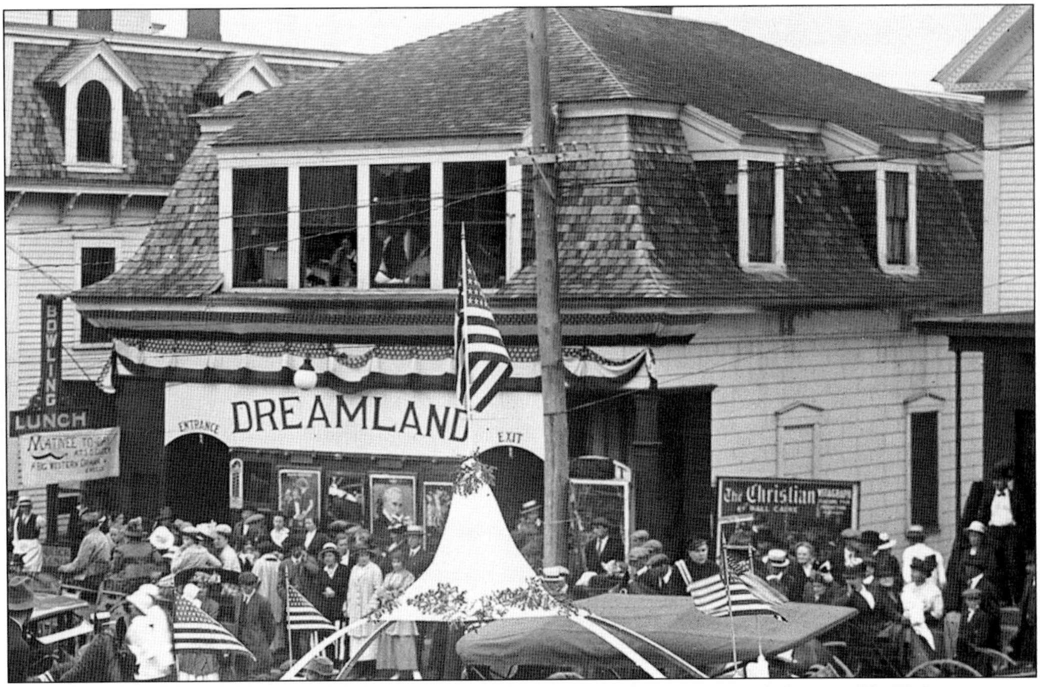

Crowds flocked to Dreamland, the movie theater in Central Square, and the pool hall downstairs. Alice Fleming and Sam Cook played the piano for silent films. While the silent film reels were being readied, a magic lantern projected local advertisements. Later, the Capitol Theater occupied the same space, closing in the 1960s. The building was destroyed by fire in January 1990.

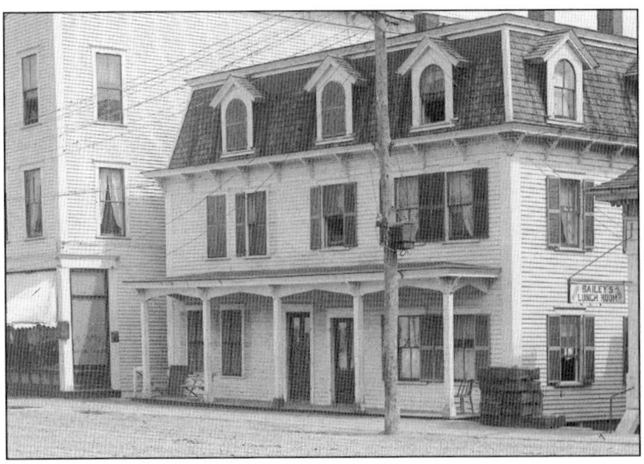

Located just beyond Dreamland, the McGreevy-Connor block was a single-family residence from 1858 to 1876. It was purchased by John McGreevy in 1880 and converted into a duplex, as shown here. Around 1915, it became a restaurant. The last remodeling occurred in 1990 by Don Knapton, who later turned it into Tookey Mills Pub, the most popular eating and drinking establishment in town. Daisy Conner ran a popular popcorn stand here for years, and Stillman Baker built a safe that still stands buried under the sidewalk.

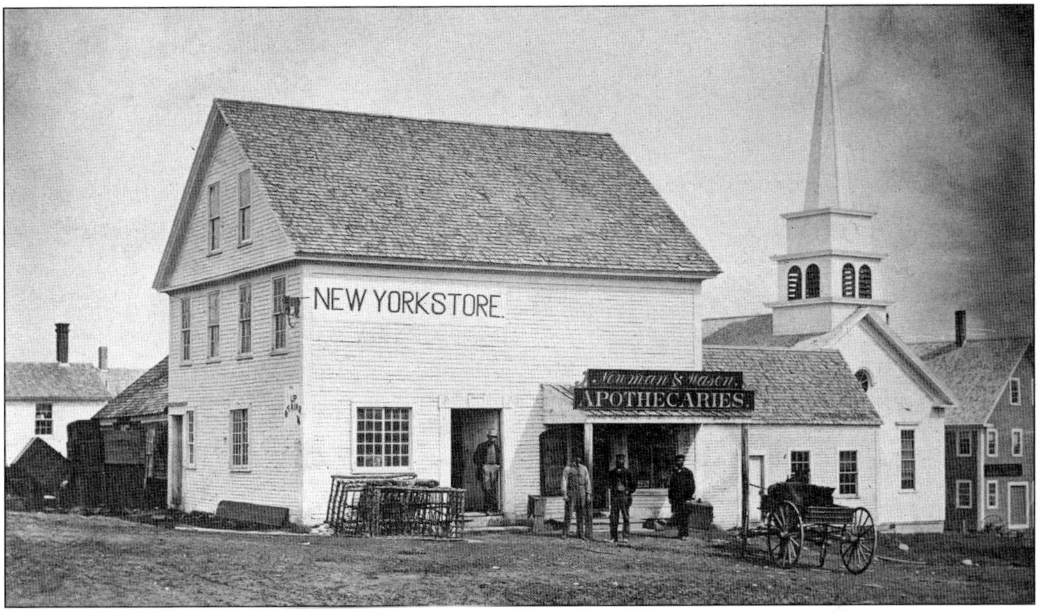

This 1866 image is the earliest known photograph in the Manahan collection. The Taggart Block, as it was known, was located at the corner of Main and School Streets and was the home of Archibald Taggart, a veteran of both the French and Indian War and the Revolutionary War and builder of the first dam across the Contoocook River. The New York Store on the second floor may have replaced the Taggart residence as early as 1810. Newman & Mason Apothecaries operated on the first floor.

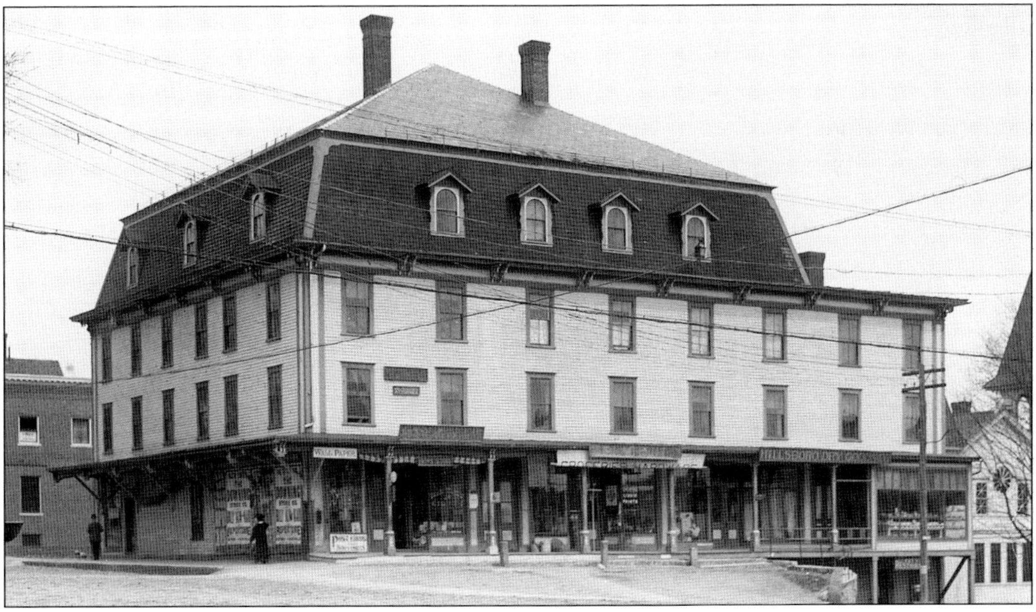

The Odd Fellows Block in Central Square, known as Alba Child's Opera House, was built in 1876–1877, replacing the New York Store. This building contained stores on the first floor, offices on the second floor, and the Odd Fellows Hall on the third floor. The hall was used for town meetings, plays, and dances. Oliver Thayer moved the first "talking films" to this location, accompanied by piano player Sam Cook.

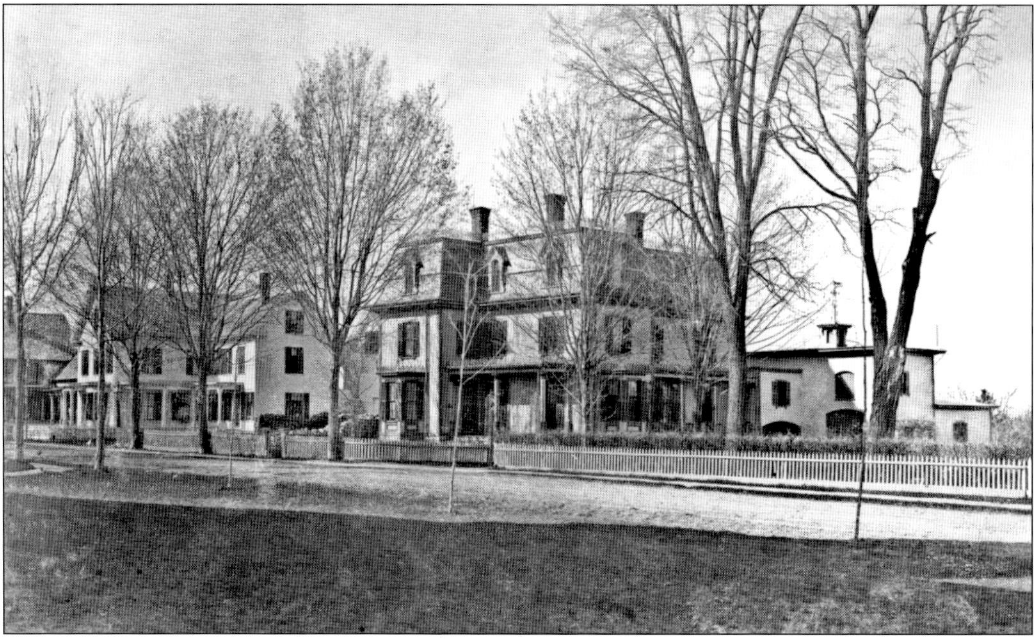

John Butler Smith, governor of New Hampshire from 1893 to 1894, lived in this Italianate-style house on School Street. Formerly the property of Hiram Bell, it was deeded to Smith in 1880. The original house was characterized by a flat roof; tall, narrow, double-paned windows with hood moldings; and a squared-off symmetrical appearance (shown above), a style popular between 1840 and 1885. Smith added a French roof to the house before remodeling and rebuilding in 1891, as shown below. It was the talk of the whole state when John Butler Smith hired E.S. Foster of Keene to build a stone mansion, designed by architect William Butterfield of Manchester, at a cost between $30,000 and $40,000. In 1924, the Governor Smith House was bought by the town for $1 and became the town library, preserving the structure. The carriage house in the rear is now home to town offices.

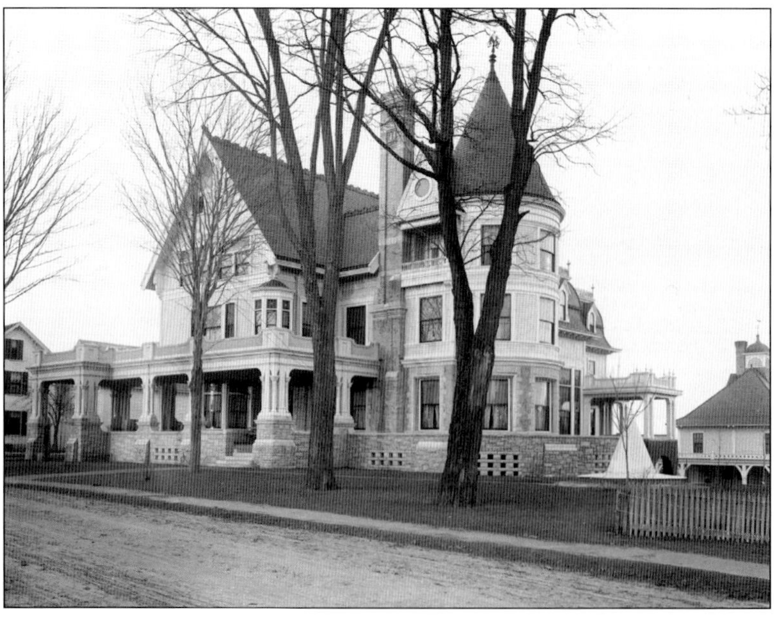

These images show the interior of the Governor Smith House at the time of the final remodeling. The photograph at right shows the main parlor and reception area. Occasionally, child prodigy Amy Beech held piano recitals there. Beech, born in the neighboring town of Henniker, was considered the top female composer of her time and spent many hours playing for the Smiths before marrying and moving to Boston. The ornate main staircase, shown below, remained unchanged during the conversion to the town library. The governor's desk, with a modern Victorian fabric lamp, and his easy chair, are seen at the foot of the staircase. Notice the Terrazo floors—a high-end option of the day. Today the former living and dining rooms are library reading rooms, but preserve most of the original detail.

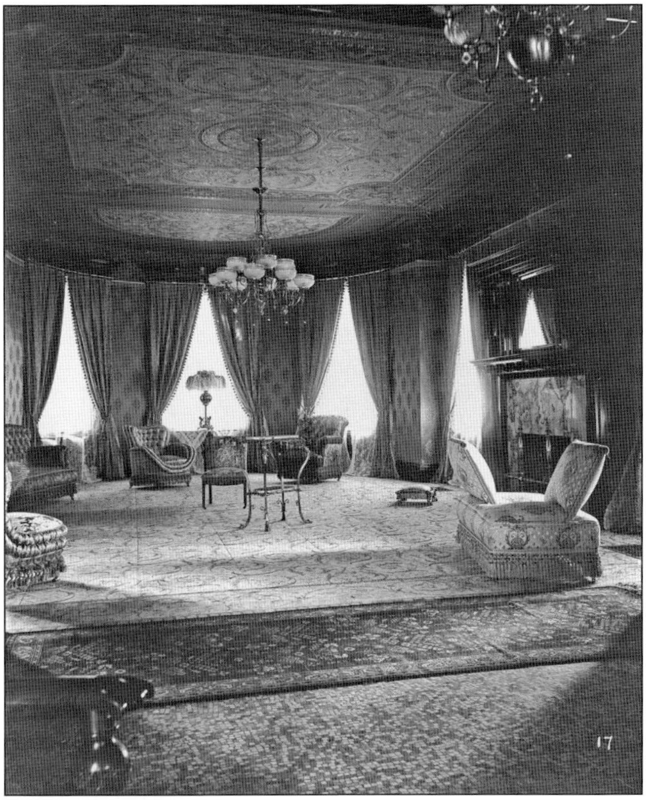

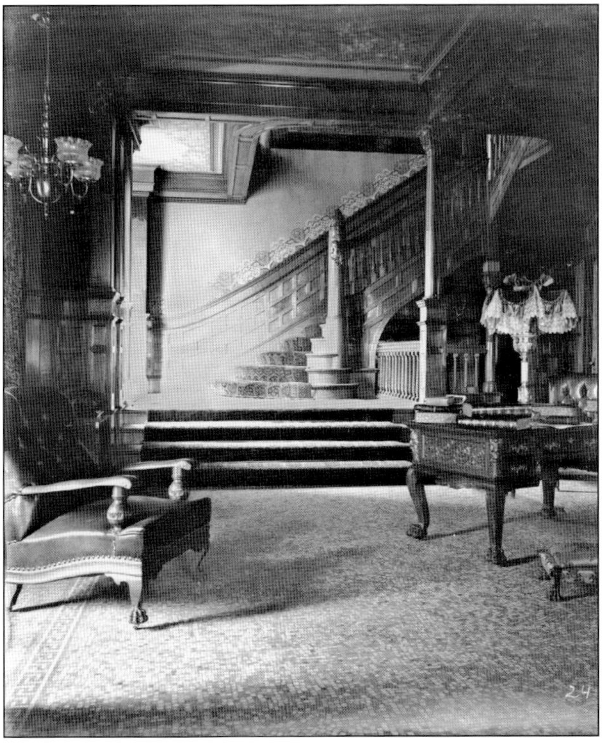

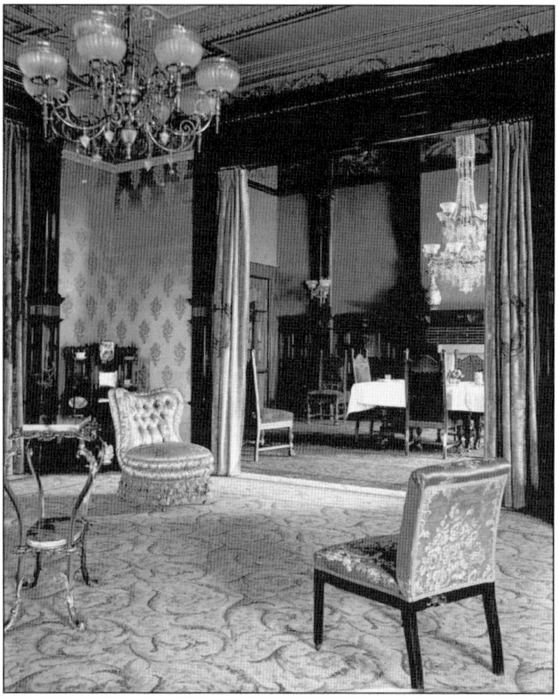

The photograph at left shows the living room in the Governor Smith House, with a view of the dining room's elegant chandeliers. Both chandeliers remained after the conversion to the town library. Governor Smith belonged to several clubs and organizations, including the Masons, and was a significant benefactor to charities, including the Smith Rifles, later known as Company K of the 2nd New Hampshire National Guard. He was also very active in the Republican Party. One of his greatest pleasures was to entertain acquaintances and friends in these rooms. The photograph below shows the "modern" bathroom, with an Italian designed bath and matching toilet, with an overhead water tank. Somehow, after town ownership, this elegant bathroom landed in Alvin Yeaton's house across from the Dutton Twins. Unfortunately, the bathroom's current whereabouts are unknown.

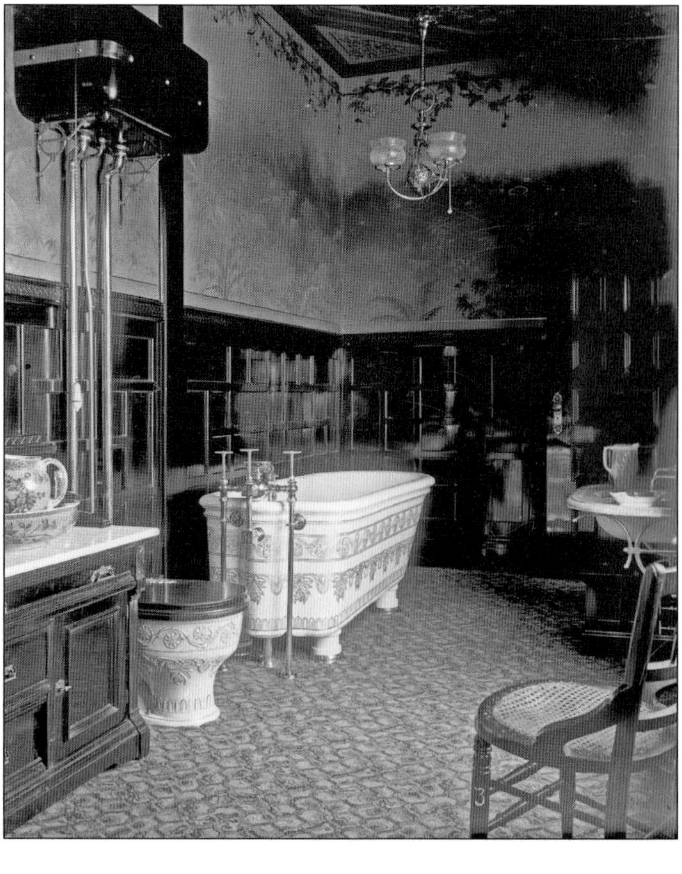

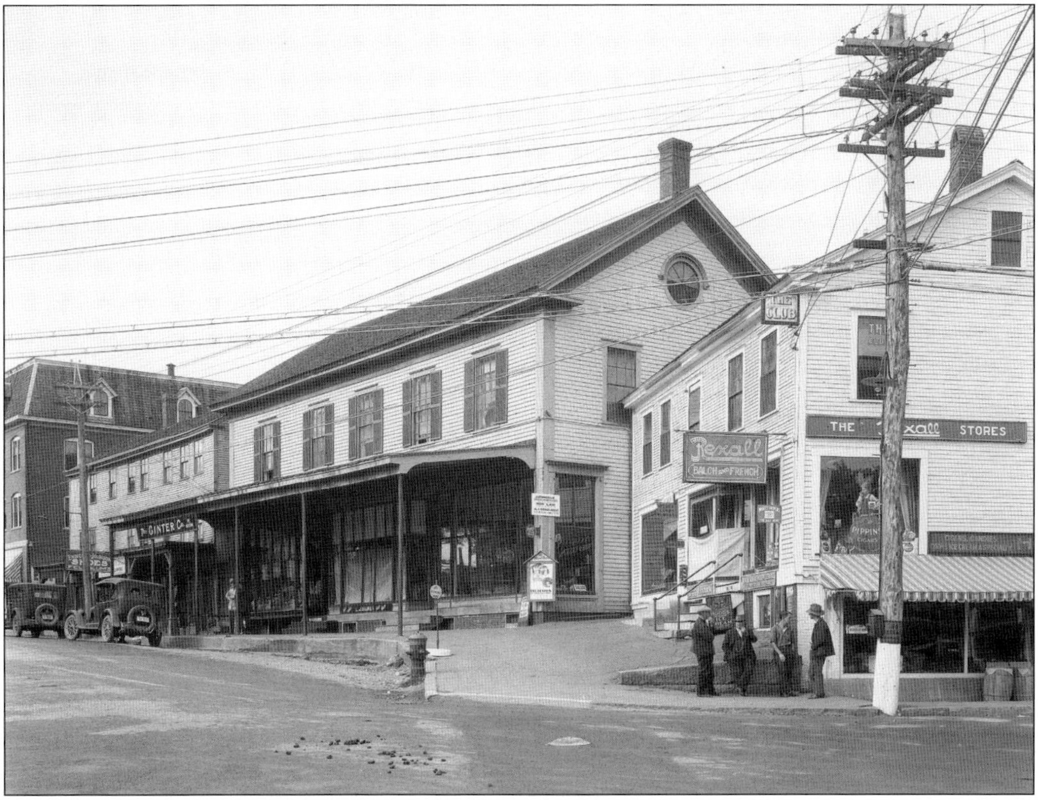

This 1926 street scene is oriented to the west on Main Street toward the Rumrill brick building. The corner building, constructed in 1820, was originally the residence of James Butler, a wealthy landowner. Adjacent to the Butler house is the Butler Block, built in 1861. This structure had been a town school. The second floor has a small hall and stage and was home to the recently restored theater curtains now on display in the Hillsborough Heritage Museum.

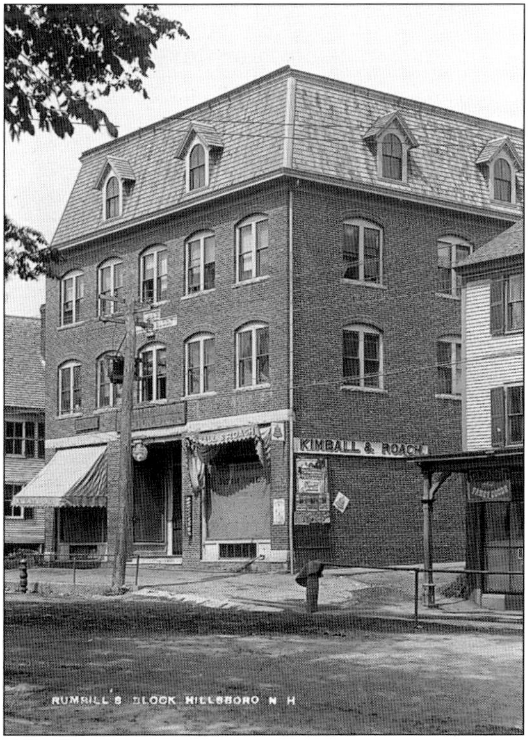

Builder Peter Rumrill constructed this three-and-a-half story brick block from 1892 to 1894. It was built on the site of the Hoyt house, which was moved directly to the back. The first floor held Civil War veteran William H. Story's Jewelry Store and a gentlemen's furnishings shop. The building is well preserved, with large plate glass windows for the two storefronts, and has been maintained without altering the proportions or the original wood and brick. It is currently in use as a restaurant.

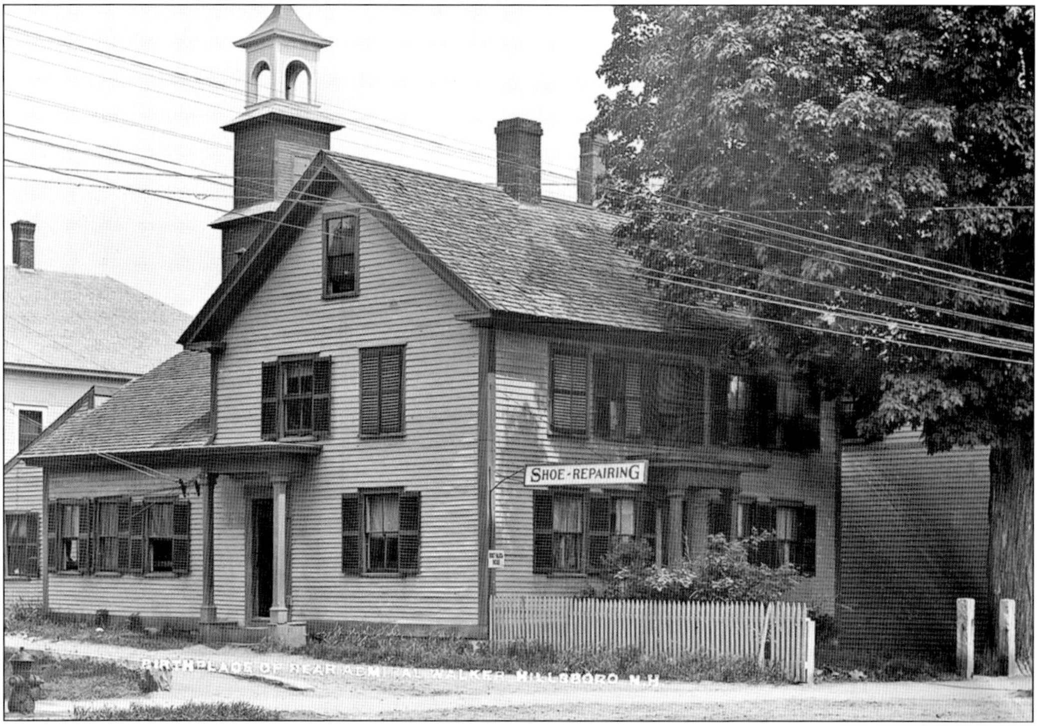

This home is the birthplace of Adm. James Grimes Walker and was adjacent to the old firehouse on the left. Admiral Walker was born in 1835, attended local schools, and was a cousin to James Butler. He graduated from the US Naval Academy in 1856 at the head of his class, and earned distinction in the Civil War at the battles of New Orleans, Vicksburg, and Wilmington. The home no longer exists, but in its place is Butler Park on land donated by Butler's daughter, Jennie.

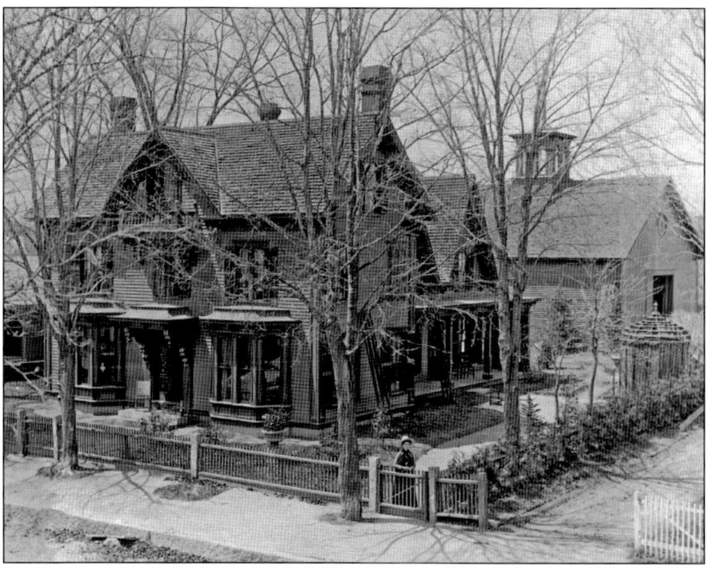

In 1953, Cyrus Phelps took over the photography business of William Manahan, whose last studio was in the Colby Block next to the Smith Church. In 1956, Phelps moved the business across the street to the Antoinette Hall residence, shown at left. Donald McCulloch served as manager and last owner of the business. Most of the early glass negatives of the Manahan Collection were stored in the barn until preserved by the historical society.

Two

Center and Village Views

From the beginning of town government up to the early 19th century, Hillsborough Center was meant to be the hub of town life. Located here were the central common, meetinghouse, animal pound, cemetery, schoolhouse, lookout tower, and early churches. Today, most of the houses that made up the original core of this area still exist. Some of the leading Hillsborough families who lived here include the Barnes, Gammel, Gilbert, Lyon, Miller, and Robbins families.

Located approximately two and a half miles southwest of Hillsborough Center is the Lower Village. At its north end is the Pierce Homestead, built by Revolutionary hero Benjamin Pierce, and its boundaries continue south down the Second New Hampshire Turnpike and east along Sawmill Road. During the stagecoach days, well located on the turnpike, it was a very lively place with two taverns, the Hillsborough Academy, the first post office in town, and the Baptist church. Notable residents included B.F. Keith, founder of continuous vaudeville; Benjamin P. Cheney, founder of the first American Express Company; and Franklin Pierce, the 14th president of the United States.

Approximately one and a half miles northwest from the Pierce Homestead on the Second New Hampshire Turnpike is the Upper Village. This part of town has that distinct small-town feel. Most of the houses, stores, and other buildings date back to the 19th century. Of note is the Pine Hill Cemetery, located just before the village, with the Pierce family plot at the forefront.

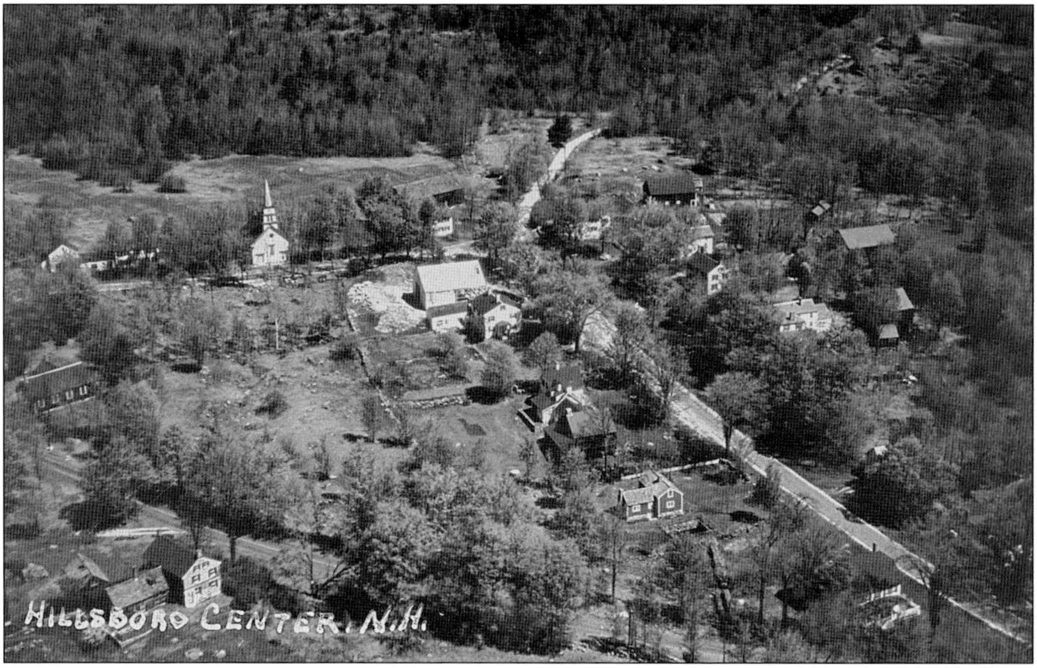

Hillsborough Center is a real New England hilltop village, becoming the center of the incorporated town in 1772. In 1779, founder Col. John Hill deeded to Jonathan Barnes 200 acres of land as inducement to come to Hillsborough as the first minister of the town. Fifteen acres of this land were reserved for a meetinghouse, school, pound, militia-training field, and burial ground. The 13 homes situated at the center have remained outwardly unchanged since the early 1800s.

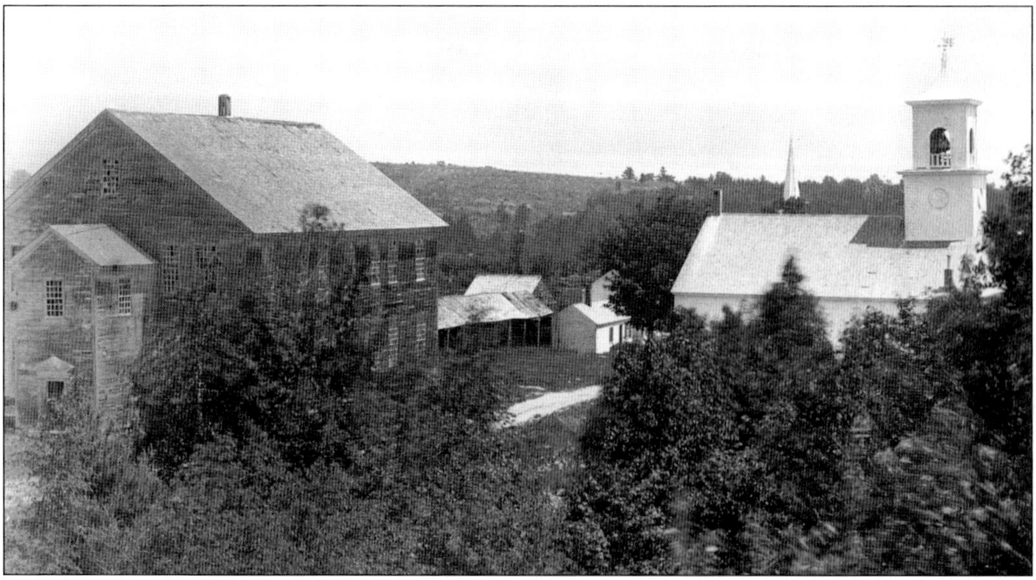

The old meetinghouse construction began with the raising of its frame in September 1789 and finished in July 1794. Until the separation of church and state, it was used for both civil and religious affairs. The meetinghouse became the town hall. The Congregational church was built in 1839, and stood on the site of the present Congregational church. Unfortunately, both structures were consumed by fire on June 19, 1892.

The Barnes homestead was built in 1773 on the most prominent site of the 200-acre tract of land "deeded forever" by Colonel Hill. The house was built by Capt. Isaac Baldwin, the second man to fall at Bunker Hill. The first occupant was Reverend Barnes, the town's first pastor, who was later struck by lightning and subsequently buried under his original pulpit in the center.

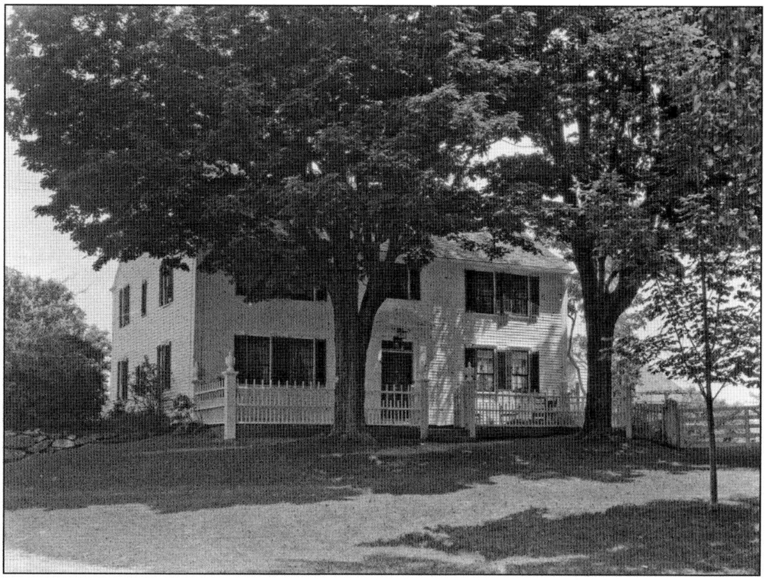

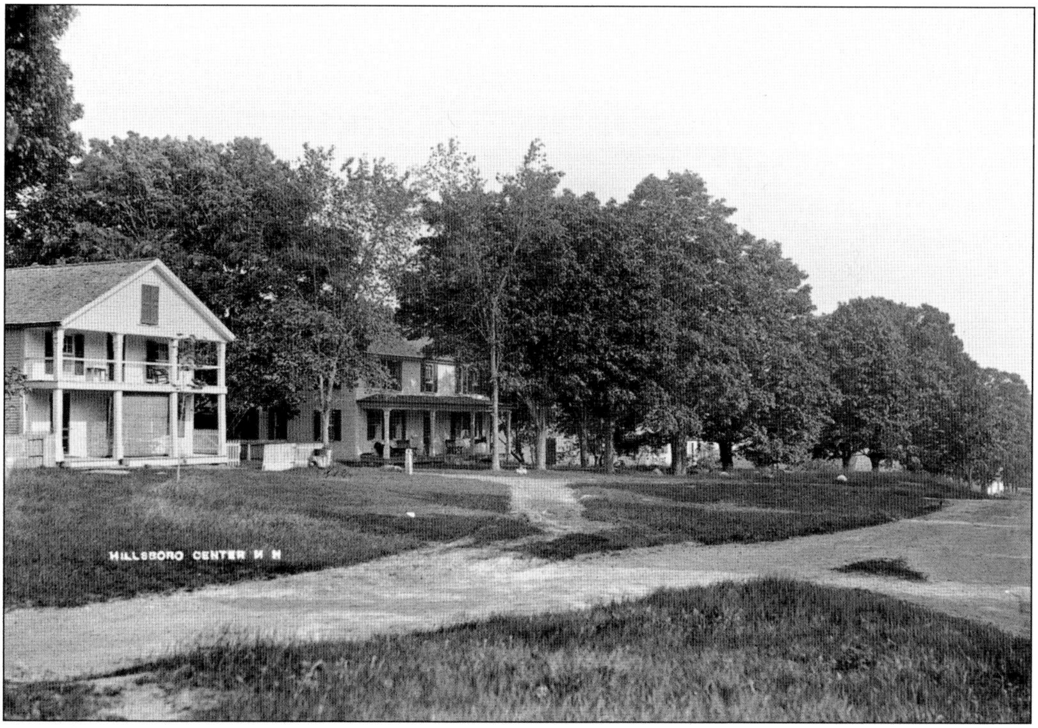

Looking south from the Barnes house is the Hearty house on the far left and the Cobb house. The Hearty house became the village store, selling dry goods, but also had an ample supply of "wet goods" as it became a general meeting place for men. The Cobb house was built in 1815, and was an early tavern called the Rising Sun. Taverns were popular in the center, as most of the surrounding communities were dry.

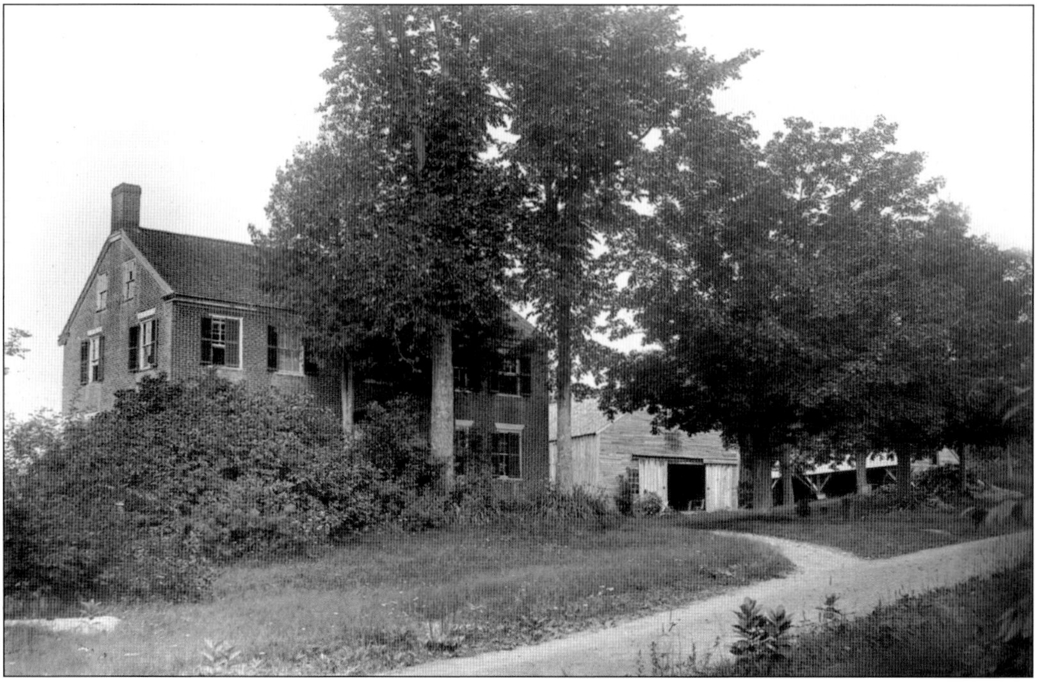

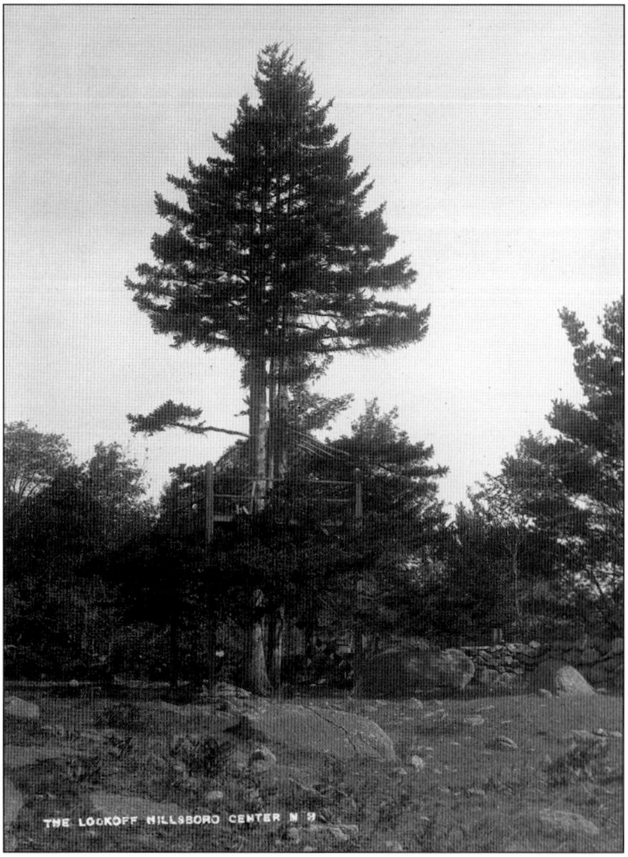

Dr. Mason Hatch built the only brick house in the center in 1817. Residents included several doctors, Barnes family descendants, and a post office. Presently, it is home to Jon Gibson's Pewter Shop, a nationally known craftsman who apprenticed with his father Raymond, who passed on the old techniques, tools, and molds.

In 1884, Elizabeth Gilbert Frost convinced neighbors to build a square, two-story platform surrounding a lookout tree. The view was spectacular with views of Monadnock, Crotched, Stow, and Lowell Mountains, as well as Loon Lake. This picture was taken around 1924, when a new structure was built. On Sundays after service, this was a popular family gathering place.

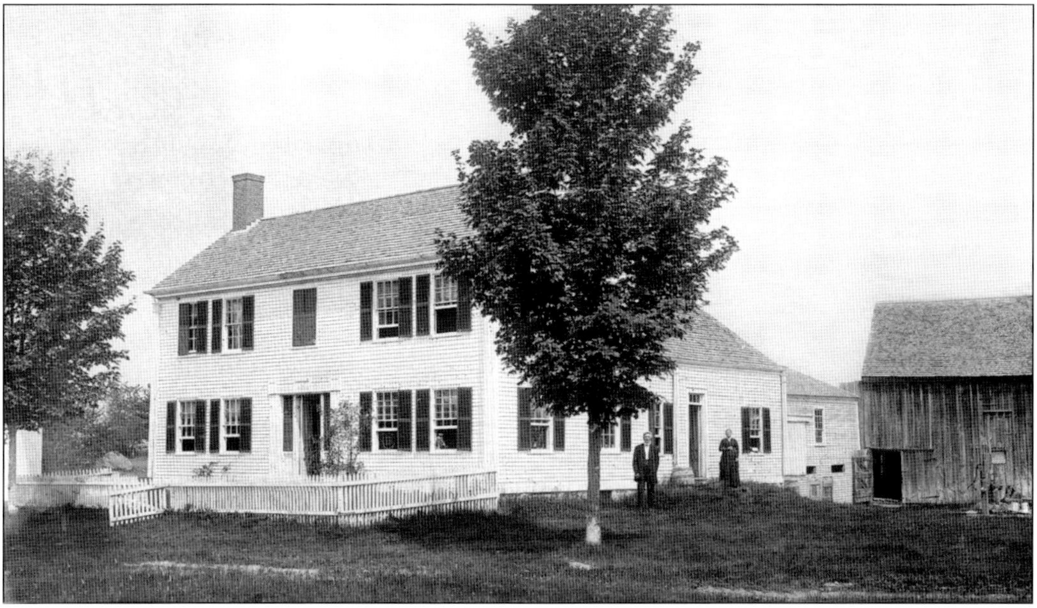

Ezra Clement built this house in 1840 at the corner of North and Center Roads. Oramel Danforth, a postmaster, lived in the house for a period in the mid-1800s. The couple pictured here is most likely Dana and Ida Powers, who moved to Hillsborough in 1865 and were both avid gardeners.

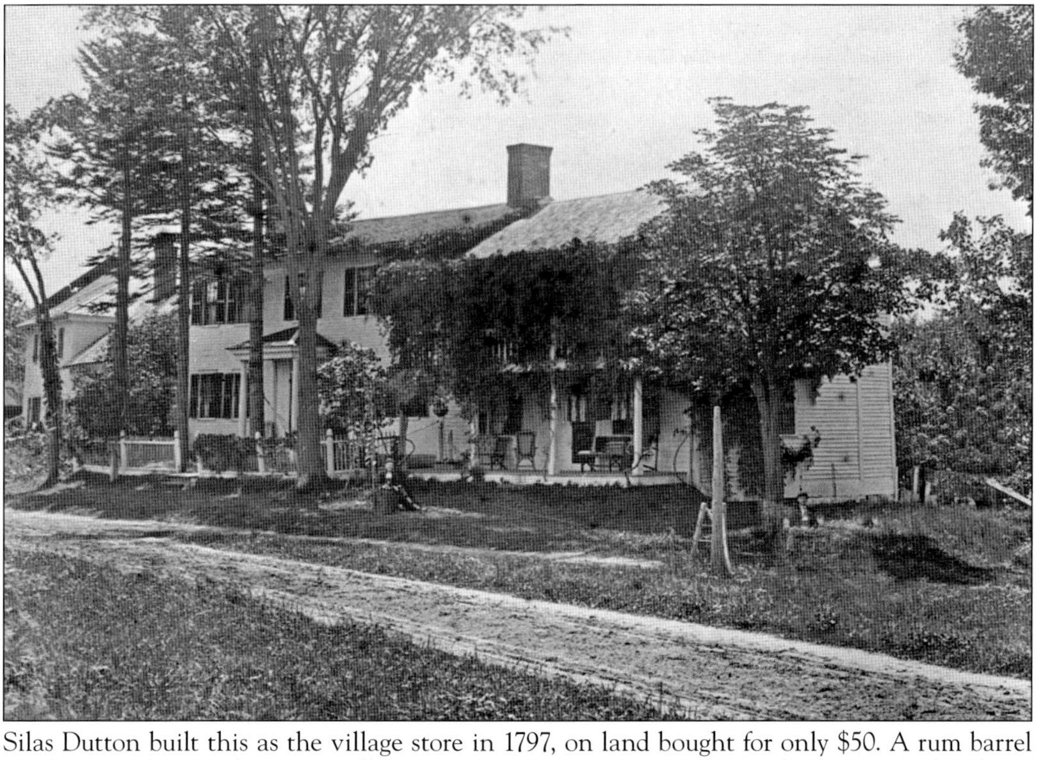

Silas Dutton built this as the village store in 1797, on land bought for only $50. A rum barrel was kept inside near the outer wall. One night a thirsty patron came to the store, found it closed for the day, and bored a hole through the wall and into the barrel, emptying its contents. The federal-style portion on the left was added later by Joseph Curtice Barnes.

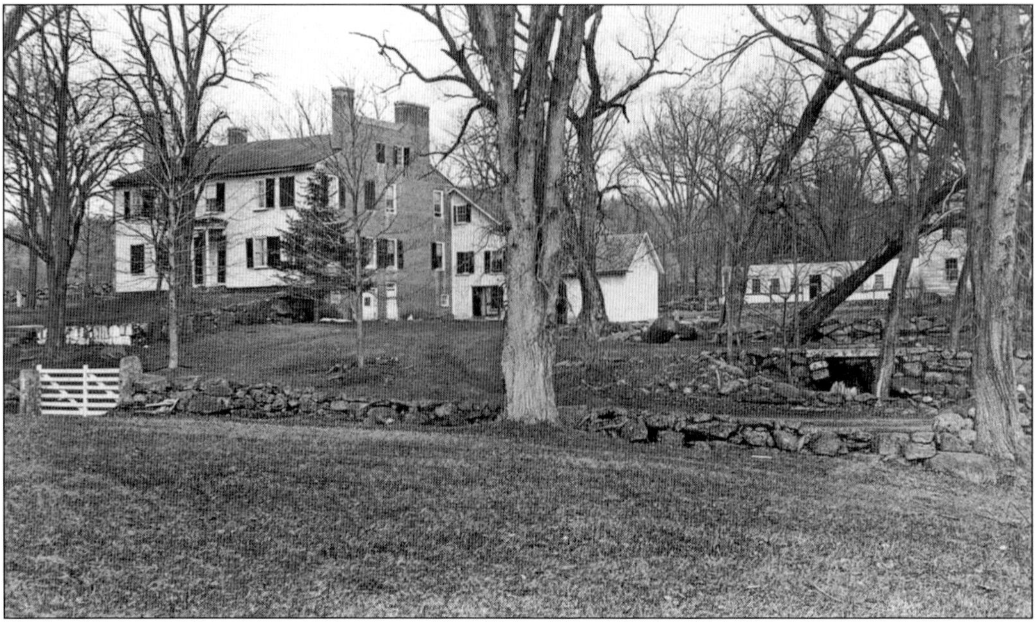

About two miles south of the center is the 1803 Jones Road house. Nathaniel Johnson built this house, which was described as the "most expensive and handsomest" house of its day, with nine working fireplaces. It was later sold to Eben Jones and remained in that family until 1913, followed by the Howards, Crooks, and the Hatfields. The current owners are Gloria and Mike Reopel, president of the Hillsborough Historical Society.

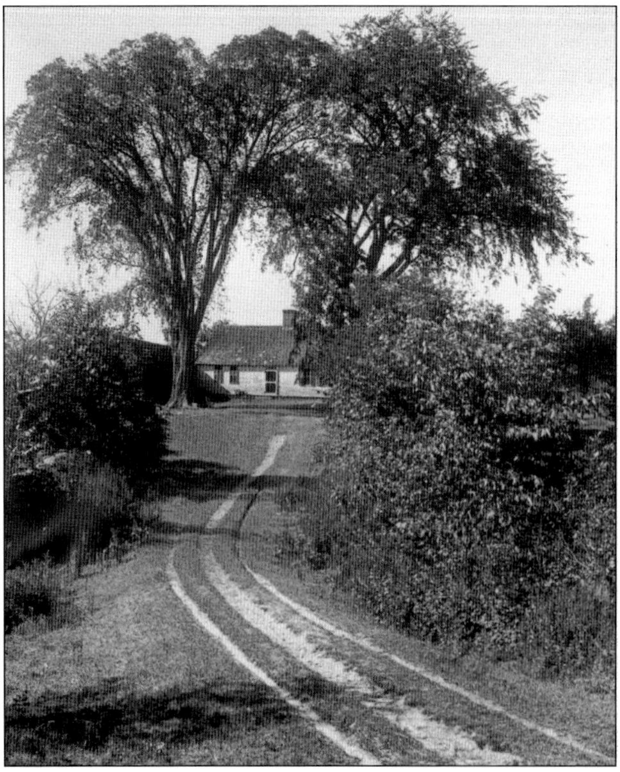

Clark Sturtevant came to Hillsborough in 1856, and settled on his farm about one mile northwest of the center. He was deacon of the Congregational church, and taught singing to schoolchildren. Note the two stately elms framing the house. Hillsborough had many elms along its main streets until the Hurricane of 1938 and later blight.

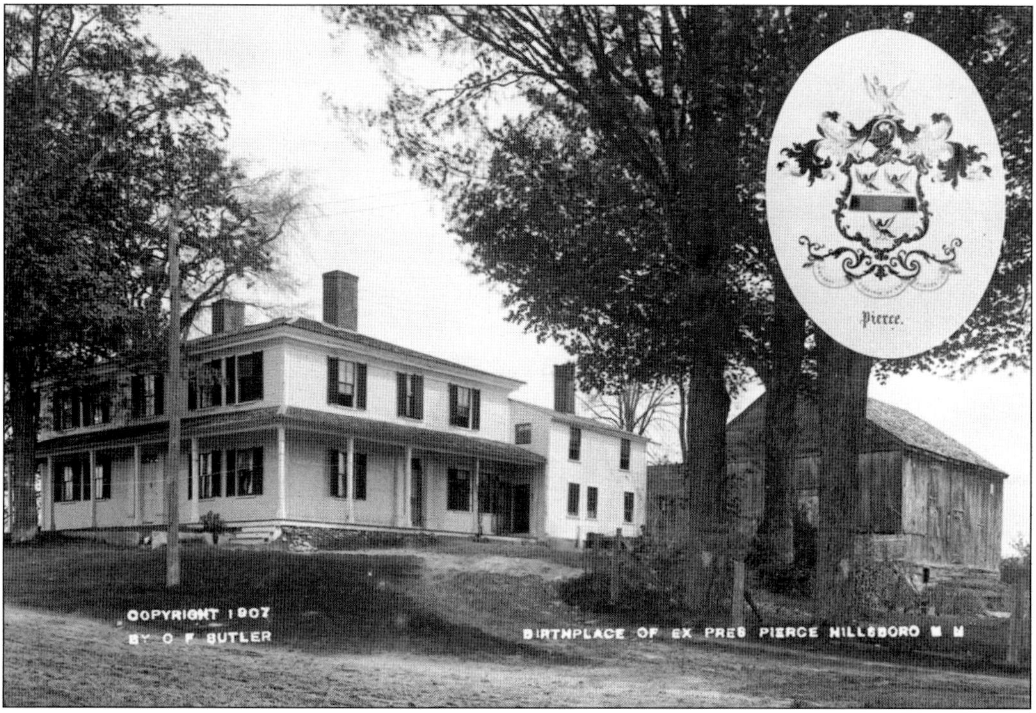

The President Franklin Pierce Homestead is one of the most historic homes in New Hampshire. This 1907 photograph includes the Pierce coat of arms and was a common postcard, copyrighted by C.F. Butler. Soon after the Second New Hampshire Turnpike was opened, Benjamin Pierce, Revolutionary War hero, future governor, and general of the New Hampshire Militia, bought 200 acres at Lower Village. Here he built a mansion and opened a tavern, which became a popular way station.

After Gov. Benjamin Pierce died in 1839, the Pierce homestead was first passed on to son-in-law Gen. John McNeil (of the War of 1812 fame), and later his daughter. Later the homestead passed through multiple owners who changed the appearance of the residence to include moving a barn to adjoin the house, removing the fence in the front yard, and adding a porch. This picture is from 1915. By 1929, the porches were removed.

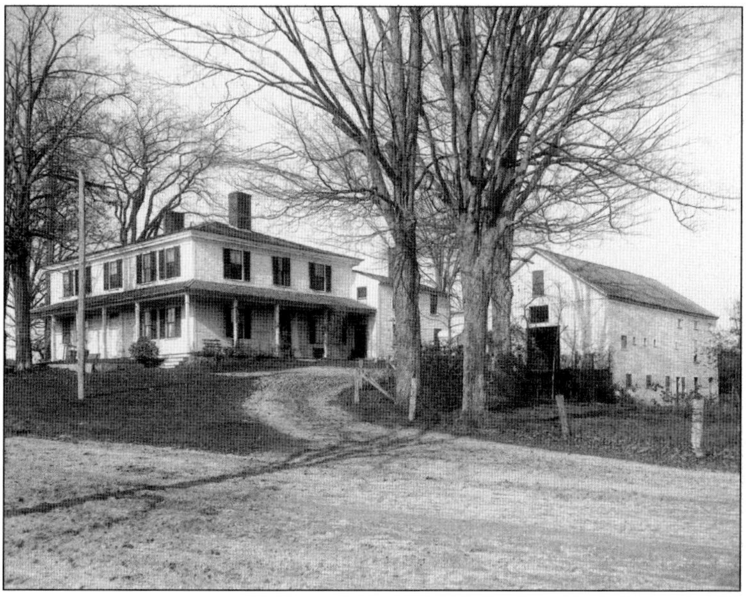

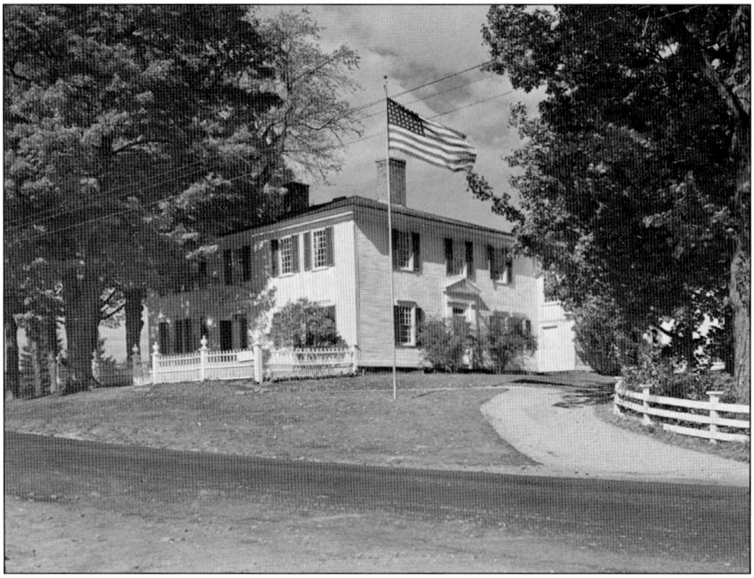

This 1952 exterior view of the Pierce homestead is remarkably similar to today's structure. The barn has become the welcome center and display area for an old postal wagon and winter sleds. The interior stenciling has been restored, and period furnishings remain throughout the house. Today, the Hillsborough Historical Society manages and preserves the property.

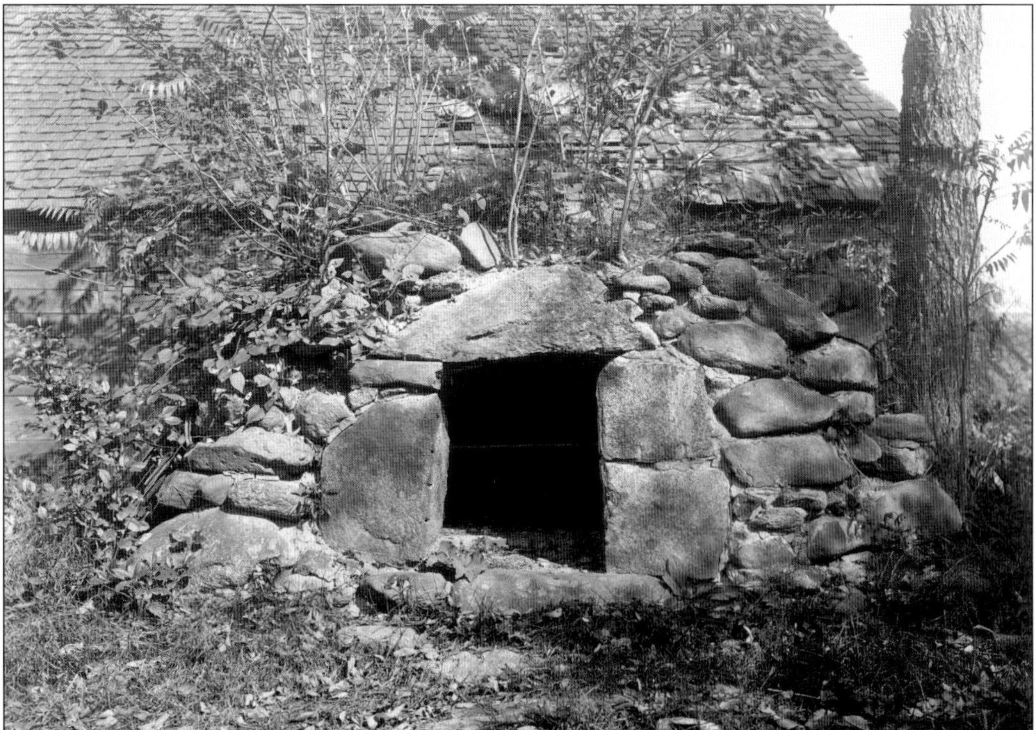

On August 19, 1852, the town of Hillsborough and the surrounding region held a mass meeting and barbeque to boost the candidacy of Franklin Pierce for the presidency. Approximately 25,000 people gathered on the banks of the Contoocook River in support of the future president, listened to speeches, and ate roasted ox prepared in this oven specially built for the occasion.

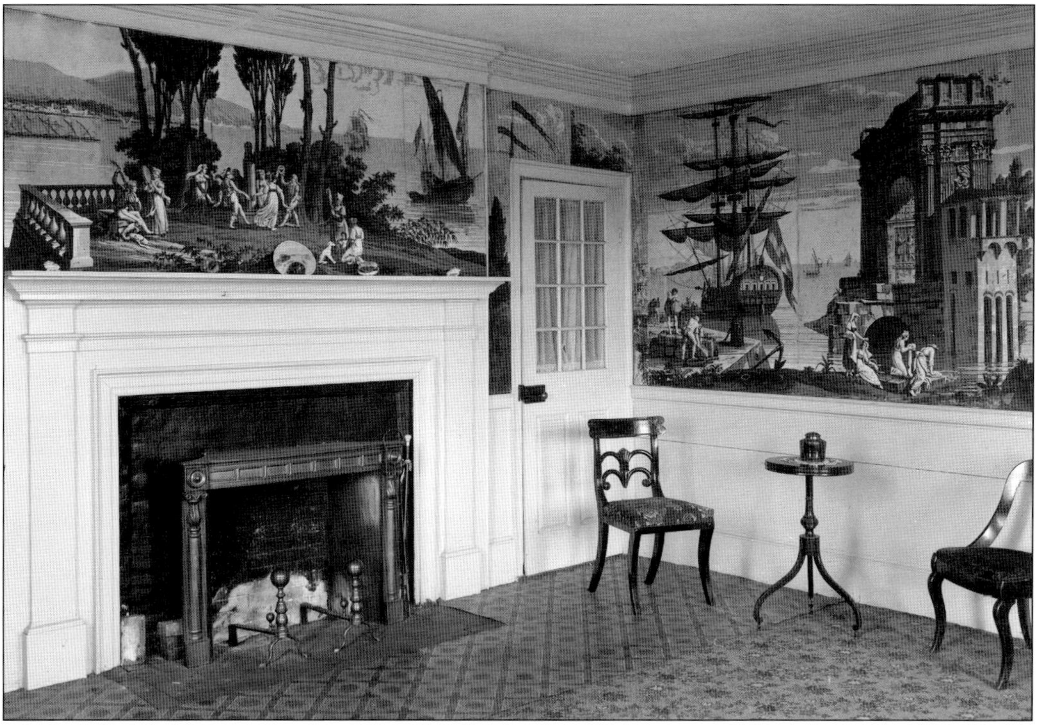

The interior of the Pierce homestead is typical of the federal period, with four rooms on both the first and second floors, and servant quarters in the second floor of the ell. The parlor front room, shown above in 1920, was quite a formal room, with original wallpaper containing a Naples scene being the distinctive feature. The other front room was normally used as the tavern. The summer kitchen (below) located in the ell had several special features including hot water from a brick-enclosed tub with a firebox underneath and convenient access to well water through a side window. The winter kitchen was a more formal room in the main building. The top floor has two bedrooms plus a large ballroom, which could be converted into two bedrooms or a large sleeping area for the tavern guests. Dances and militia drills were often held there.

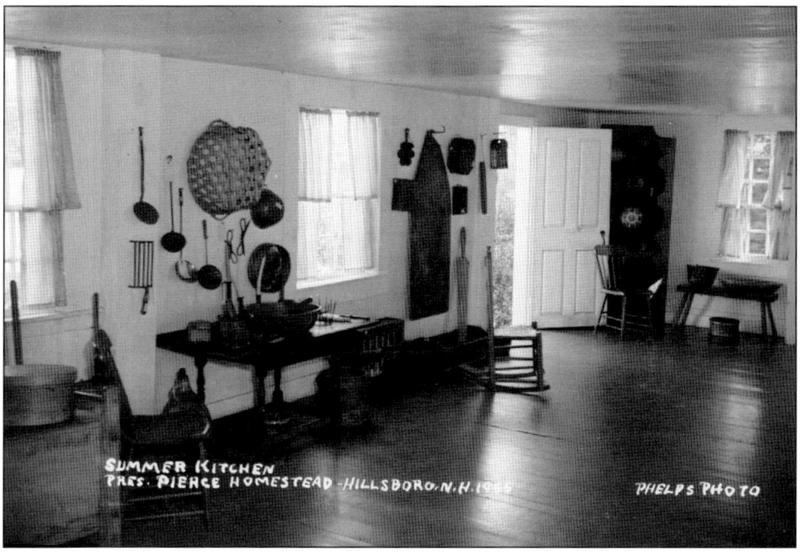

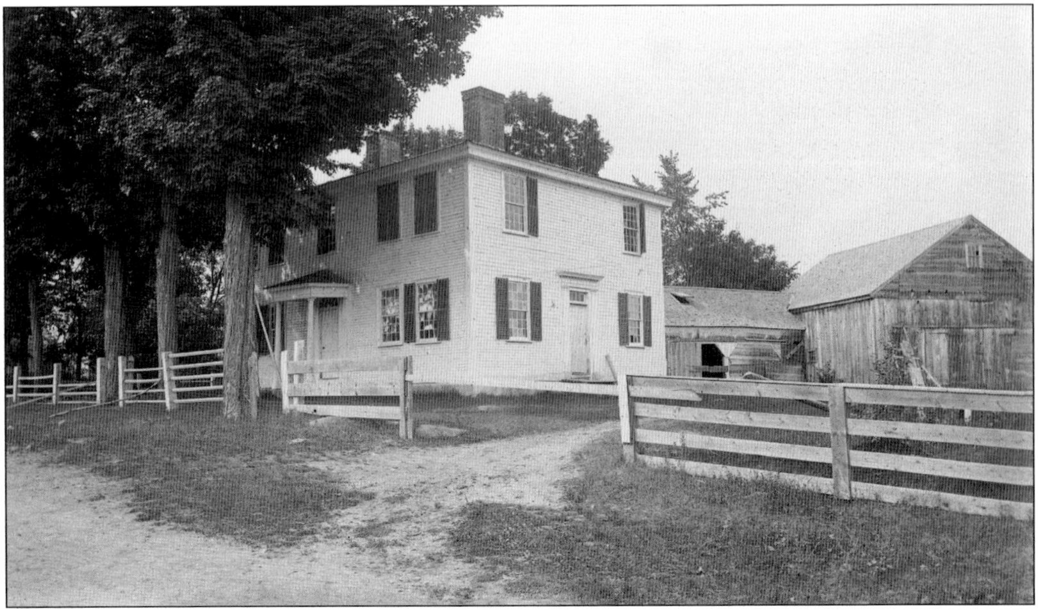

The Elizabeth Pierce house was built in 1807 next to the homestead and with a similar floor plan. Elizabeth was the first child of Benjamin Pierce, and married Gen. John McNeil. The house still retains much of its original stenciling, which is similar, if not identical to, that found in the Pierce homestead. For the last few decades, the home has served as an antique shop for a number of proprietors including Dick Withington, famed country auctioneer and the No. 1 New Hampshire license holder.

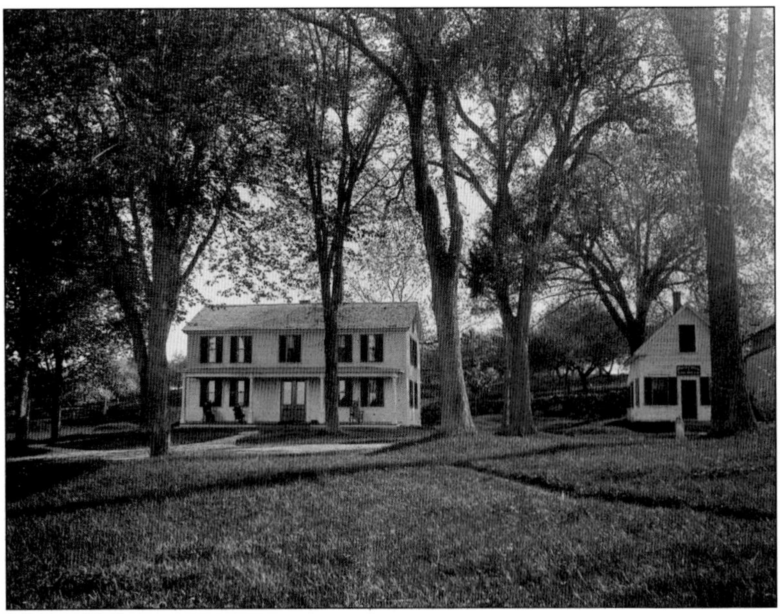

This is the Kirk Dearborn Pierce home in the Lower Village. Pierce was admitted to the bar and opened an office in the small building on the right. He was a successful town lawyer and an excellent debater, a trait inherited from his illustrious relatives. Franklin Pierce lived here with Jane Appleton as newlyweds from 1834 to 1838.

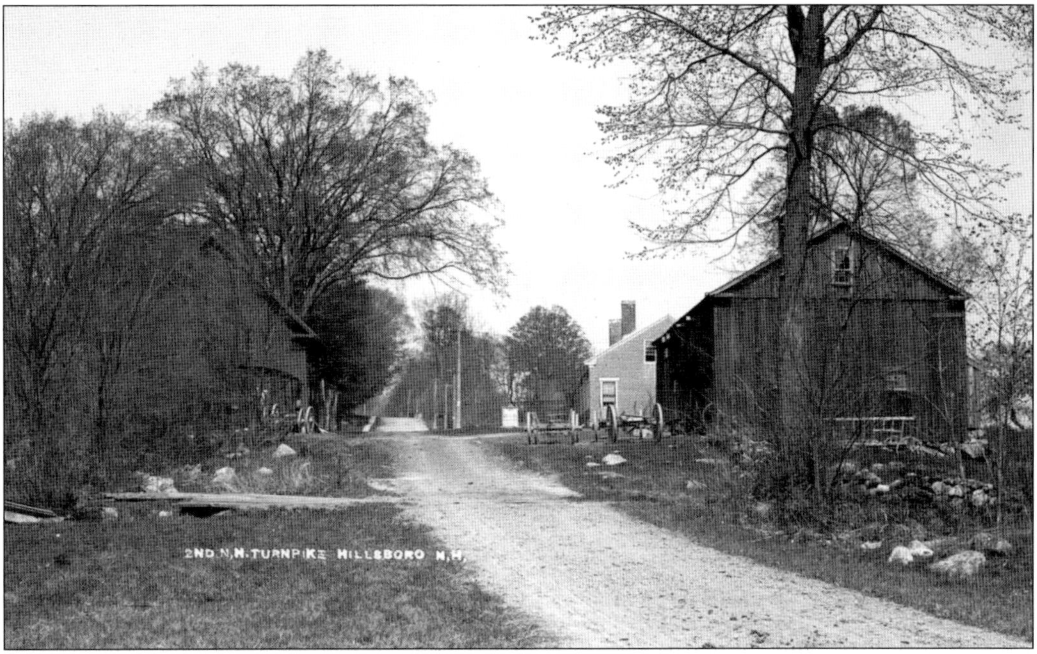

The Lower Village stands on a high rise of land on both sides of the Second New Hampshire Turnpike, as shown in this photograph from the early 1900s. In its heyday, Lower Village had two taverns, one store, an academy, and about two dozen dwellings and offices. Additionally, due to the close proximity to waterpower, sawmills, gristmills, a foundry, and tannery formed a prosperous industrial base. The tannery office was in the barn on the left.

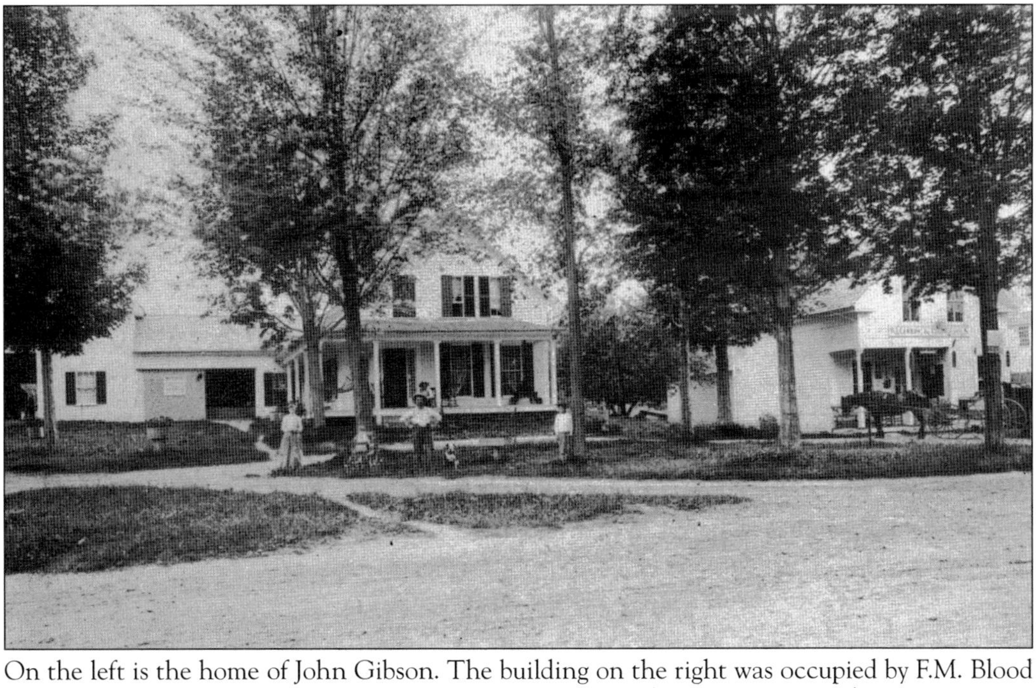

On the left is the home of John Gibson. The building on the right was occupied by F.M. Blood and later by Brooks Webber's law office. John Gibson opened up a store across the street. His son Fred took over the store in 1891. Fred's daughter Bernice is in the baby carriage.

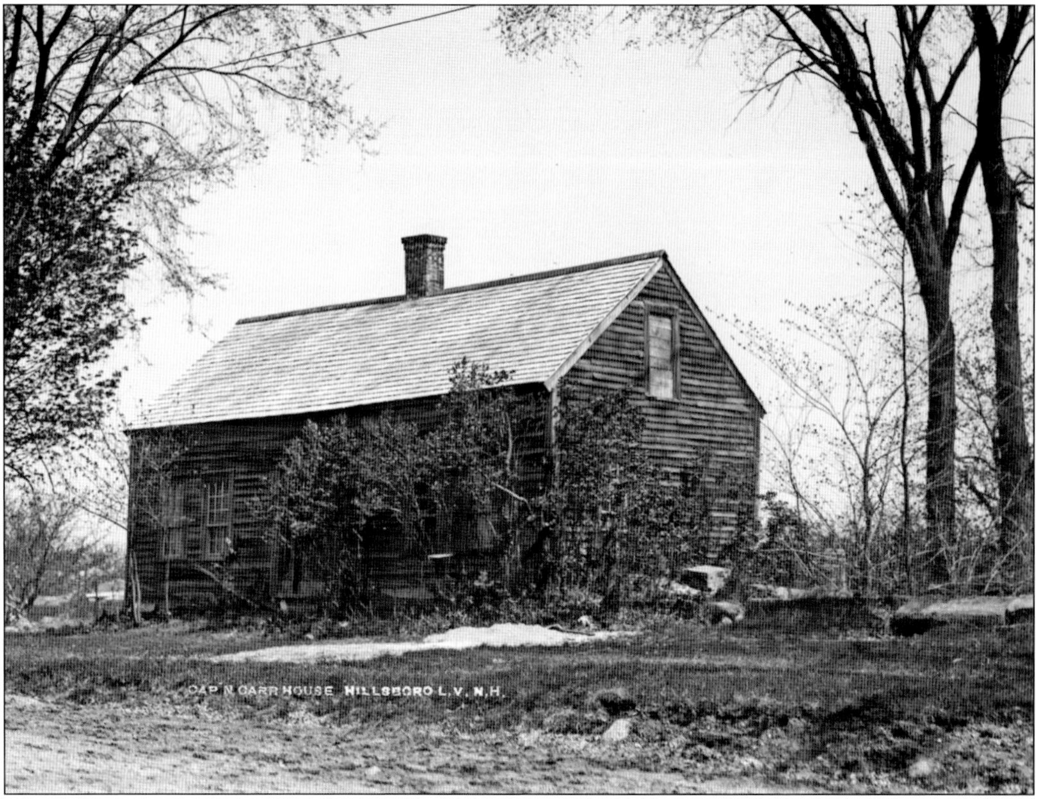

Nathan Carr's house, pictured here, was located next to the schoolhouse in the Lower Village. Carr was a captain in the militia and had a desire to be rich in an era when imitating currency was relatively easy. Captain Carr was caught and sent to state prison for counterfeiting. Nearly all the brick houses in both villages, and possibly the stone arch bridge on Jones Road, were made with counterfeit money, including Carr's former brick house on Jones Road.

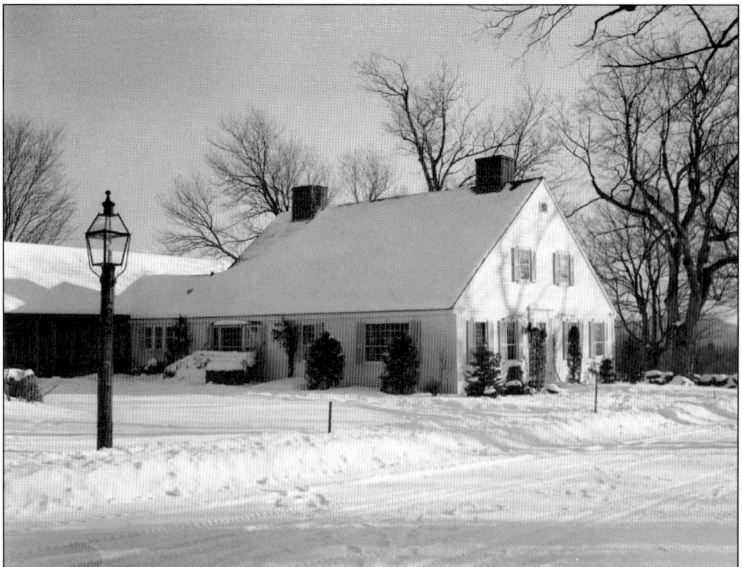

Capt. Samuel Bradford built the Samuel Bradford Tavern in 1765. The tavern is located on Bible Hill, at the time a simple trail almost equidistant from Hillsborough Bridge, the Center, and the Upper and Lower Villages. It was the site of the first town meeting. The families of George Tuttle, Harold Harvey, Earl Bennett, and Henry Clapp have all been residents at one time.

Three

Stone Arch Bridges

Among Hillsborough's treasures, and sources of real architectural pride, are the old granite stone arch bridges erected by Scotch-Irish stonemasons in the early 19th century. These old bridges, built from the same granite that gave the state of New Hampshire its nickname, blend in beautifully around the picturesque landscape of Hillsborough. It is a testament to the strength of the granite and well-built construction of these arches that these old structures have lasted well over a century in New England weather.

Early bridges built in Hillsborough were typically wooden and crude. They frequently washed out with floods, and were subject to decay unless covered with roofs. Stone arch bridges were a solution to the weaknesses of wooden bridges. The early Scotch-Irish settlers in Hillsborough had the necessary stone splitting skills to erect these structures. Hiram Monroe proposed building stone arch bridges, saying that they "would be cheaper in the long run." The permanence of stone arch bridges was very appealing. The higher initial cost was offset by a longer lifespan and higher load capacity than wooden bridges. Granite boulders, scattered widely by ice age glaciers, were plentiful in Hillsborough for construction. This stone can be split precisely and has a high friction coefficient—an ideal material for arch construction.

Eventually, 12 stone arch bridges were built in Hillsborough from the 1830s to the 1860s. Each bridge differed in various ways. Typically, the basic design was adapted to the requirements of individual sites. There was wide variation in length, number of arches, shape of the arches, design of approaches, and type of facing and railings. Of the 12 bridges, eight are still in service today. Of the other four, one was destroyed for replacement, one was destroyed with the building of the Pierce Lake dam, one was destroyed by flood but replaced, and one still exists but is not accessible by vehicular traffic.

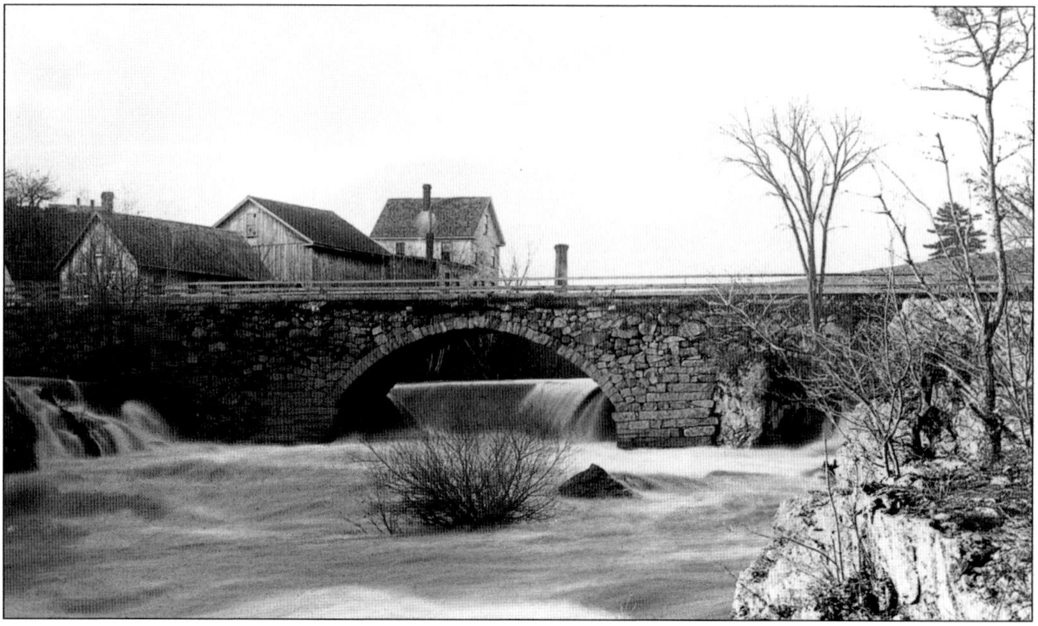

This bridge carries Bridge Street over the Contoocook River just south of Central Square. It was the first of all the stone arch bridges and is the most massive. Substantial construction was required because of traffic volume as well as water volume. The bridge has a single large arch together with headrace openings at both ends. It was built without mortar and had rubble facing.

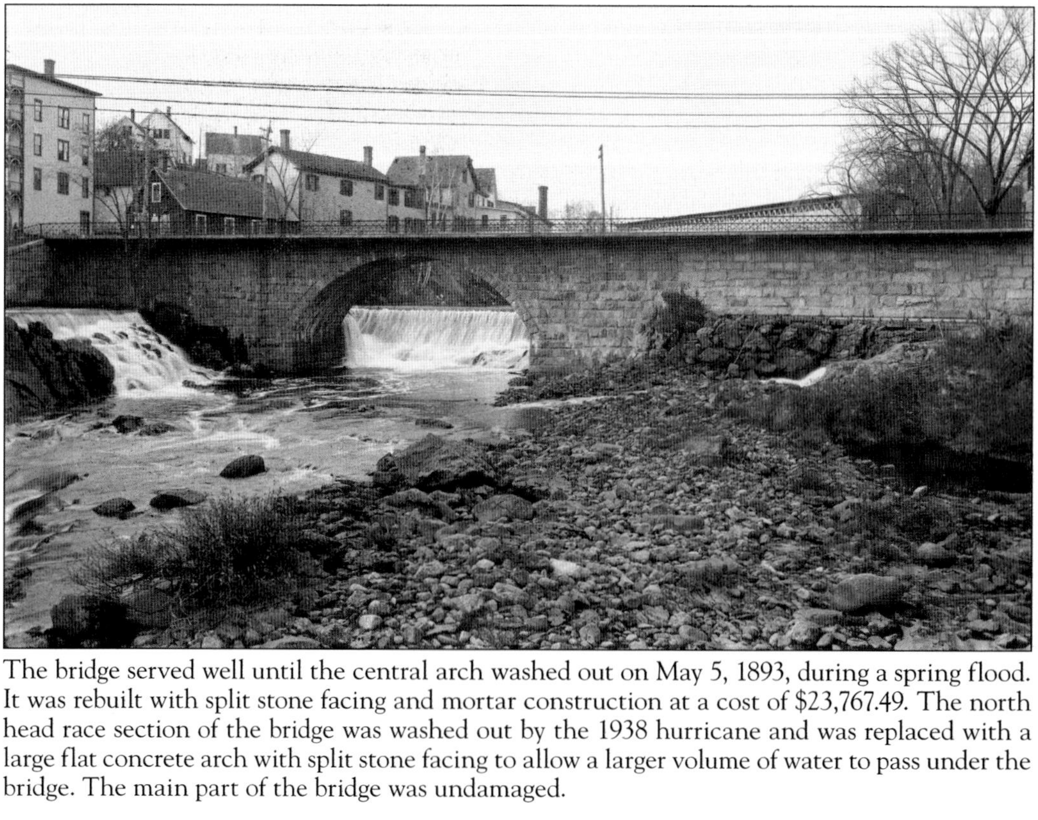

The bridge served well until the central arch washed out on May 5, 1893, during a spring flood. It was rebuilt with split stone facing and mortar construction at a cost of $23,767.49. The north head race section of the bridge was washed out by the 1938 hurricane and was replaced with a large flat concrete arch with split stone facing to allow a larger volume of water to pass under the bridge. The main part of the bridge was undamaged.

The Gleason Falls Bridge, built around 1830, carries Beard Road over Beard Brook just south of the intersection with Gleason Falls Road. This bridge has the most picturesque setting of all the bridges. Beard Brook falls sharply down through a short, narrow, rocky chasm just below the bridge. Walking carefully down the south edge of the chasm reveals gorgeous views of the bridge.

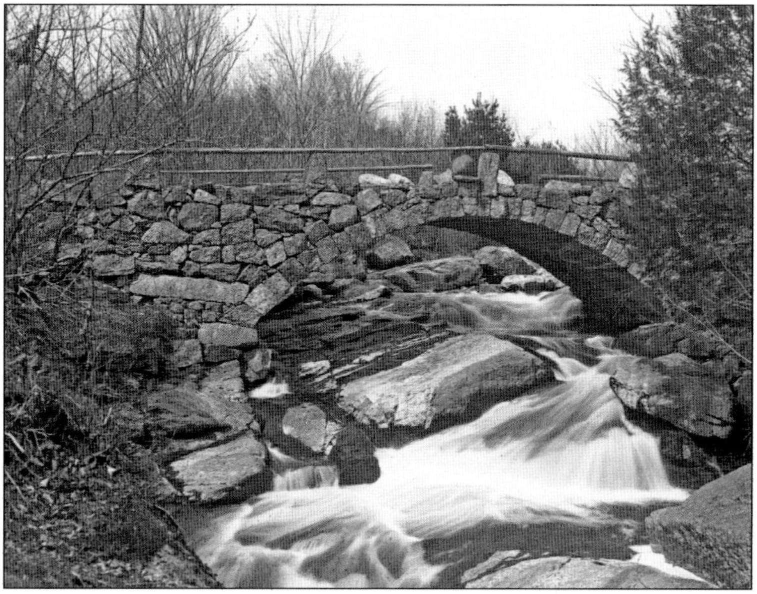

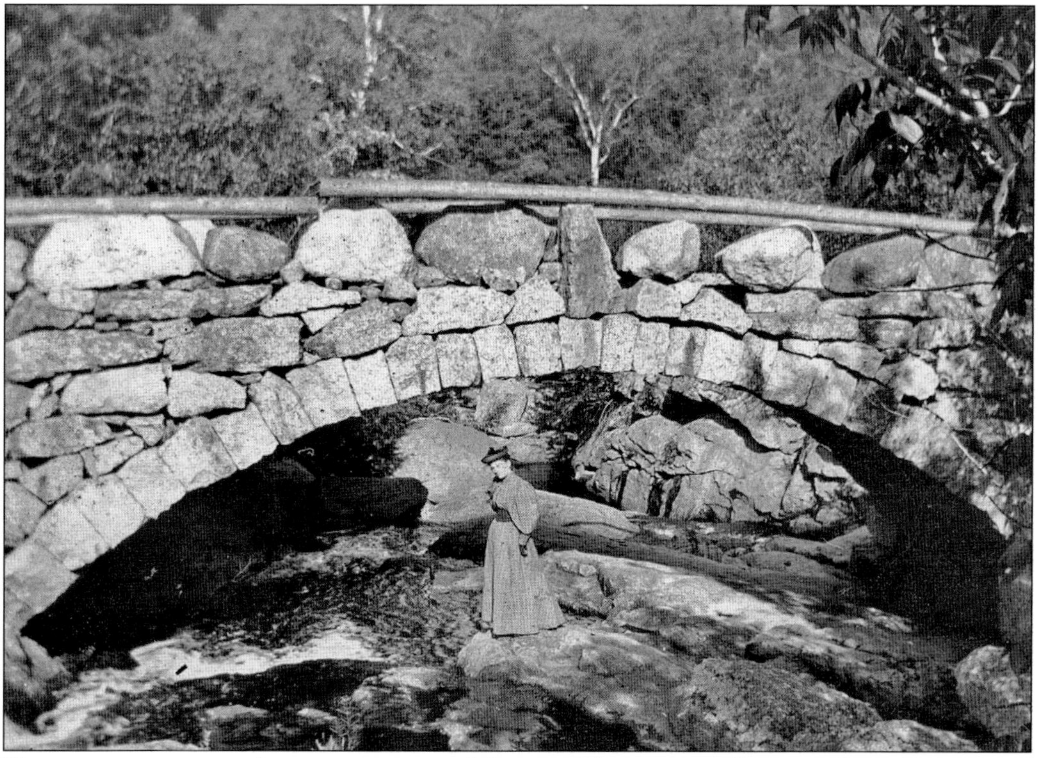

The views are spectacular in any season of the year. This is an early image from the upstream side. During the peak of the October 9, 2005, flood that devastated the western area of the state, water flowed over the top of the bridge and the roadway. Twenty-four hours later, the water level was still up to the top of the arch. Only minor damage was done to the facing on the south side of the bridge.

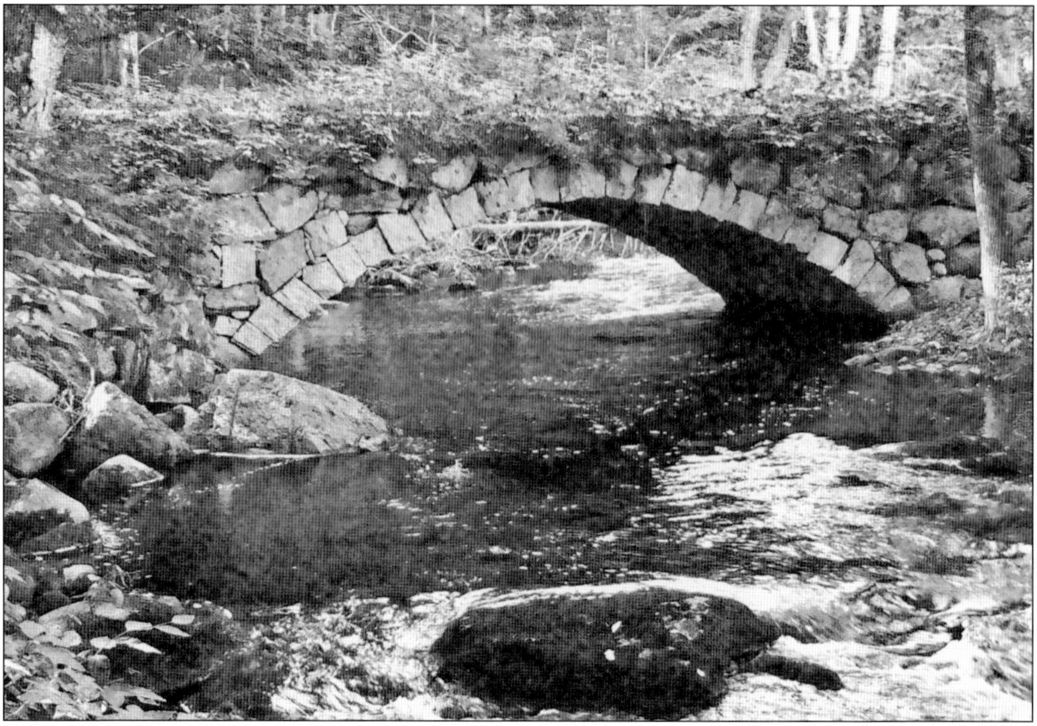

The two Gleason Falls Road bridges, built around 1830, carry Gleason Falls Road over Beard Brook just to the west of the intersection with Beard Road. Wharfing over an island separates these bridges. The two are very different in appearance and function. The western bridge has a much wider and flatter span to accommodate the greater flow of the main stream. The eastern bridge has a much narrower arch, and probably served as the tailrace for a mill located just above the bridge.

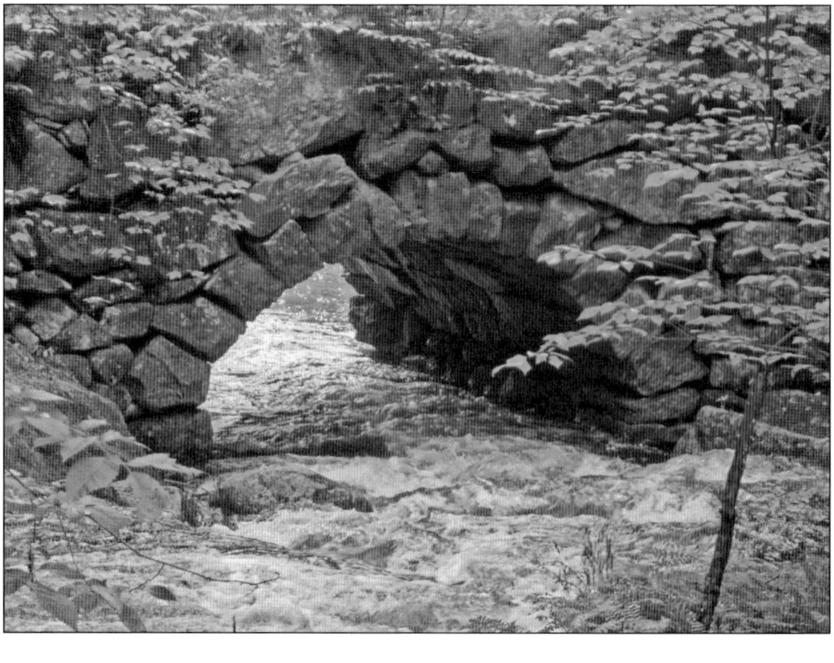

The Foundry Bridge carried Sawmill Road over Beard Brook at the intersection of West Main Street and Beard Road. This was a single-arch bridge. It was destroyed in 1931 when the Franklin Pierce Highway, Route 9, was built as an extension of West Main Street up Penstock Hill.

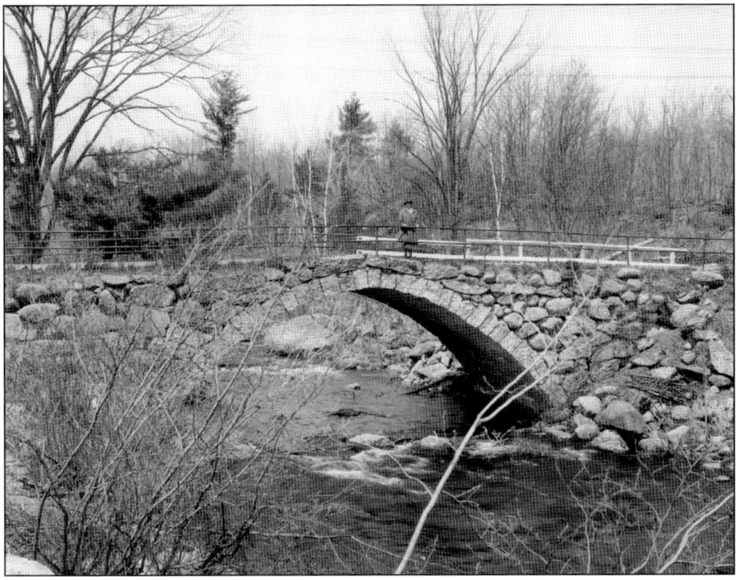

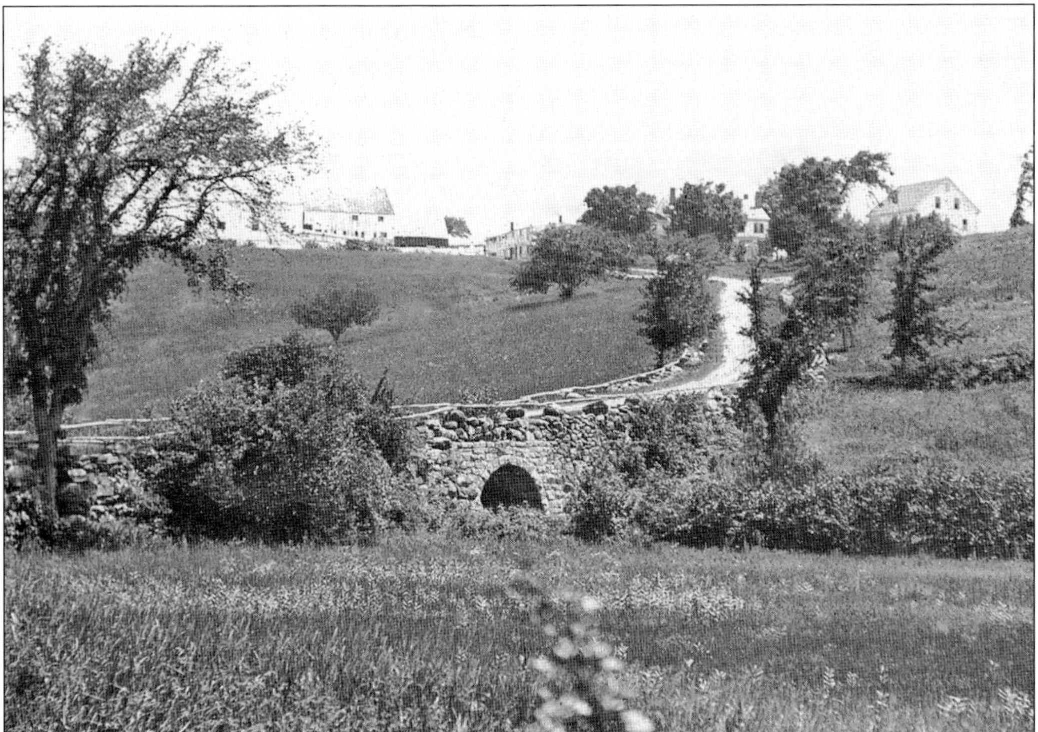

The Shedd Brook Bridge, built in 1859, carried Shedd Road over this brook, just east of the cemeteries on the Second New Hampshire Turnpike. It had a relatively small arch since the brook is not a large stream, but the bridge had a very high roadway because of the steep banks of the brook. After being washed out, the bridge was replaced by a simple, modern bridge.

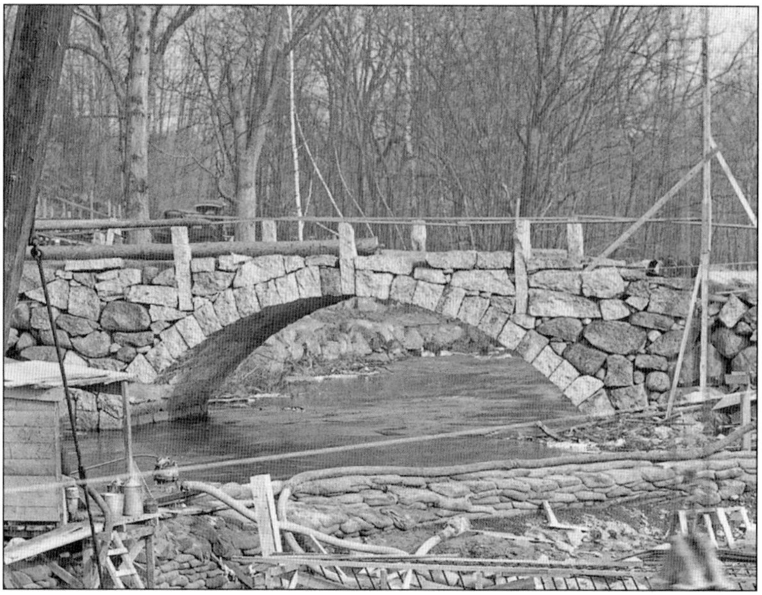

The Crooker Bridge carried Barden Hill Road over the North Branch River, just below the location of the Pierce Lake Dam spillway. This bridge was beautifully proportioned with a flat arch. Many considered this the most beautiful of all the bridges. This bridge was carefully constructed with arch segments of precisely split stones. The keystone also serves as one of the support posts for the railings.

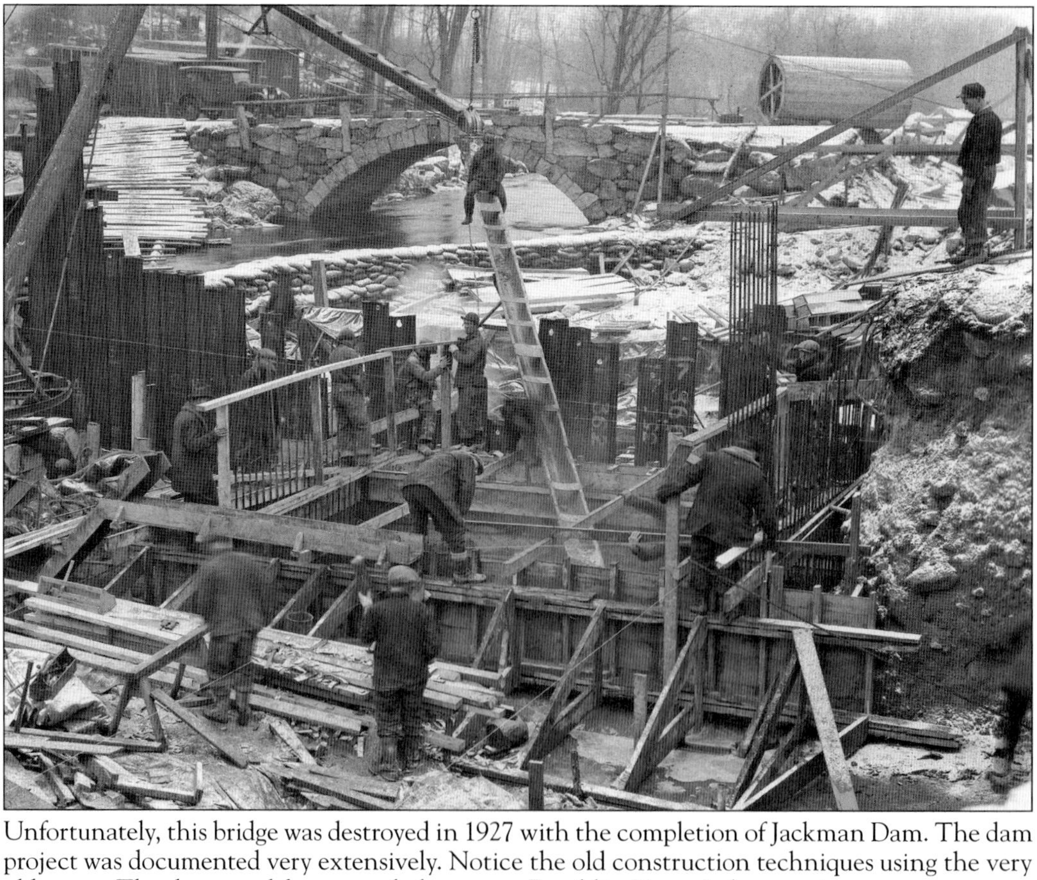

Unfortunately, this bridge was destroyed in 1927 with the completion of Jackman Dam. The dam project was documented very extensively. Notice the old construction techniques using the very old crane. The dam, used for power, helps create Franklin Pierce Lake, a major recreation area.

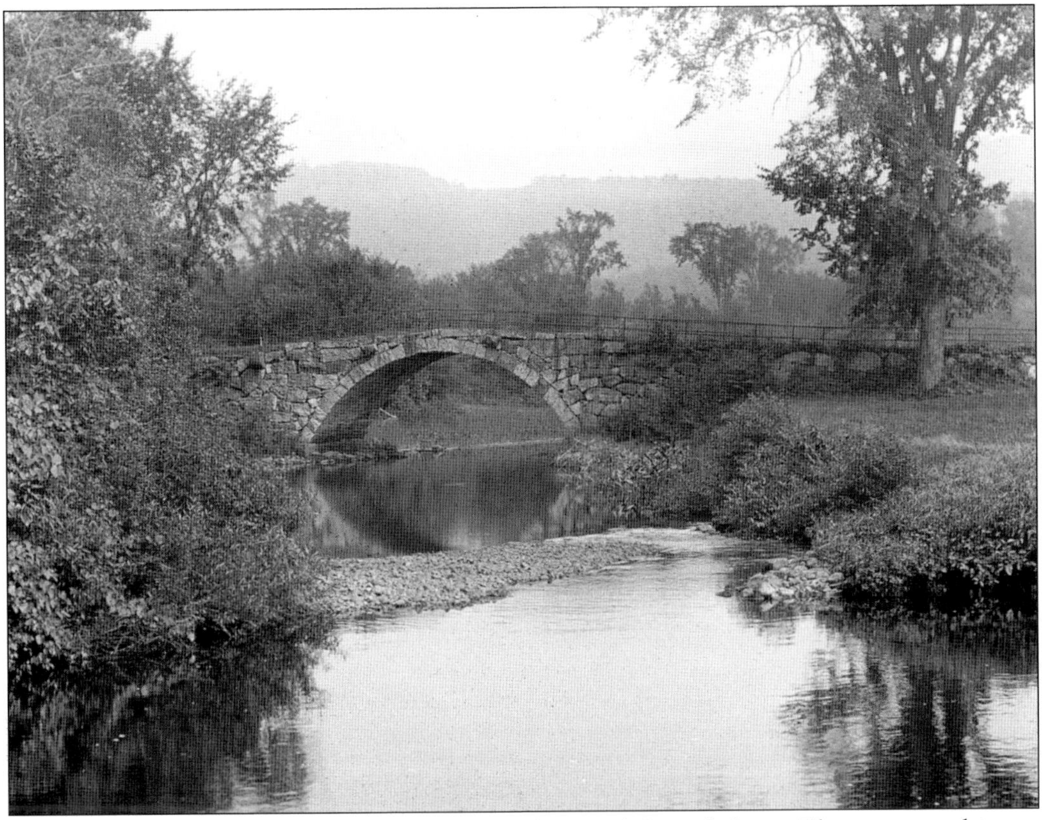

The Tuttle Bridge carried Old Keene Road over the North Branch River. Then, as now, this was the main road across southwest New Hampshire from Concord to Brattleborough, Vermont. This was also the crossroads for a road to Antrim Center and another road leading to the Sulphur Hill area. It is not clear when this bridge was built.

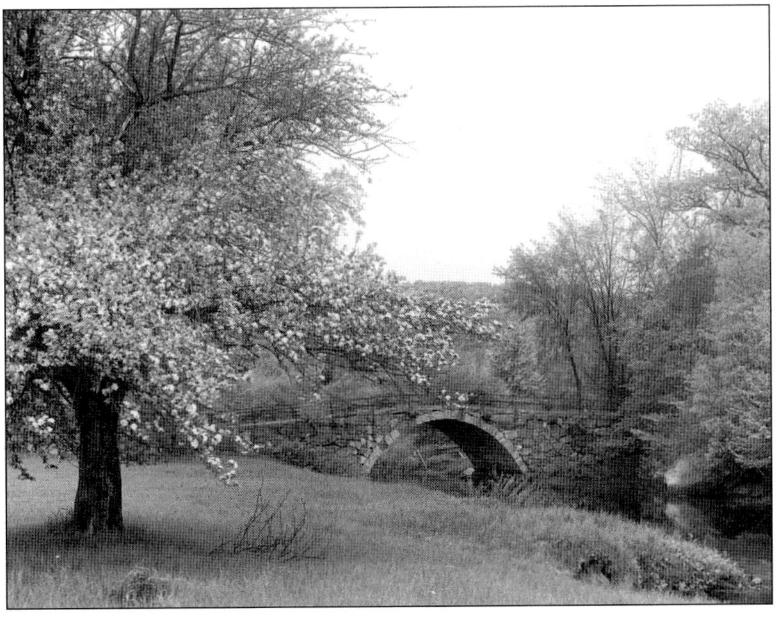

The Tuttle Bridge remains in excellent condition; the only problem is that it is now underwater in the middle of Pierce Lake. When the water in the lake is lowered at times, the bridge reappears out of the depths like the Loch Ness monster. When the water is lowered enough, it is still possible to travel over the bridge.

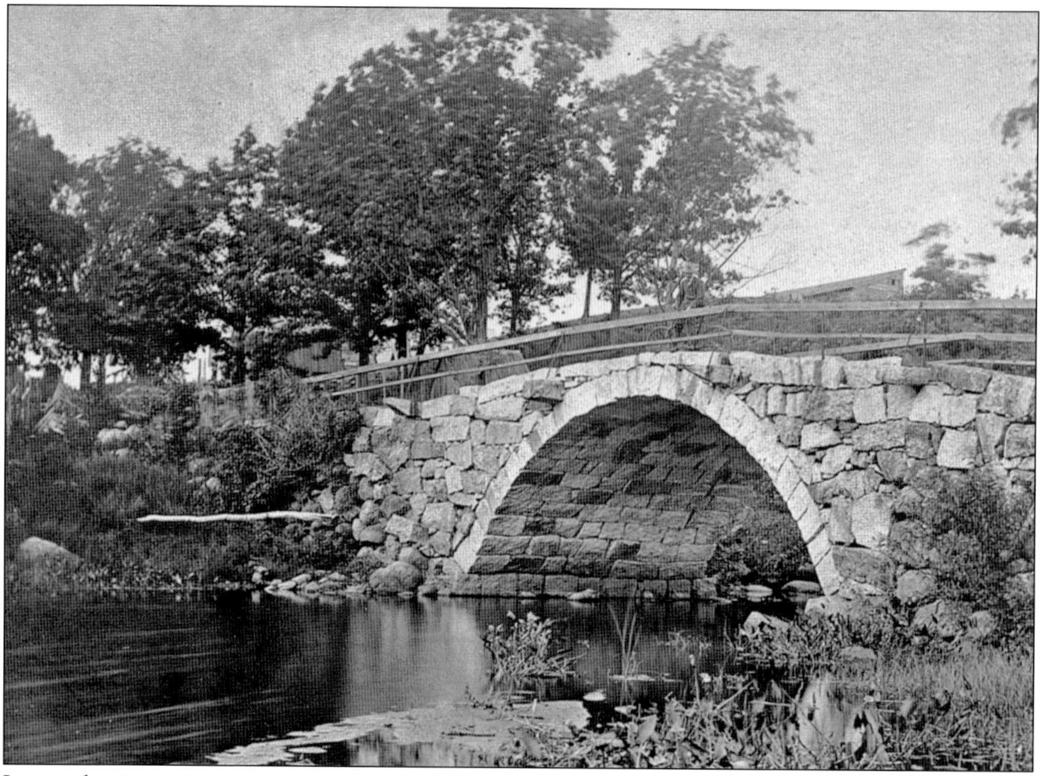

Located as it was at an important crossroads, an inn was conveniently located here by the bridge. Horse-drawn travel over this route took days, so inns flourished not too many miles apart. Today similar journeys just take hours, but even with the advent of travel by automobile, the inn continued in business until recently, nicely situated on the shore of Pierce Lake. This area was rich farmland cultivated for many generations and was settled early because of this river bottomland. Now the shores of Pierce Lake are the attractive setting for many homes.

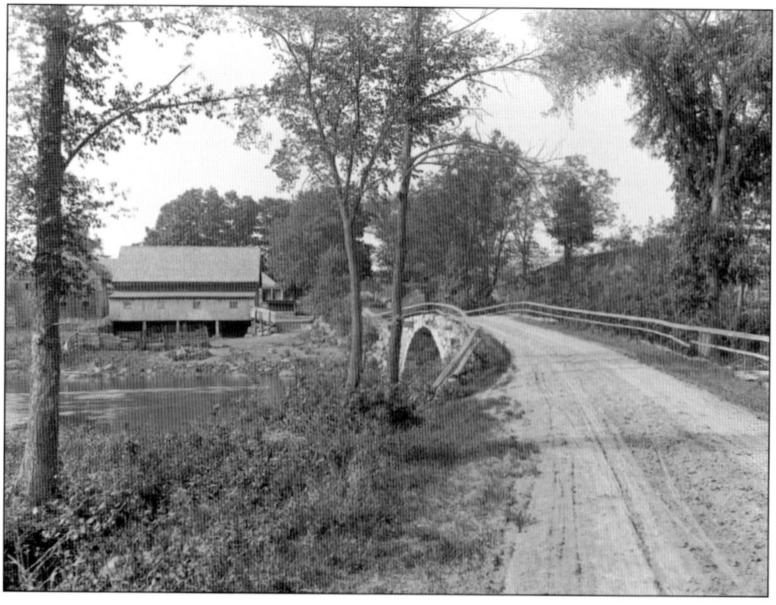

The Carr Bridge, built in the mid-1800s, carries Jones Road over Beard Brook at the intersection of Beard Road. This is a two-arch bridge of pleasing proportions. It is characterized by short, steep approaches at both ends. They have helped prevent damage to the bridge in times of high water because water can pass around the bridge.

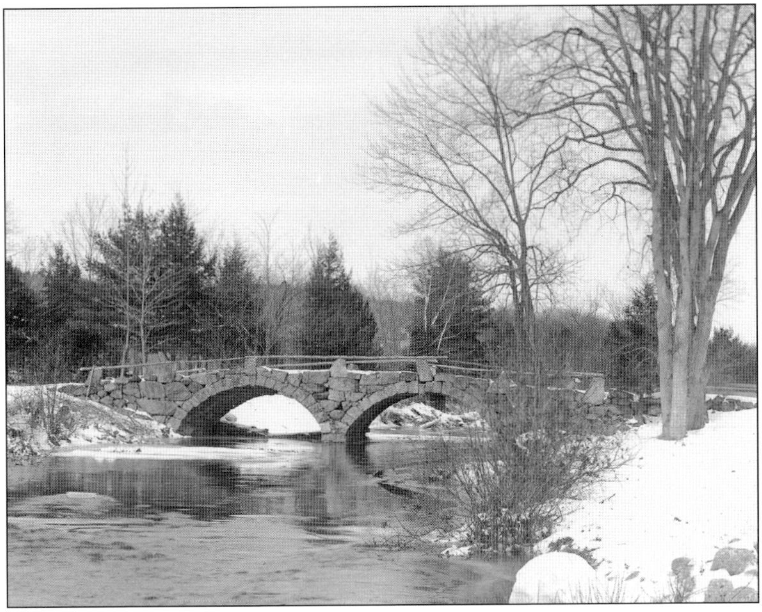

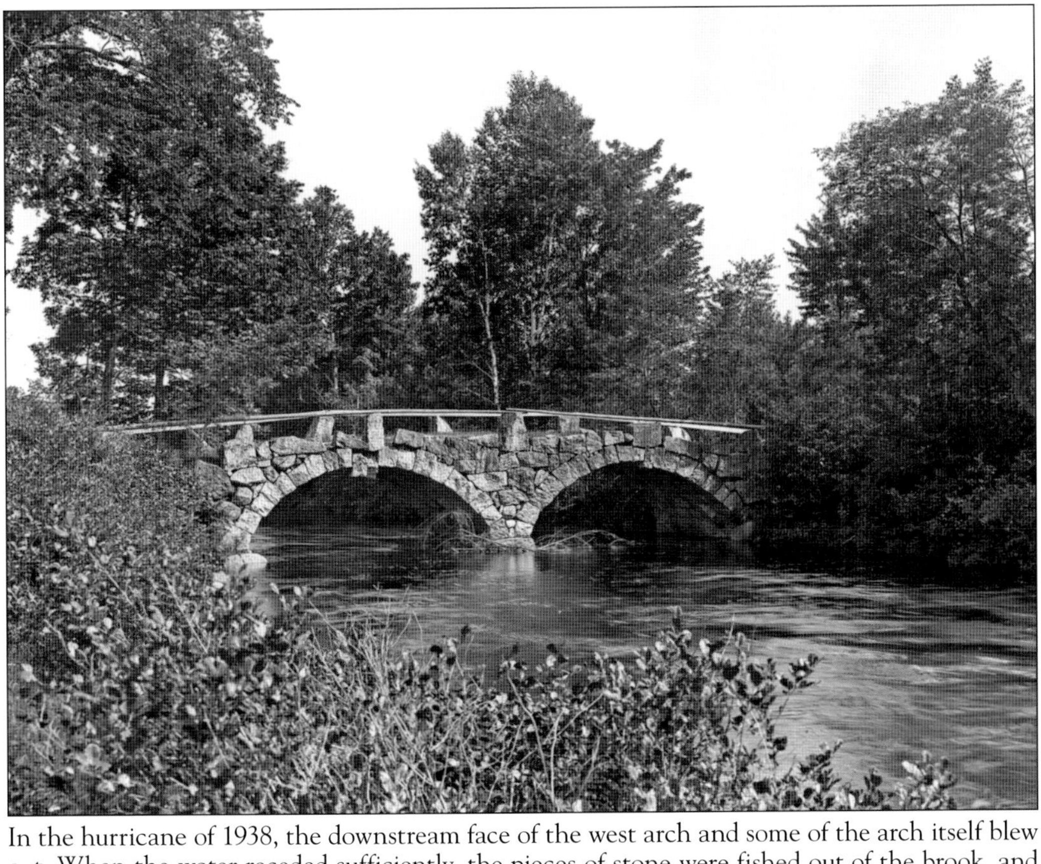

In the hurricane of 1938, the downstream face of the west arch and some of the arch itself blew out. When the water receded sufficiently, the pieces of stone were fished out of the brook, and the bridge was put back together. The New Hampshire Department of Transportation rates this bridge at six tons capacity. A computer study done by an MIT student rates it at 69 tons.

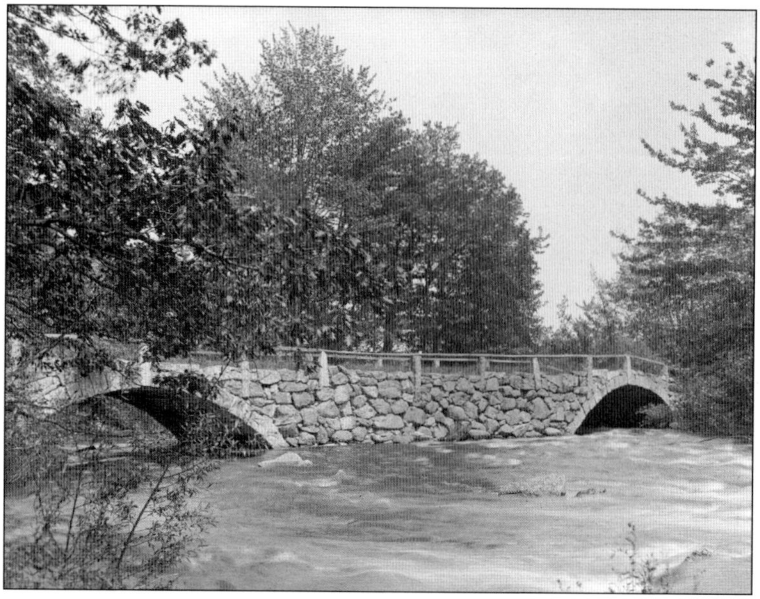

The Second New Hampshire Turnpike Bridges, built in 1864, carry the turnpike over the North Branch River, just south of the intersection with Sawmill Road near the Fuller Tannery. These are two separate bridges connected by wharfing over a small island.

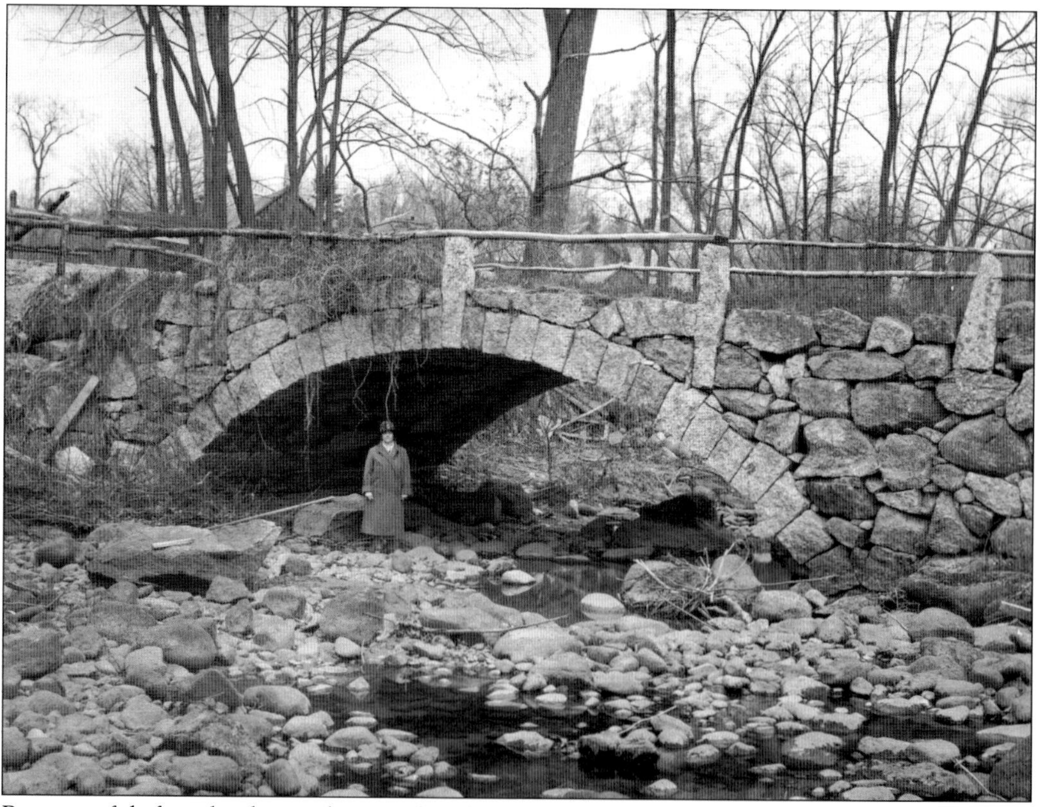

Because of shifting by the southern end of the northern span, the arch became very asymmetric to the point of probable collapse. The two spans were totally rebuilt in 2001 using reinforced concrete construction, but with a very careful reconstruction using the original split-stone facing. The result is a bridge very closely resembling the original, but with a much higher capacity to carry the heavy traffic loads on the road.

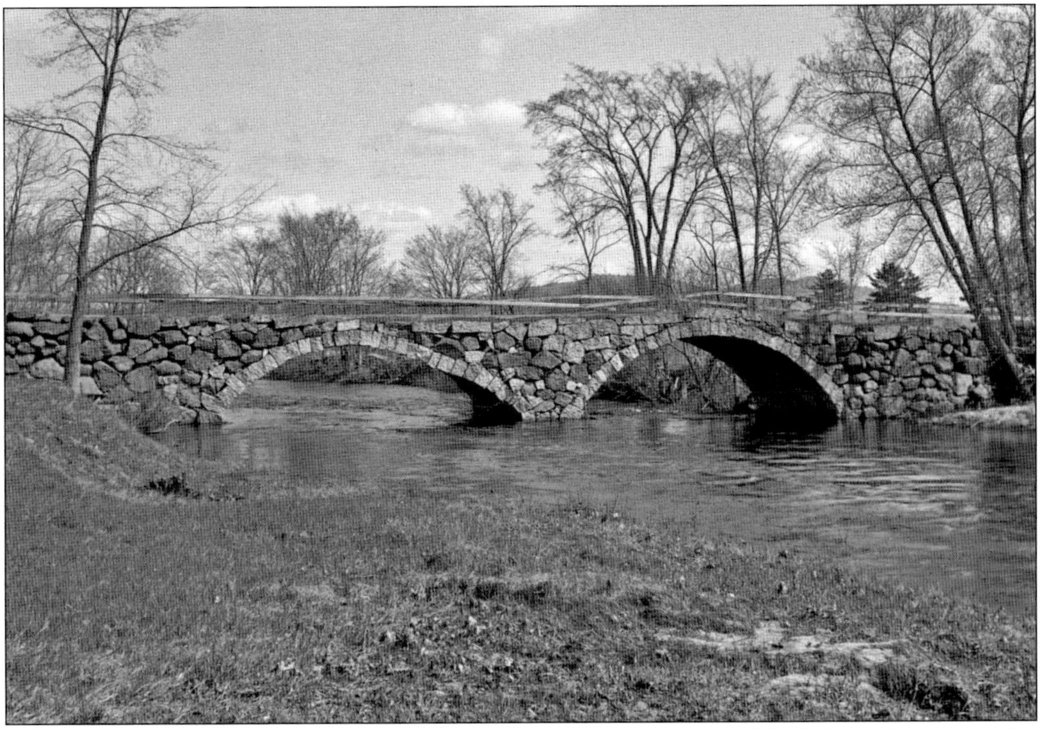

The Sawyer Bridge, built around 1866, carries Antrim Road over the North Branch River at the West Main Street intersection. It was the last stone arch bridge to be built in Hillsborough. This bridge provided a much shorter and less roundabout route between Hillsborough Bridge Village and the rapidly growing and quaintly named Antrim P.O. Village. This is a double-arch bridge with flat arches. Such arches are considered more aesthetically pleasing, but are subject to shifting and failure because of the higher lateral forces on the abutments. It was critical that abutments be very substantial. Due to such shifting, the northern arch of the bridge became very asymmetrical over time. Nonetheless, this bridge continued in service until it was rebuilt many years later.

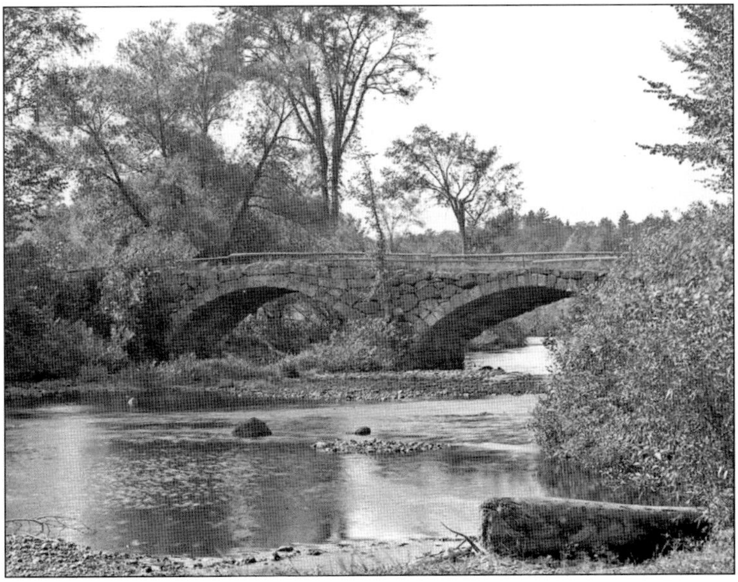

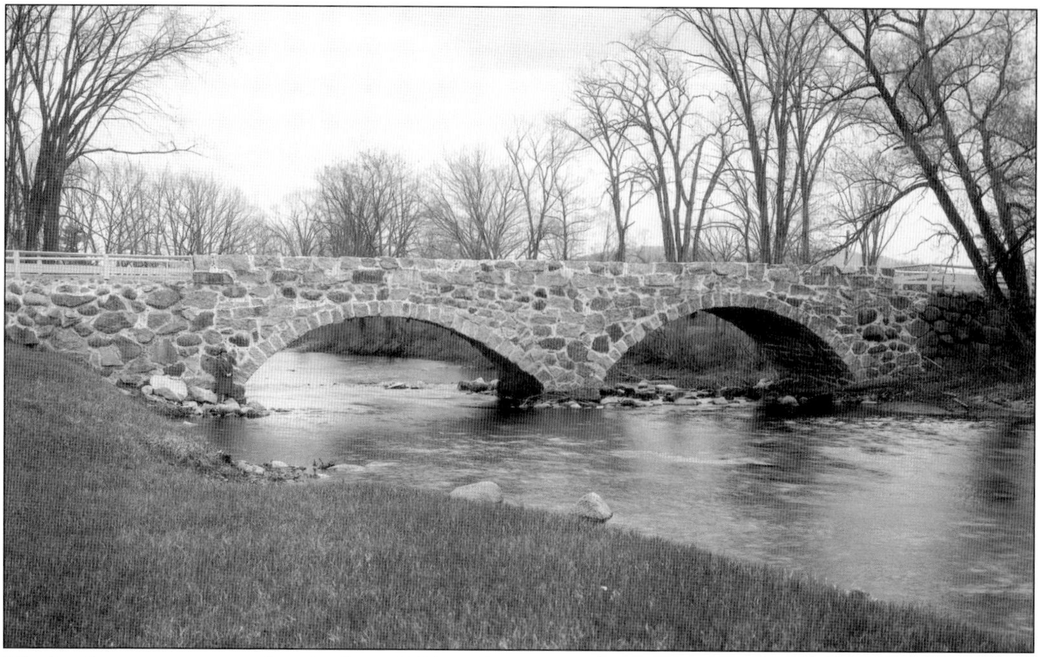

The bridge was extensively rebuilt in 1926 with mortared construction. Stone railings were added, so the appearance of the bridge changed significantly. This bridge was bypassed in 1988 by a modern bridge of reinforced concrete construction with split-stone facing. The old bridge has been recently repaired and restored much closer to its original appearance with the stone railings removed. Pictured at left is Mrs. Shutliff, whose husband, Arthur, took the photograph.

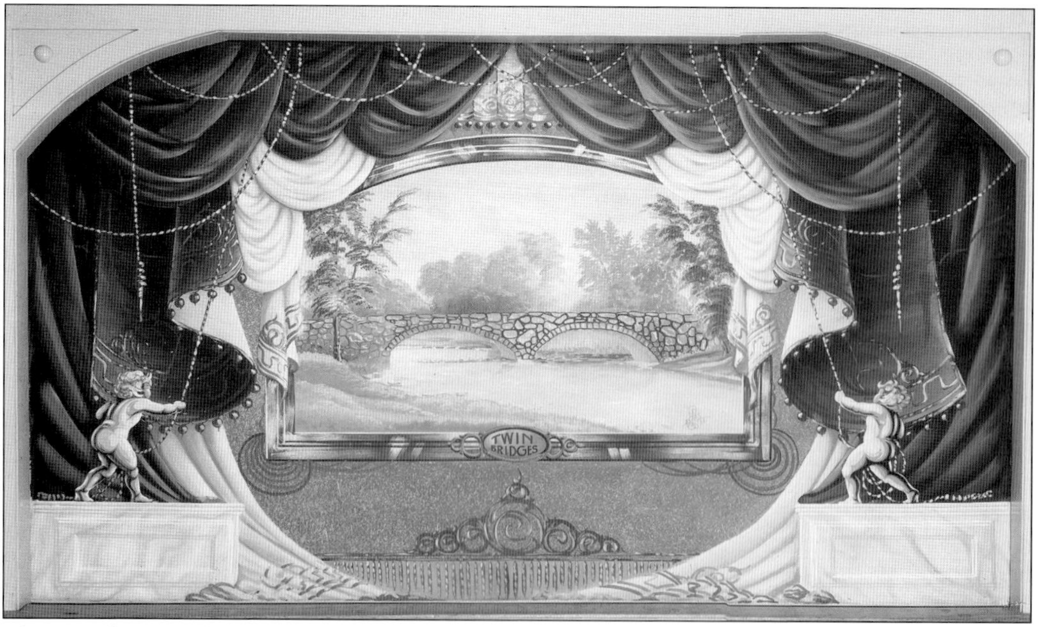

This is a photograph of the Twin Bridge stage curtain in use at the grange hall over the ice cream parlor in Central Square. Three curtains were found and rescued by Art and Bea Gillette and eventually restored, two of which are displayed in the Heritage Museum in the old firehouse including Twin Bridge and a curtain advertising local businesses in Hillsborough.

Four

MILLS AND RAILS

With the dawn of the industrial era, Hillsborough became known for nearly a century as a mill town and railroad center. The center of Hillsborough's industrial success was the Contoocook River. The town's growth can be attributed to the ingenuity of industrious men who were able to harness the power of the river water and utilize it to power mills. Gersham Keyes constructed the first sawmill built along the river in 1739. With its success, other sawmills and gristmills soon followed, including Archibald Taggart's, Charles Hartwell's at the foot of Loon pond, William Rumrill's at Bridge Village, and the Jackman Brothers' Mill in Lower Village.

At the turn of the 19th century, Hillsborough was one of a handful of towns to pioneer in the manufacturing of cotton and wool. The third cotton mill ever built in the state, the New Hampshire Cotton and Woolen factory, was incorporated in Hillsborough in 1811. Along the south bank of the river, Joshua Marcy built a mill in 1828 that manufactured cotton cloth, shirting, and sheeting, and was where the first ever cotton-wrapping twine was made in America. In 1865, John B. Smith purchased the Marcy Mill and founded the Contoocook Mill, where knit woolen hosiery, shirts, and undergarments were manufactured. In 1875, the Hillsboro Woolen Mill was built. High-quality woven woolen cloth for suiting, cloaking, and overcoats were manufactured here. By the middle of the 20th century, the mills became obsolete and were closed down, and the properties sold.

A major factor in the industrial boom was the arrival of the railroad in Hillsborough. The Contoocook Valley Railroad was incorporated on June 4, 1848, and soon thereafter, tracks connected to the cities of New Hampshire and with the major hubs in Massachusetts. In 1849, the Hillsborough Railroad Depot opened. On average, nine trains would leave the station every day with the same number arriving daily. Later, the railroad was extended to Peterborough and beyond. For almost a century, the Hillsboro Railroad Depot was the gateway to the town, but in 1938, floods destroyed the track to Henniker and the little old depot closed down forever.

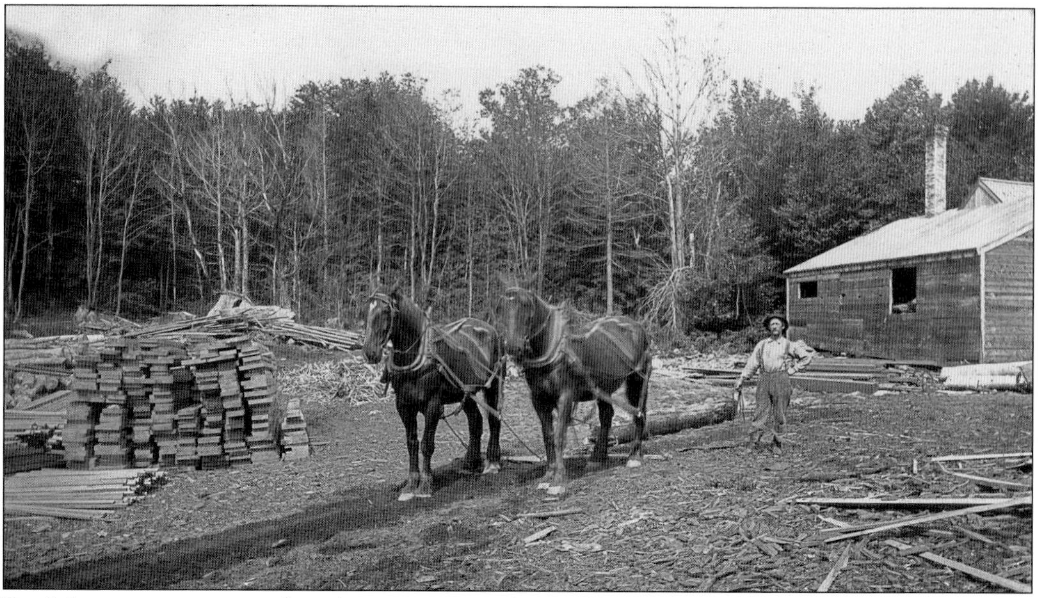

Draft horses were essential in the operations of sawmills. They were used to drag fresh-cut logs from the forest to the river for transport or to the mill directly. They also pulled wagons filled with the finished products to their final destination. Here a proud sawmill worker is posing with his team of horses.

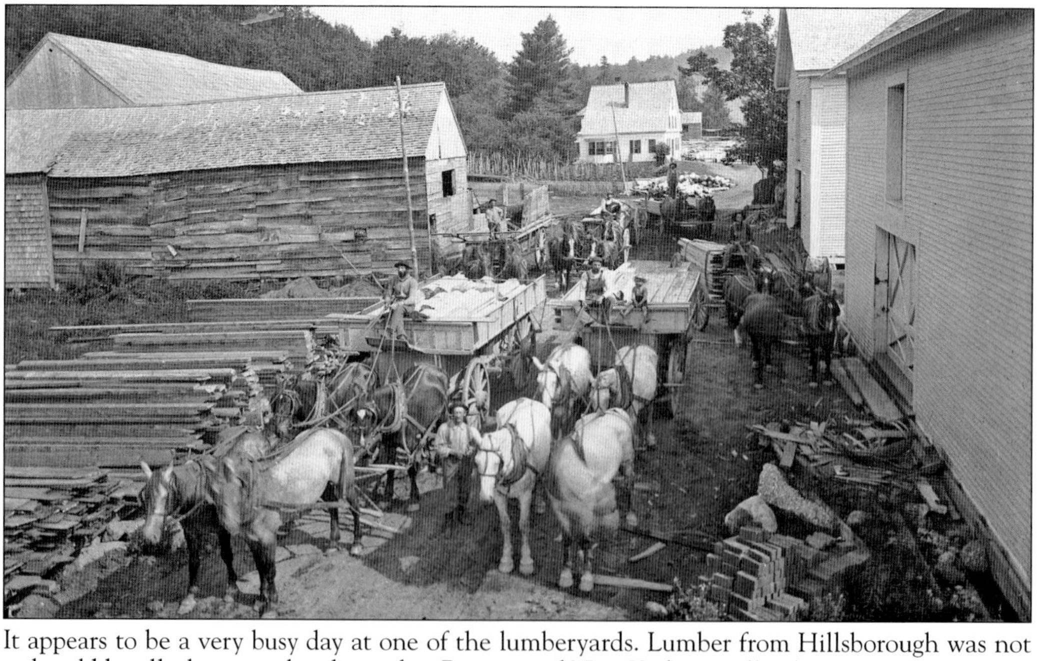

It appears to be a very busy day at one of the lumberyards. Lumber from Hillsborough was not only sold locally, but was also shipped to Boston and New York. Locally, the lumber was used to build farmhouses, to supply the box making operations at the Marcy Mill, and to make carriages and furniture.

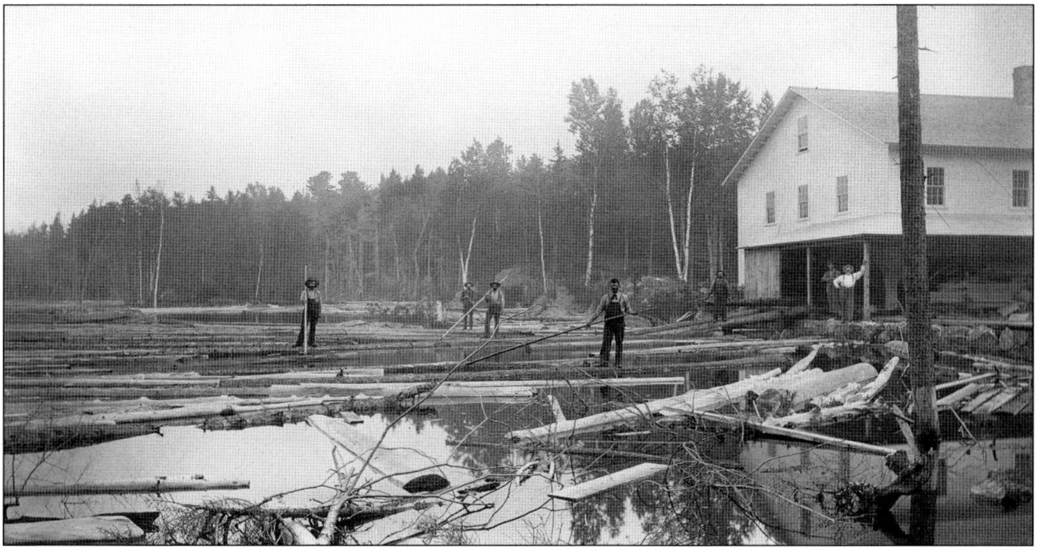

Sawmill workers would sort logs on the millpond. This could be a dangerous job for the rookie, but the experienced man worked the logs with speed, ease, and agility. The men posing here appear to be masters at jumping from log to log and keeping their balance as they push logs into the sawmill.

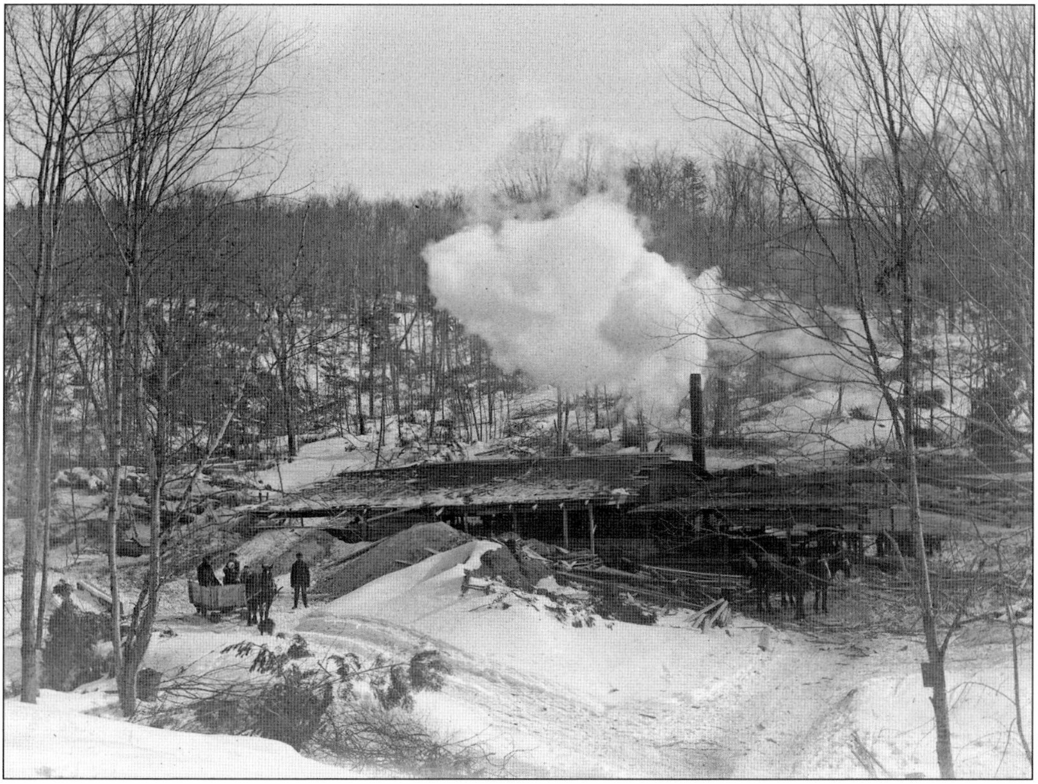

This steam sawmill operated near the farms of John Davis and Richard Crane on East Washington Road. Even during the wintertime, the mill was in full operation as it was easier to bring logs out of the woods.

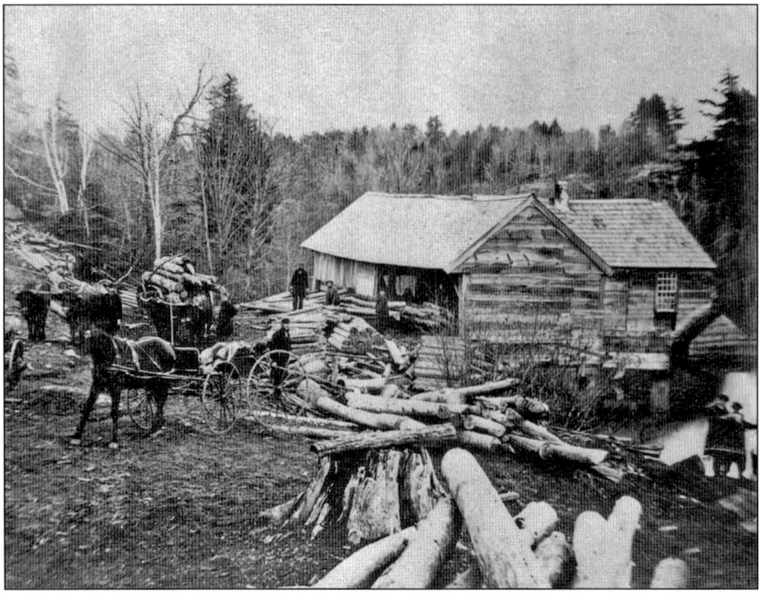

Along the North Branch River in the Lower Village was the Grimes-Manahan sawmill. The Jackman Brothers, very capable construction contractors of that time, later acquired it. They built many of the farmhouses in Hillsborough, as well as the Union Chapel and Saint Mary's Catholic Church.

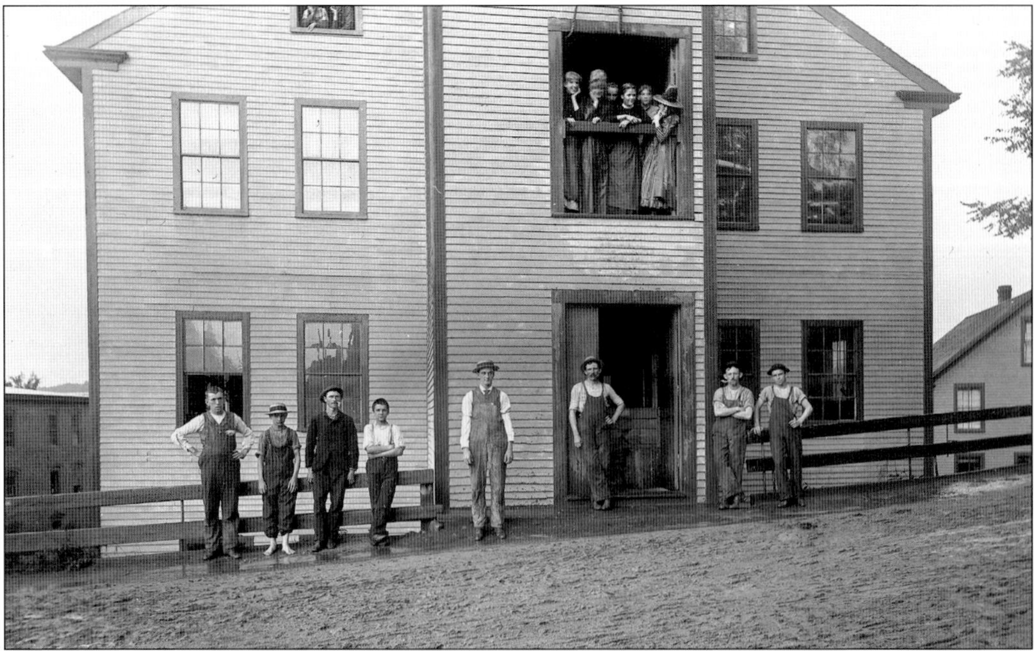

The Albion Mill, seen here with mill workers posing in front, was built in 1870. The granite and brick basement housed a water wheel that was powered from the Contoocook River. The second floor contained the carding operations. Often the owner, George McDonnell, would throw handfuls of pennies from the top floor of the Albion building down to kids outside when they got out of school.

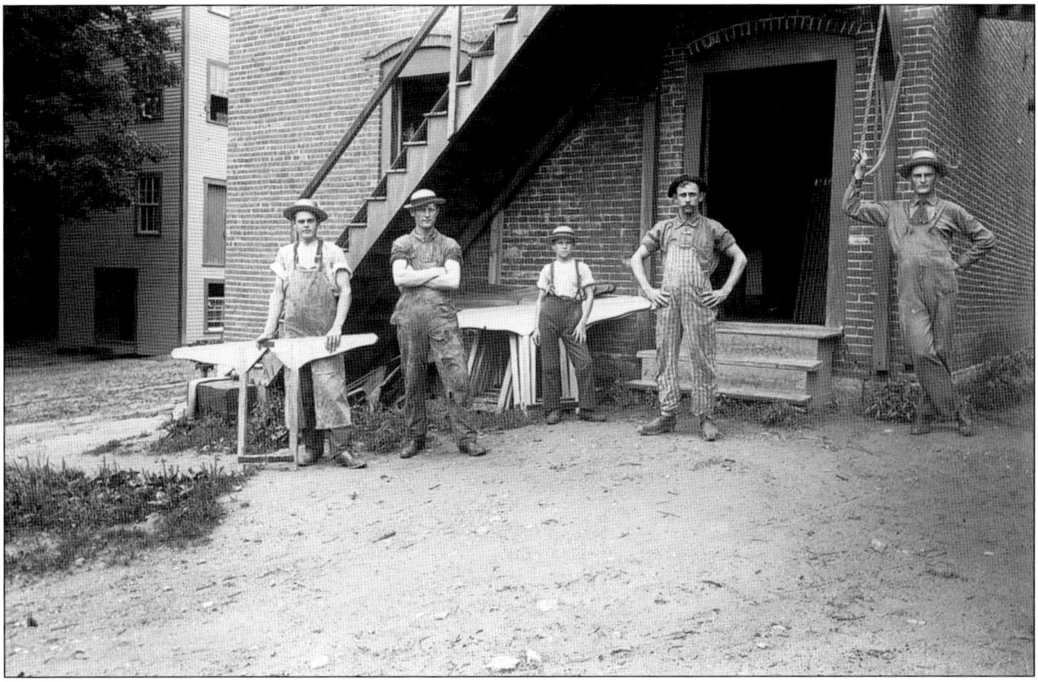

A mill yard crew, including Charles Nelson on the left, poses with shirt forms behind the Marcy Mill's office. Some of these men appear to be wearing wooden-soled clogs with leather uppers. Clogs were favored by those working in damp or wet conditions, and may indicate these workmen labored in the dye house.

This image captured a great view of the J.B. Smith complex. Pictured from left to right are the Hosiery Mill, the brick management office, the brick picker house, and the dye house. The location of each building was imperative to the orderly operations of the manufacturing production line.

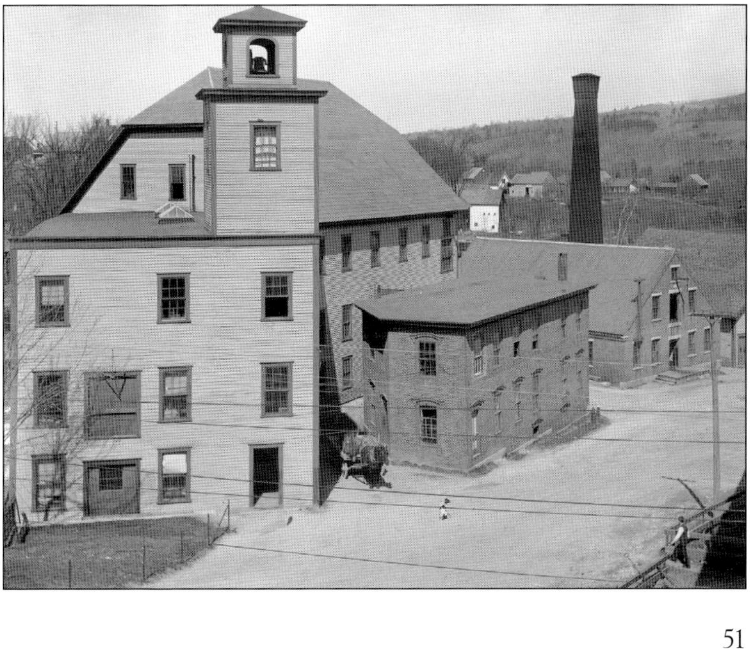

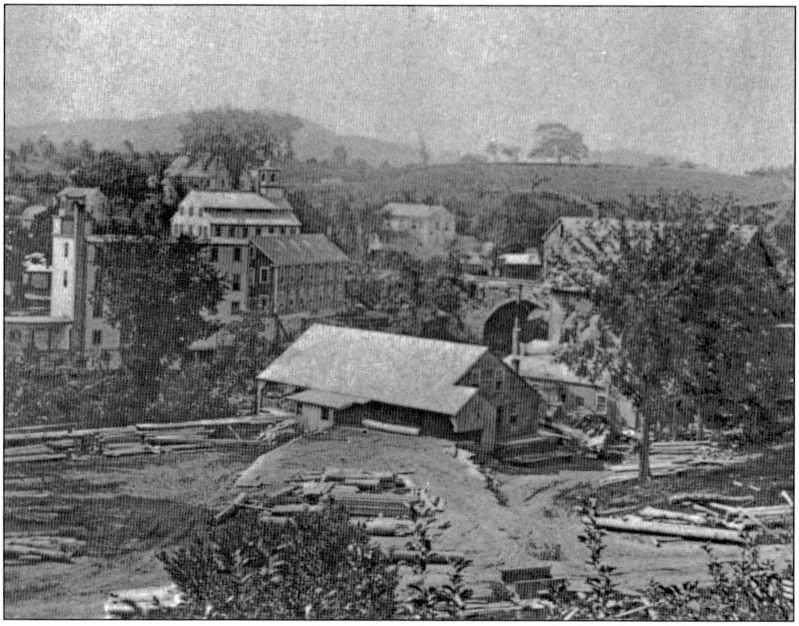

This panoramic view from atop a hill in Bridge Village includes the Hosiery Mill, the lumber mill owned by Samuel Clement, and the stone arch bridge spanning the Contoocook River. When the mill was closed, several Hillsborough kids used to fish for trout through the floorboards.

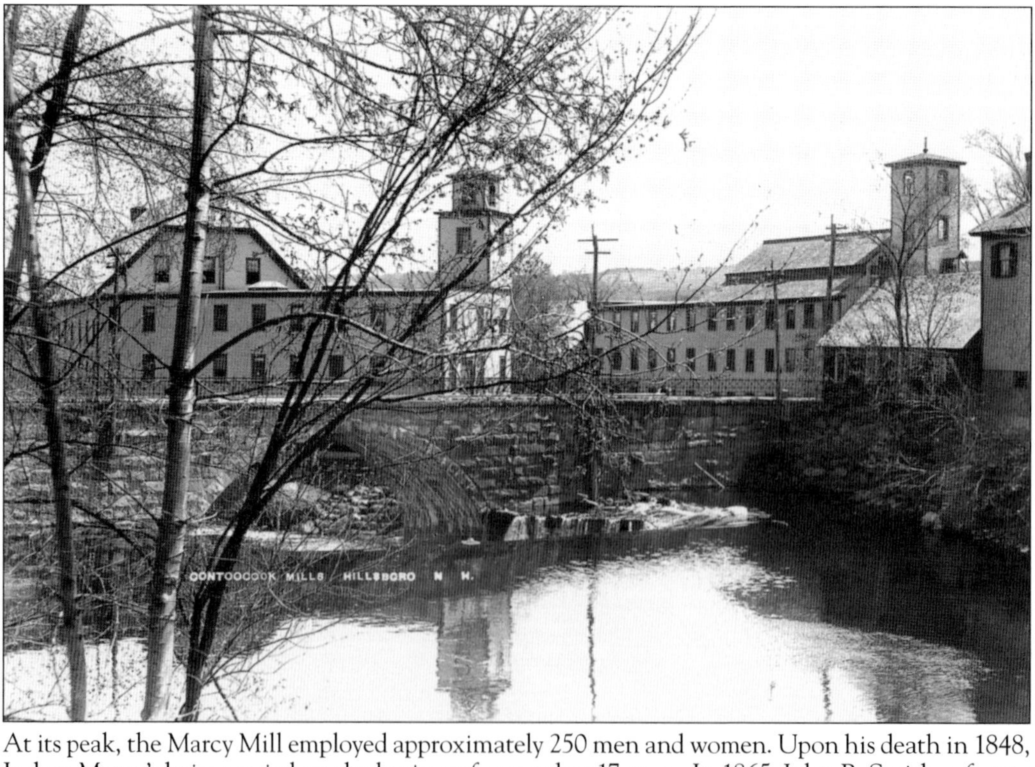

At its peak, the Marcy Mill employed approximately 250 men and women. Upon his death in 1848, Joshua Marcy's heirs carried on the business for another 17 years. In 1865, John B. Smith, a future New Hampshire governor, purchased the mill. He was successful from the start, and installed new knitting machinery and continued to build additions throughout his tenure as owner.

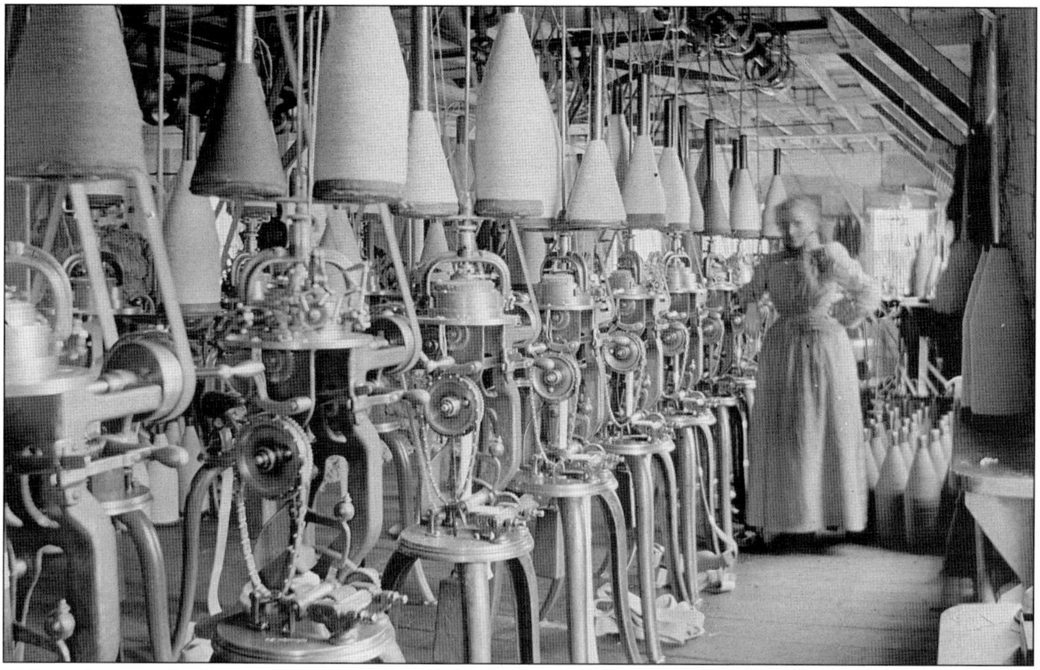

Taken during the late 1800s or early 1900s, this photograph shows machinery in the Hosiery Mill that made knit tubes for stockings. At the next stage in production, heels and toes were added in the looper room. Pictured here are top knitters—circular knitting machines run by a belt-and-pulley system.

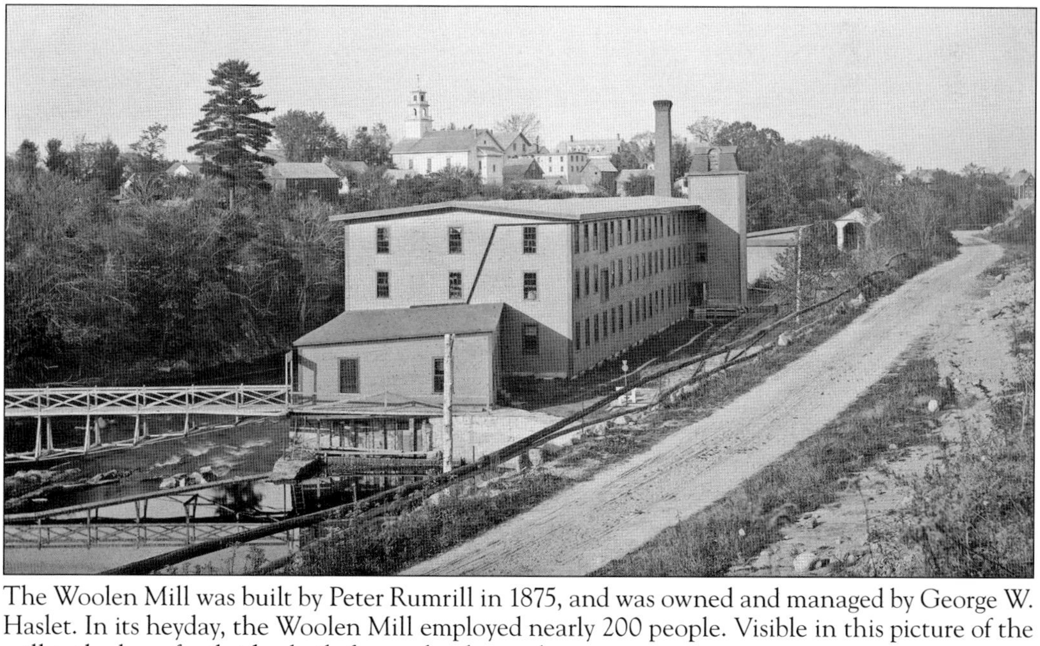

The Woolen Mill was built by Peter Rumrill in 1875, and was owned and managed by George W. Haslet. In its heyday, the Woolen Mill employed nearly 200 people. Visible in this picture of the mill is the long footbridge built for use by the workers.

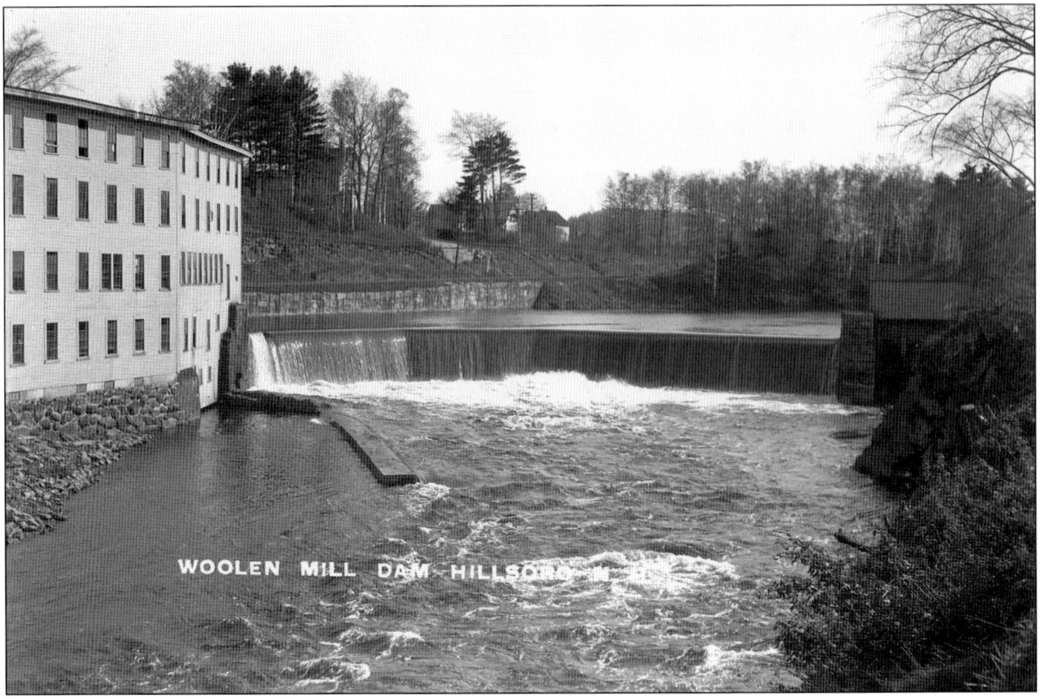

This picture of the Woolen Mill crib dam was taken in May 1927. The water of the Contoocook River was diverted to the water wheel located just under this building, providing power to the mill. Eldon "Dude" Kemp removed the dam in 1939 after it was damaged in the 1938 hurricane.

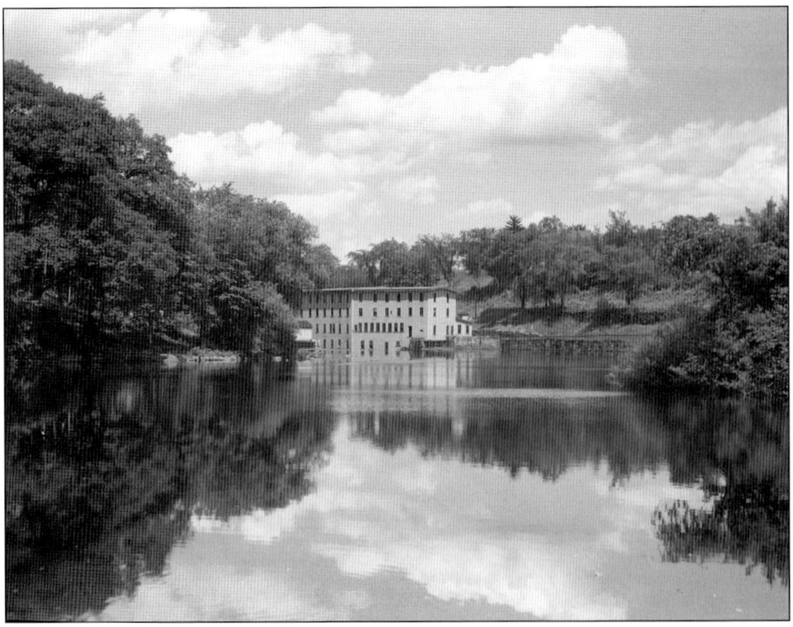

It was a quiet day on the Contoocook River when this photograph was taken in June 1934, upstream from the Woolen Mill. Normally, the mill whistle sounded two distinct long blasts at 5:00 a.m., six days a week. The typical schedule for a worker was Monday through Friday from 7:00 a.m. to 6:00 p.m., and Saturdays from 7:00 a.m. to noon.

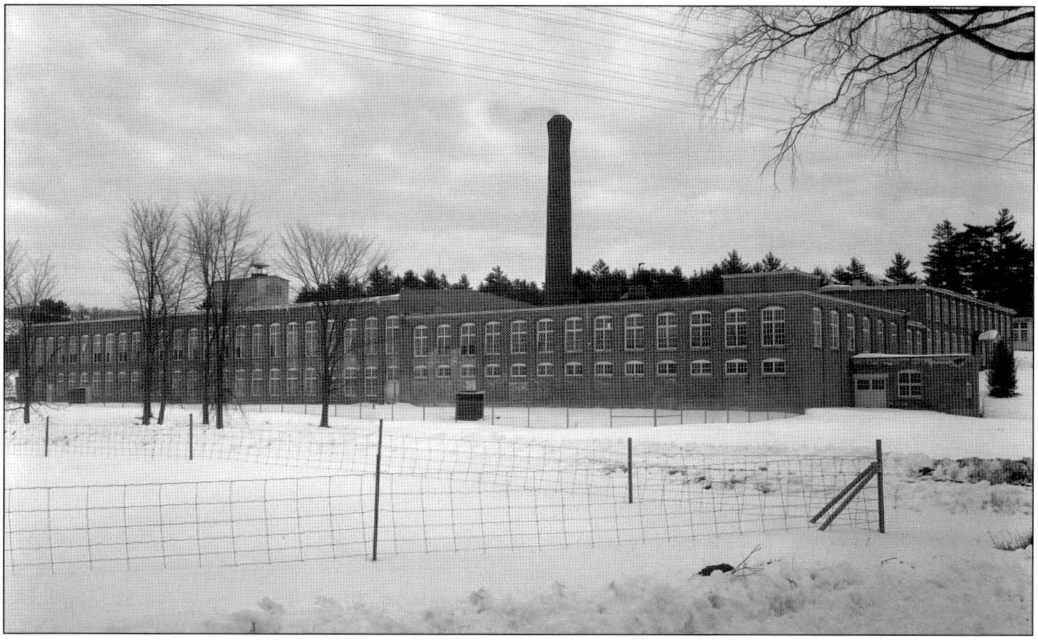

In 1782, Joseph Putnam established a grist and sawmill businesses near the Great Falls of the Contoocook River, located just south of Hillsborough. In 1819, Moody Butler acquired the site and converted the mill into a papermaking facility. The main ingredients for this venture were readily available—an abundant supply of flax from the neighboring farms and plentiful clear, soft mountain water. In 1832, John W. Flagg, Butler's descendant, installed the latest papermaking machinery, the British Fourdrinier machines, becoming the first American paper mill to use machines to make paper. In 1870, the mill was renamed Monadnock Paper Mills and became known for its high-quality paper products. Pictured above is a c. 1930 panoramic winter view of the paper mill. Since it first opened, many residents of Hillsborough have been employed there and some appear in the 1887 group picture below.

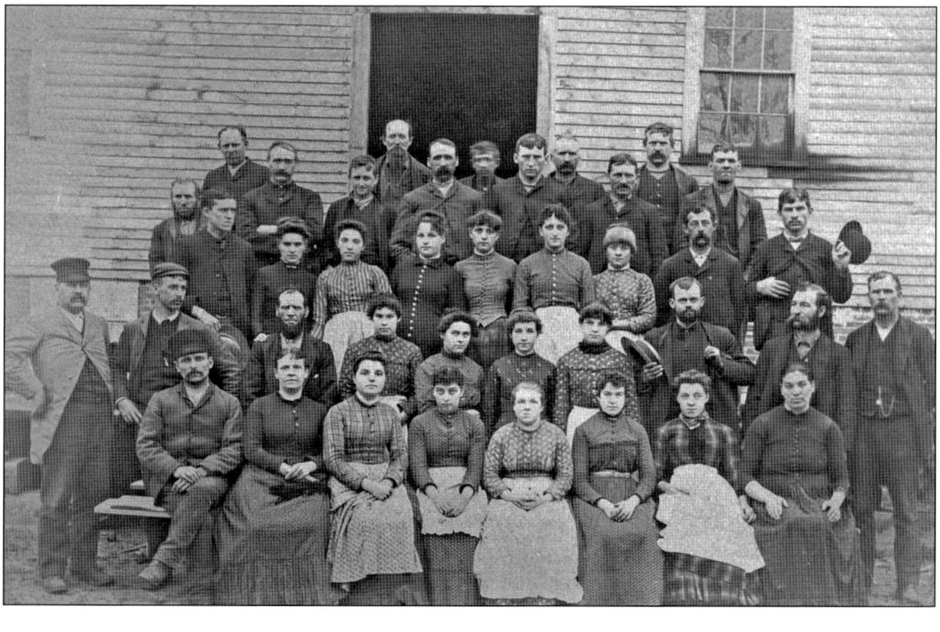

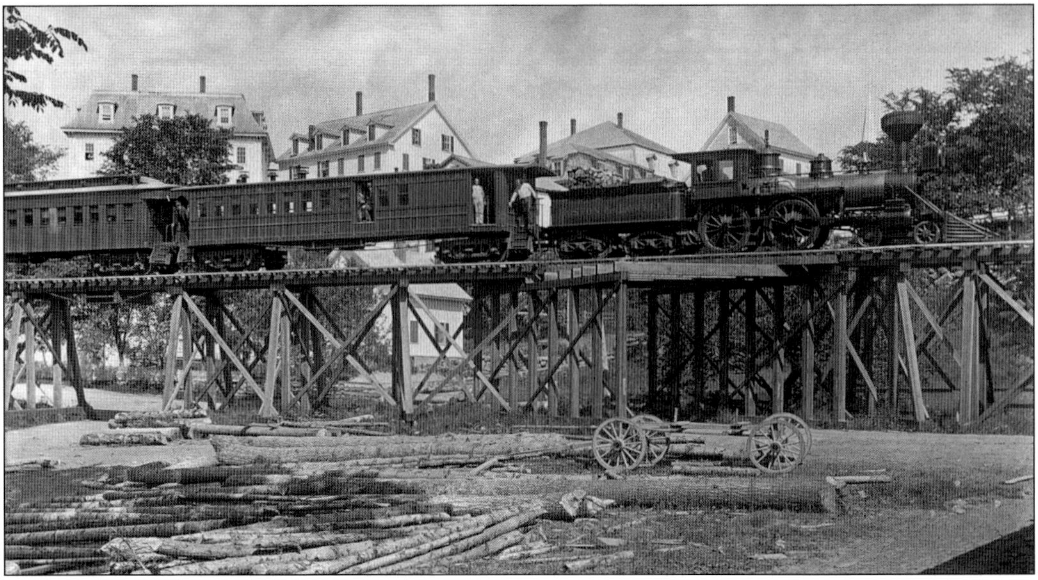

This photograph captures the Boston and Lowell train as it is crossing over the 1870-built trestle through Bridge Village. The train trestle through Hillsborough was unique because it was one of only a few that actually had curved tracks along its route. In the background are the mills and tenement buildings that housed the workers. The locomotive is an early wood-burning engine typical of the mid-19th century.

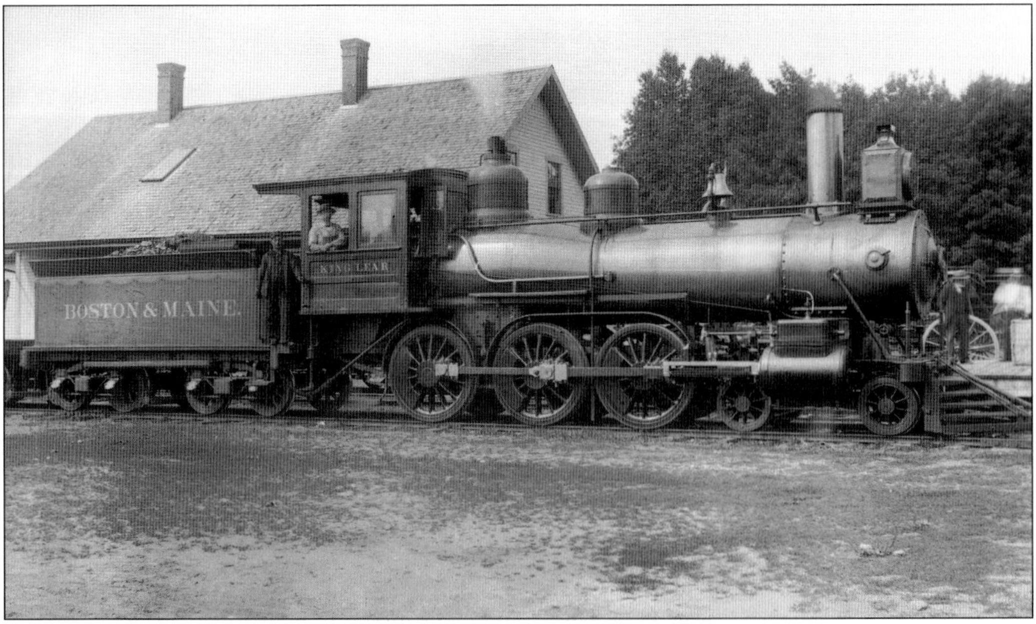

Stopped at the station is the Boston and Maine locomotive named the *King Lear*, a 4-6-0 ten-wheeler. Attached behind it is the tender filled with coal and water to power the steam engine. Other locomotives plying this torturous and mountainous branch were the *General Pierce* and the *Contoocook*.

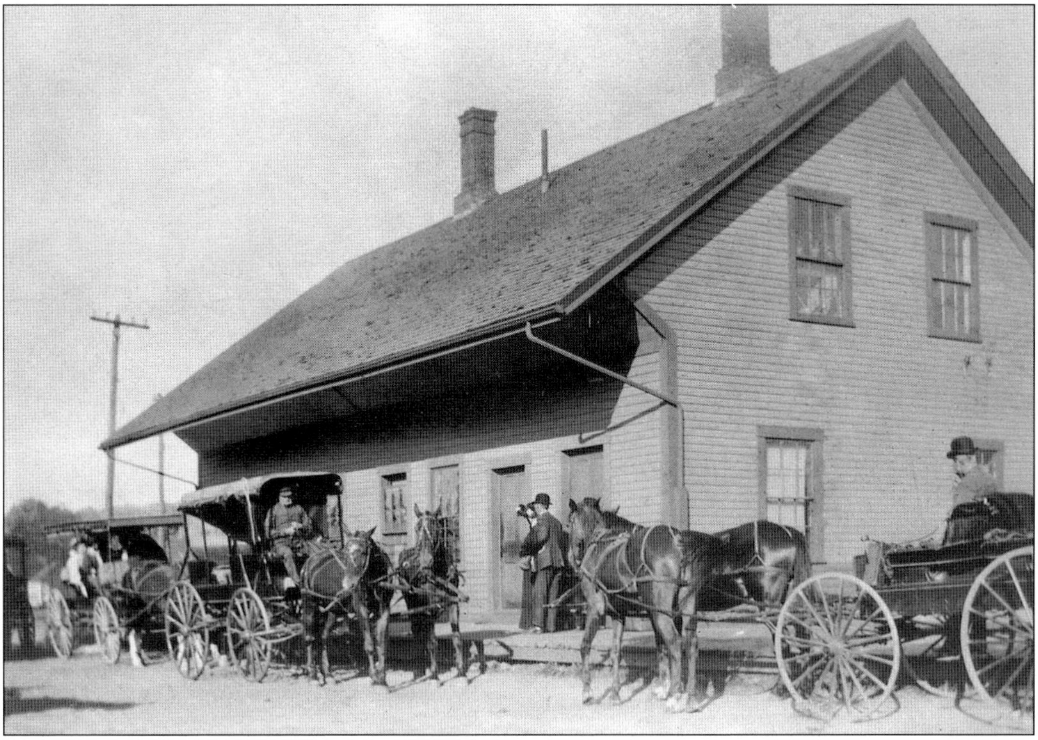

On this side of the railroad depot, horse-drawn carriages from the Valley Hotel would wait daily for guests, no matter the season or weather. In 1921, Leon Hill was the station agent at the depot, Joe Vaillancourt was the night man who cared for the engines in the roundhouse, and Joe Stock was a train conductor for many years.

The Hillsborough Railroad Depot had two sets of tracks. The tracks on the left were for freight trains, which were unloaded and loaded in a building behind the depot. The tracks on the right were for passenger trains. There was a telegraph office a short distance down the tracks, and a Railway Express office affiliated with the railroad in a separate building adjacent to the depot.

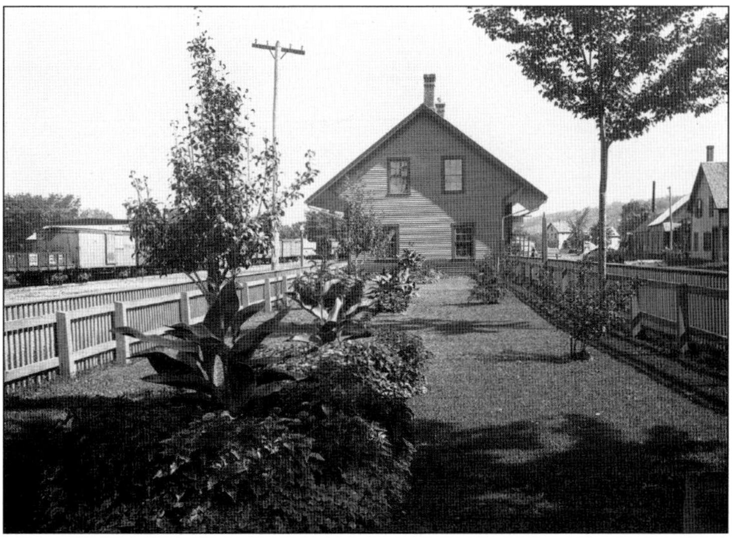

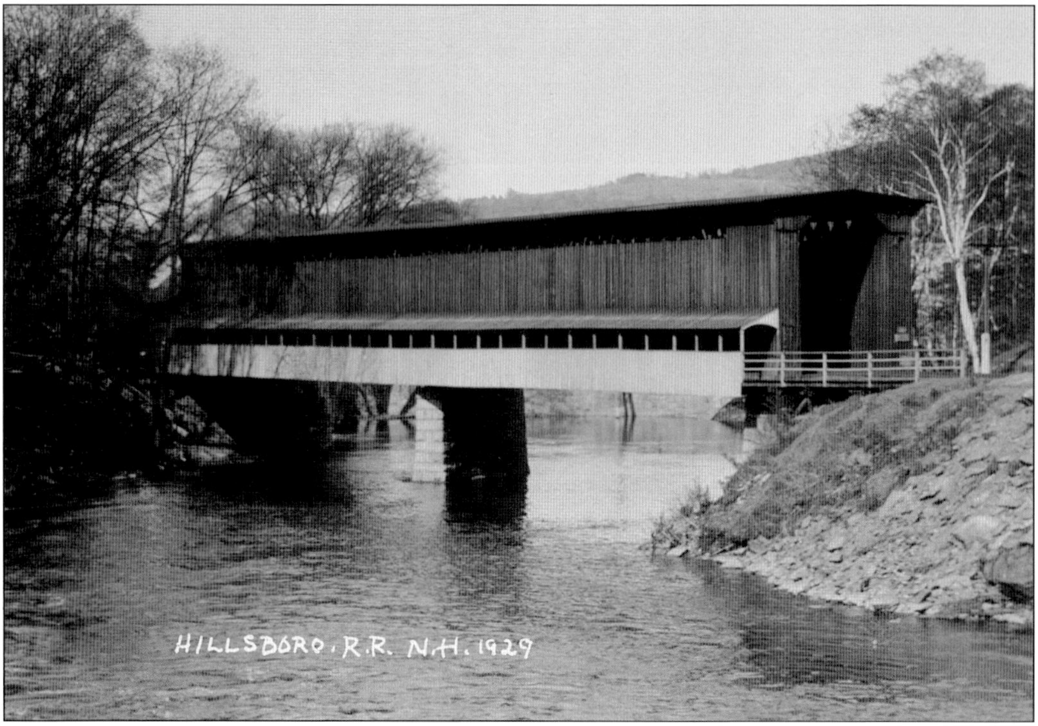

Whitney and Childs of Henniker built the original covered bridge in 1878 at a cost of $1,097.66. However, it was destroyed on July 2, 1899, by a fire with an unknown cause. It was rebuilt and completed in October 1899 by the Berlin Bridge Company at a cost of $7,147.48. The c. 1929 picture above shows the rebuilt bridge, with a span over the Contoocook of 134 feet and a clearance of 23 feet above the water. Below is a closer look at the covered pedestrian walkway. It is said that the young Frankie Camera would often bet children 10¢ that he could run across the pedestrian walkway roof faster than someone could run along the tracks inside. Frankie always won.

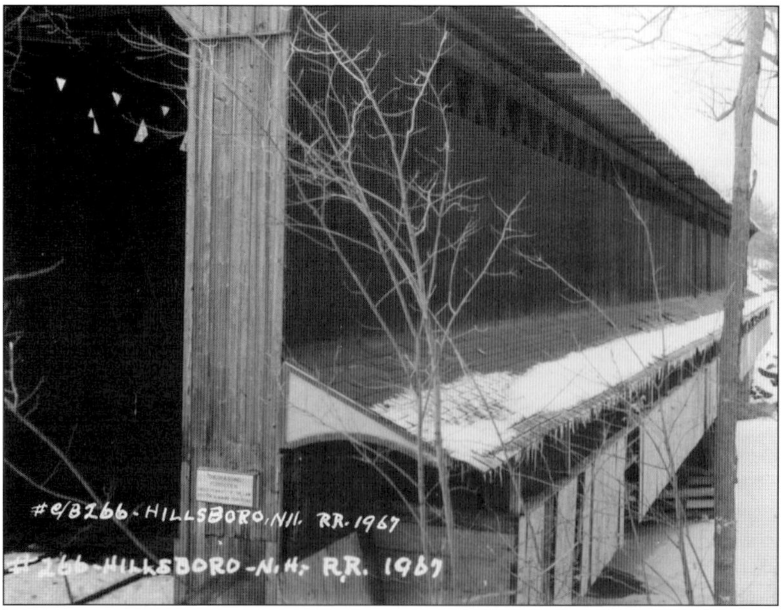

Running past the Woods Woolen Mill in March 1963 was a diesel-switching locomotive with snowplow clearing the tracks, with Clarence Spaulding as engineer. Even though the hurricane of 1938 destroyed a large portion of the railroad track to Henniker, for just over two decades some portions still had limited use.

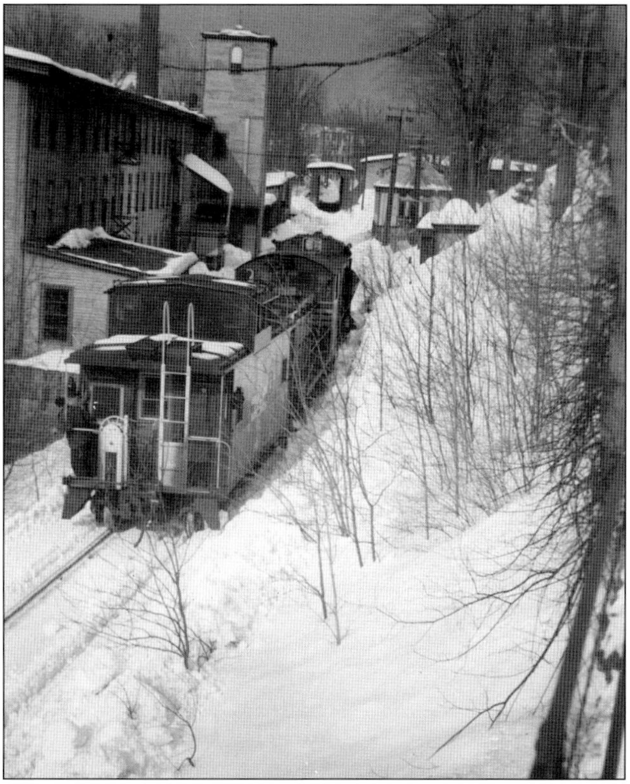

The flagman pictured here was Civil War veteran Mr. Blanchard. It was his responsibility to signal the approach of trains at the Bridge Street grade crossing. Many positions offered by the railroads were occupied by veterans of the Civil War.

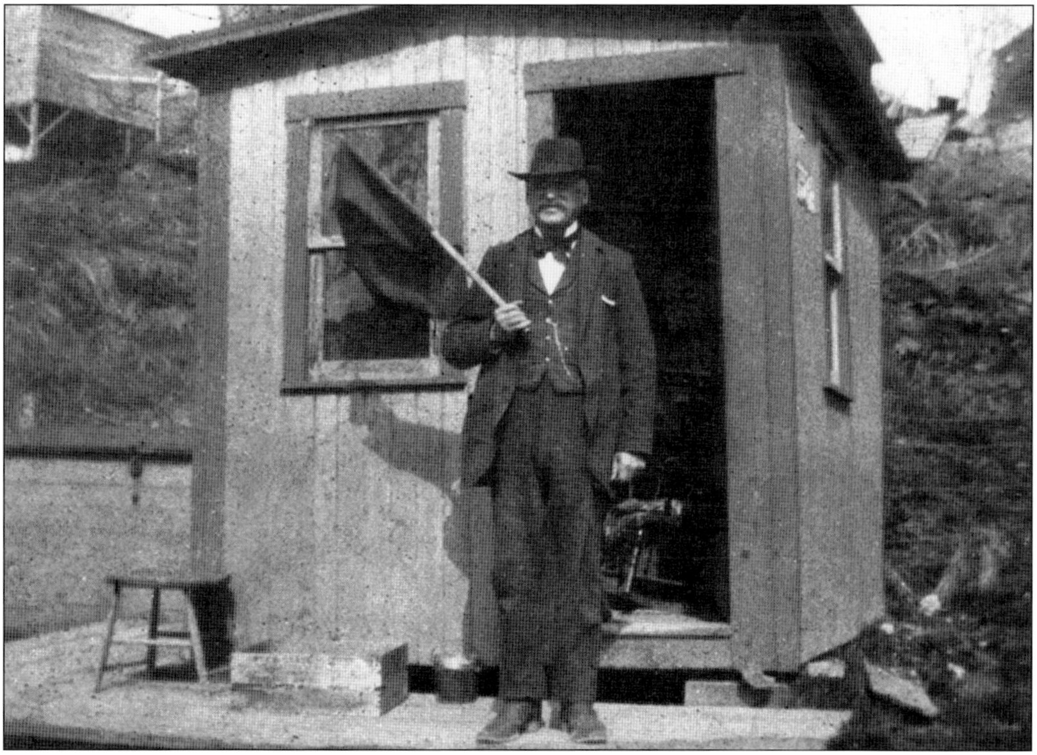

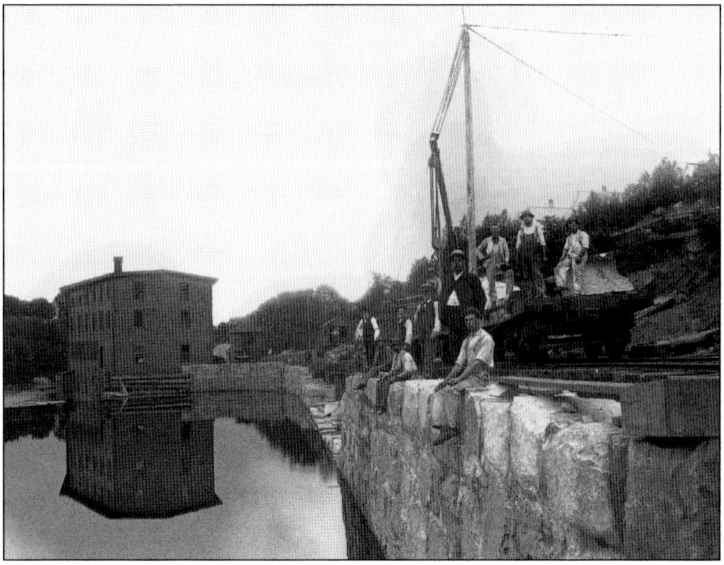

Workmen near the Woods Woolen Mill build a new split-granite-faced embankment to support the railroad track to replace the old wooden viaduct. When initially built, railroads in rural areas used less-expensive wooden construction, as was done for the viaduct at this location, as well as for the nearby bridge. If the rail line prospered, wooden construction was often replaced by more substantial stonework.

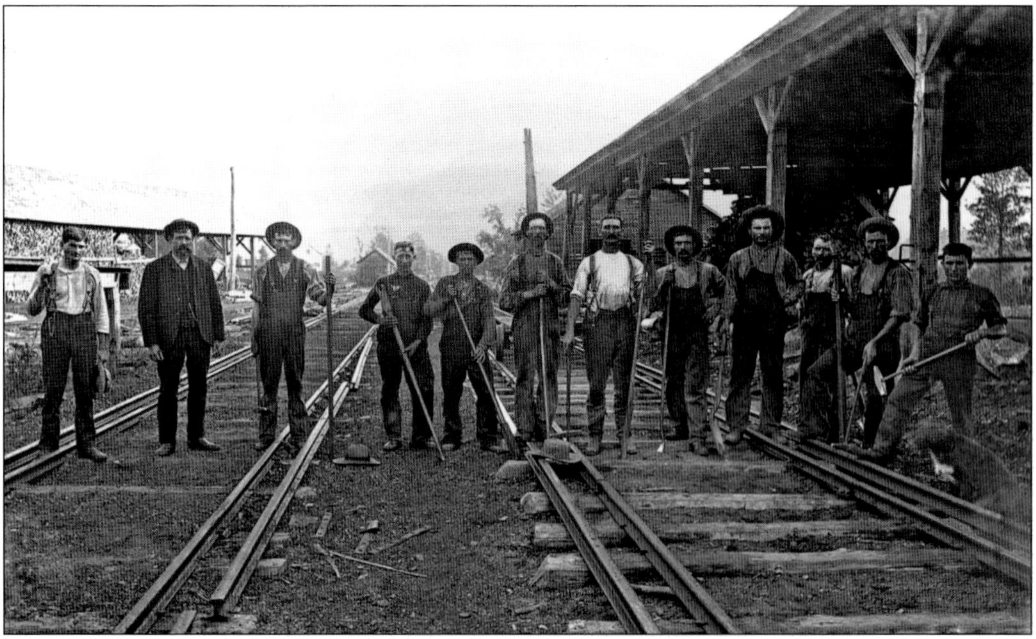

These railroad workers have been hard at work repairing the tracks at the Hillsborough depot. They are replacing badly worn rails. This work was all done by hand labor. The old rails had to be manhandled out and the replacement rails put in. Then the rails were bolted using long wrenches. Finally, the new rails had to be set to the proper width and fastened to the wooden ties with large spikes.

Five

On the Farm and at Work

Like most early settlements in New England, Hillsborough started out as a farming community. Early settlers cleared small plots of land and built one- or two-story farmhouses. Farmers were self-sufficient and were required to be jacks-of-all-trades. They made their own tools and did most work by hand. There was little need to go into town or to buy something from the general store. The wives of farmers made their own milk, butter, cheese, bread, and soap. Nothing was ever thrown away because it could always be put to good use in some way or another.

Most of the farms in Hillsborough were plotted on the side hills. The soil was hard to cultivate, but it did produce a decent crop every season. The most successful crops in town were potatoes, corn, wheat, barley, rye, oats, apples, and garden vegetables. With plenty of fields to pasture, settlers brought with them their cattle, sheep, chickens, and hogs. However, by the 1840s, the industrial boom had hit the town. With more and more farming machinery being introduced, there was less of a need for help on the farm. Also, with the emergence of manufacturing along the rivers and the inability to compete with the farms of the Midwest, the traditional family farm increasingly fell to the wayside in Hillsborough.

By the mid-1800s, various businesses and other enterprises developed in Hillsborough. Along the riverside, the mills, tanneries, machine shops, and manufactories were thriving. With a large growth in population, Bridge Village began to rapidly develop. Hotels, taverns, banks, drug stores, meat markets, dairies, and grocery stores lined the streets. People in service occupations, like physicians, dentists, and lawyers, were starting to settle in Hillsborough. Eventually, public services like post offices, fire precincts, water and sewer systems, and power and telephone lines were established in the town. Even with this growth that was on par with any major city in New Hampshire at the time, Hillsborough still had, and hopefully always will have, that small-town feel.

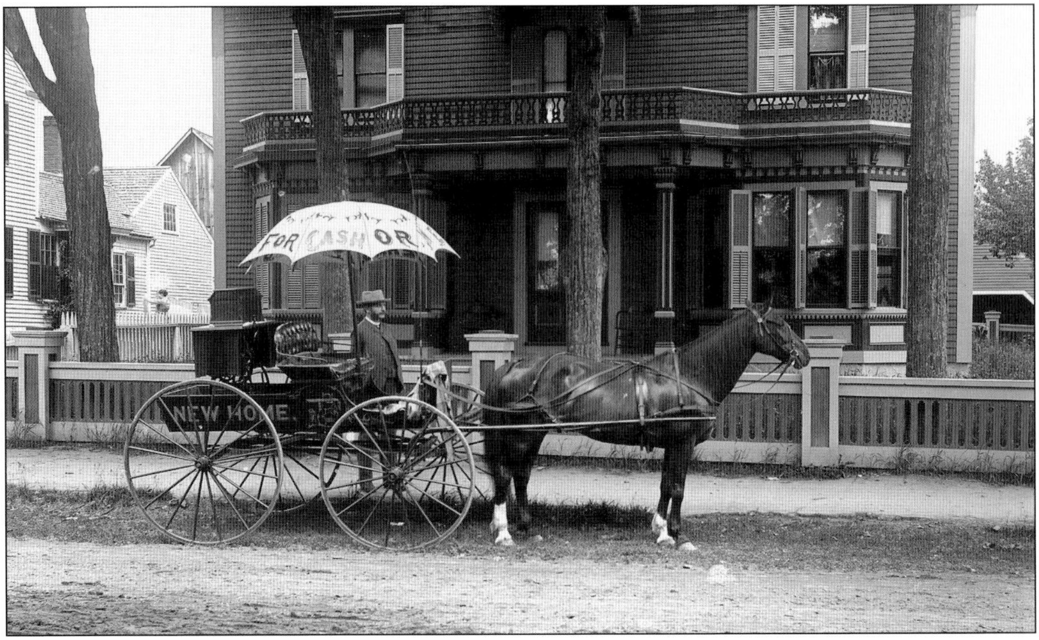

Given the ability to move product from Boston and New York by rail, traveling salesmen were able to market and sell merchandise as long as they had a horse and carriage. This door-to-door salesman is pitching the "Light running New Home Sewing Machine" by Leavitt and Brant of Boston, targeting young Hillsborough maidens with marriage prospects.

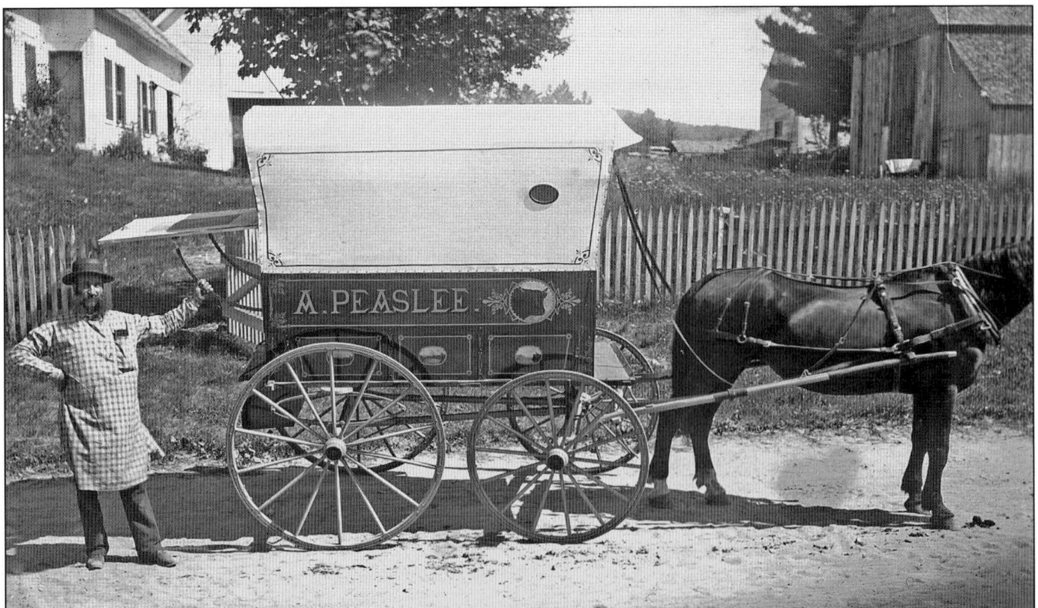

Meat products could also be distributed by horse and carriage. A.W. Peaslee, the town butcher, has readied his rig for morning deliveries. The Peaslee family of Hillsborough was also active in blacksmithing and axe-making until 1836, when their building was destroyed by fire.

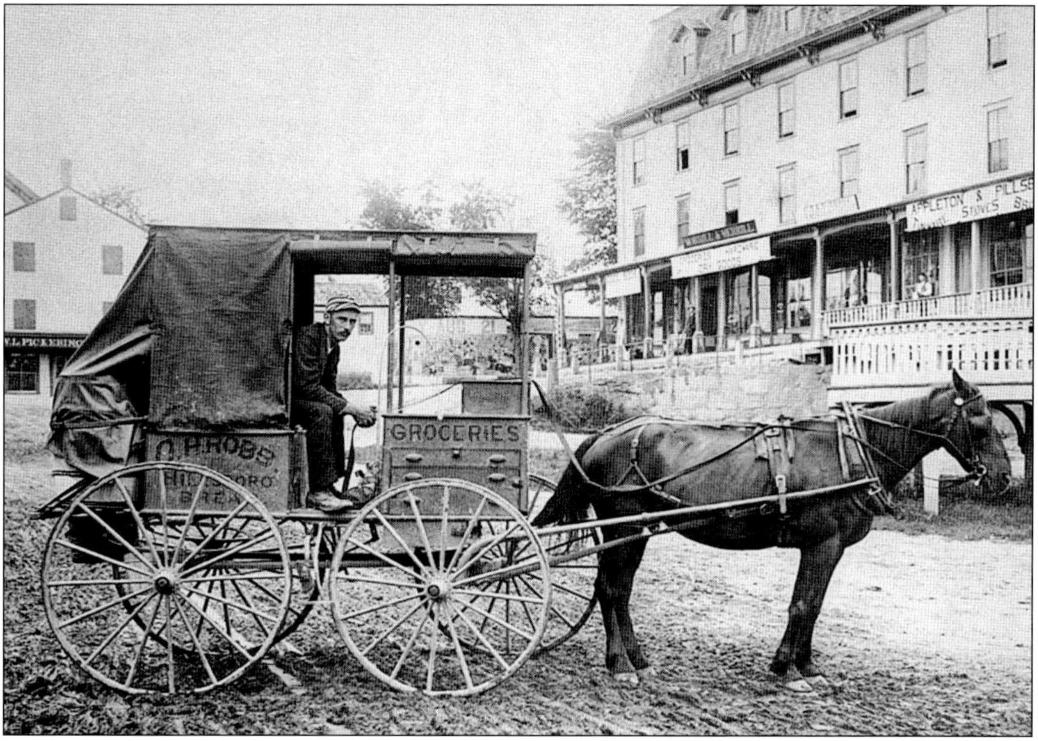

Every morning merchants would arrange transport on Main Street. Hillsborough was a distribution center for a large portion of the Contoocook Valley that was too distant from the larger cities of Manchester, Concord, and Keene. This c. 1890 photograph of O.H. Robb's grocery wagon was taken near the Opera House Block.

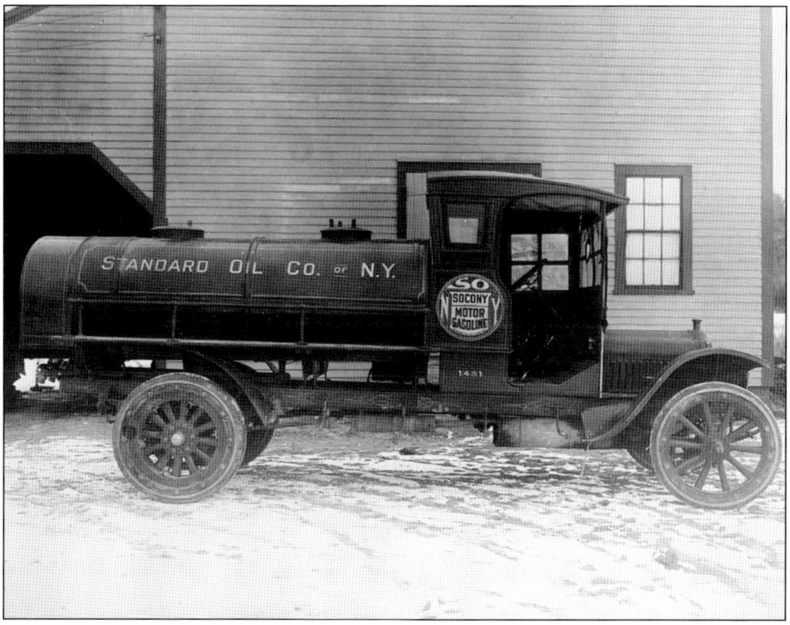

In the late 1800s and early 1900s, kerosene was the common fuel for kitchen stoves and lighting. This Hillsborough oil truck was part of the Standard Oil Company of New York distribution system. This photograph was taken in November 1917, just before the onslaught of winter.

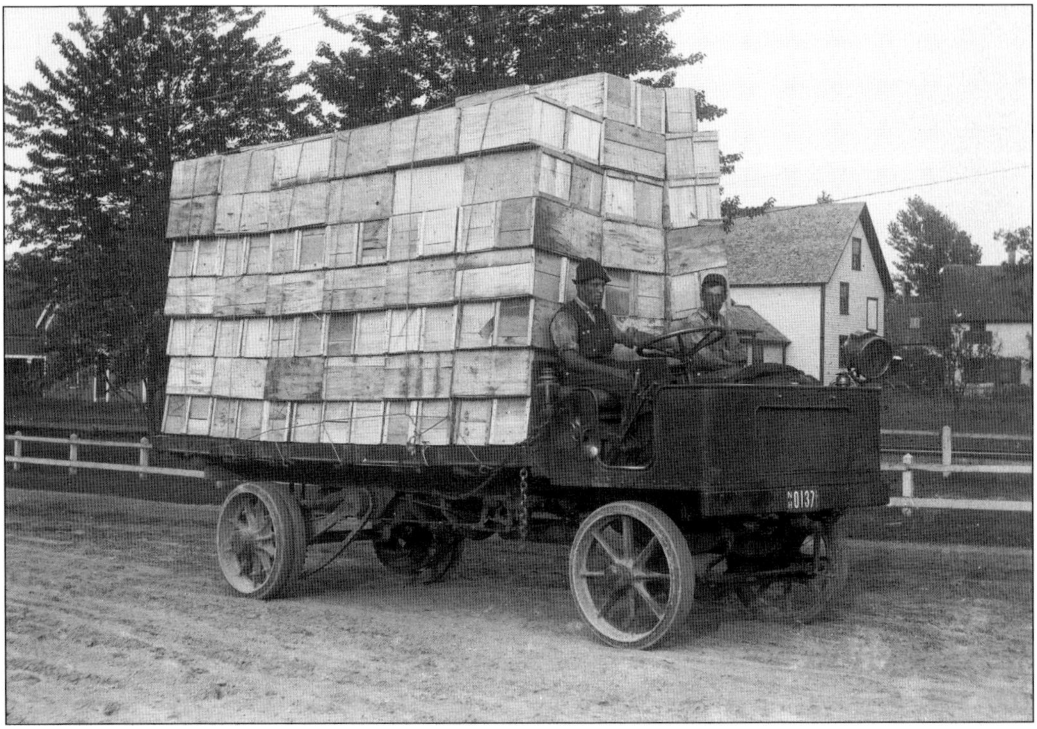

This early chain-driven truck, shown here delivering boxes from the Hosiery Mill, was a regular at the Hillsborough freight station. In support of the mill, boxes were made in Hillsborough as early as 1887 to hold hosiery, shirts, and apples from the orchards. Excess lumber was staged at the railroad freight yard and eventually shipped to Boston and New York.

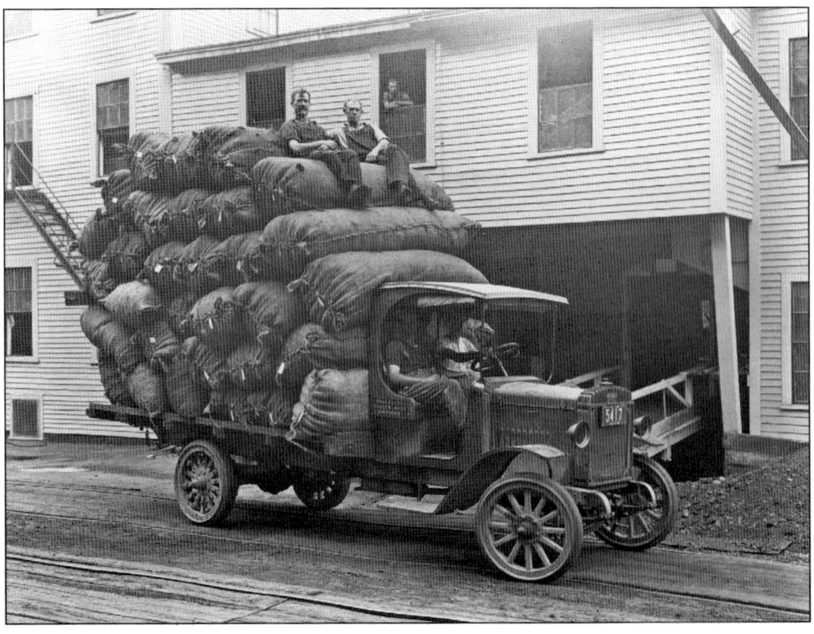

This heavily-loaded truck was driven by Pop McNally in support of the old Woolen Mill. When this photograph was taken in 1920, it is quite obvious that truck regulations were not yet developed or enforced in town. In all likelihood, the truck, carrying its cargo of raw wool, was en route to the Picking House.

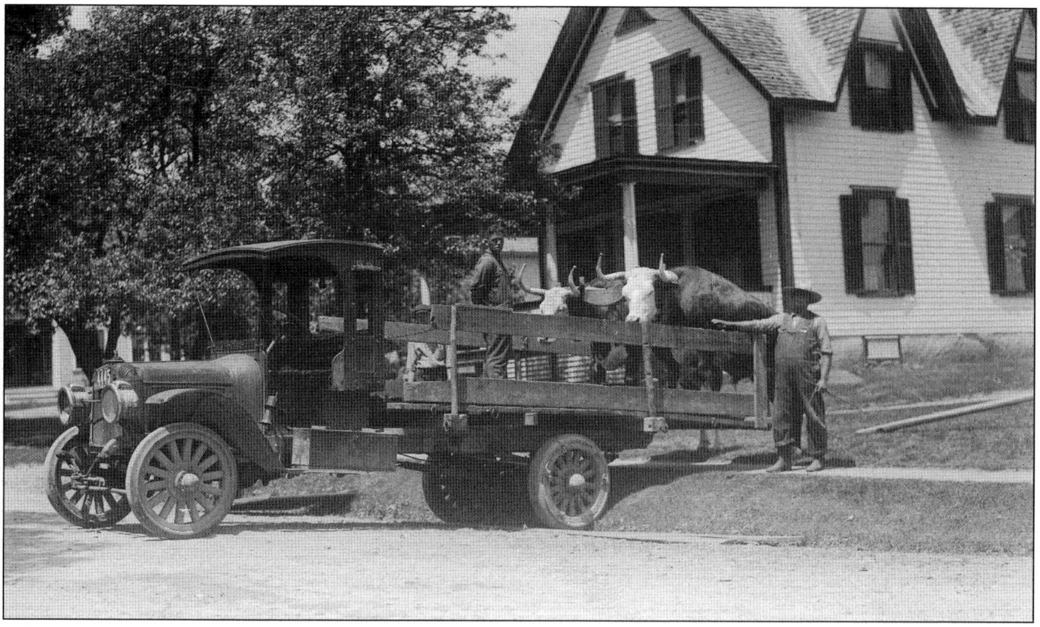

This 1920s photograph shows Frank Gay loading oxen into a truck at his home on School Street. Oxen were still in use as beasts of burden for large loads and earth-moving projects. Gay was a real party animal, organizing the winter carnival, Old Homes Day, and a masquerade ball that was advertised as the "wildest party ever held in Hillsborough County!"

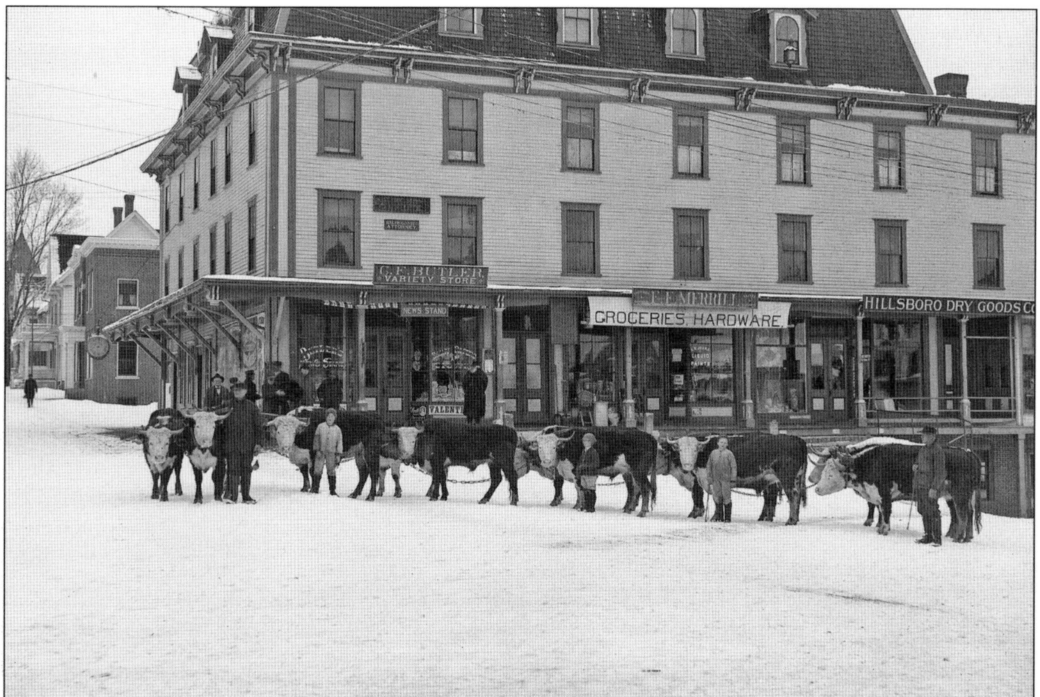

This 1927 image shows Edwin Dutton's large oxen teams in front of the Child's Opera House in Central Square. Each oxen team is being escorted by Dutton's sons: Walter, Leon, Harry, and Archie. Dutton's oxen tipped the scales at 3,000 pounds each and were renowned statewide.

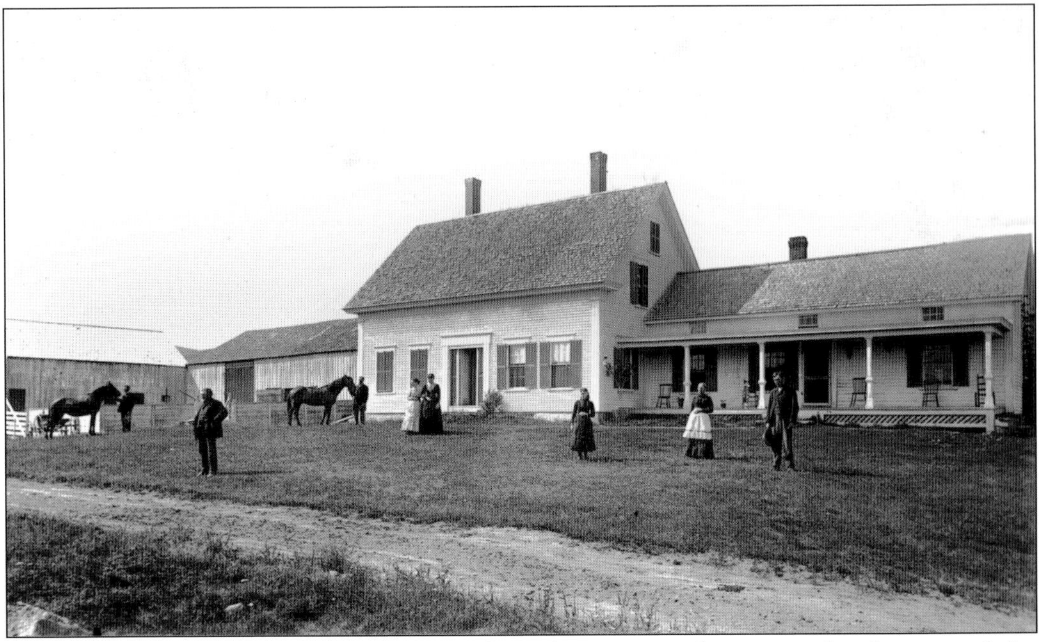

For most rural communities in New Hampshire, farming was the principal industry until the advent of mill employment. Farmers in Hillsborough were quite proud of their homesteads, and often posed in front of their farmhouses and outbuildings with their prize horses and livestock. The phrase "call out" was given to this genre of photography in rural New Hampshire. This call out is of a farm along Old Sawmill Road in the Lower Village.

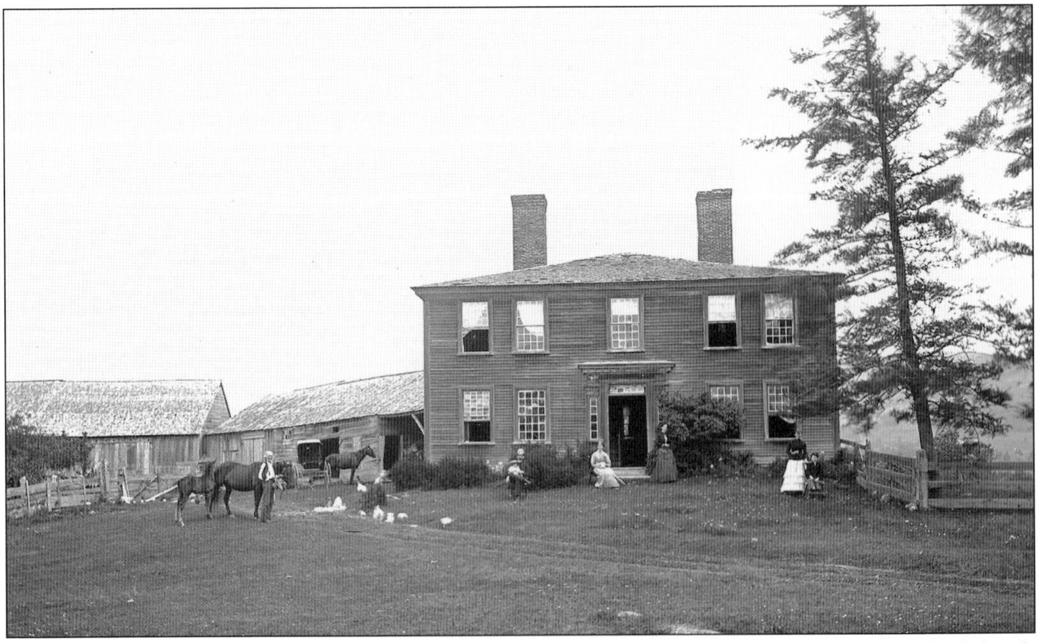

In the traditional farmstead pose, this Hillsborough family is standing in front of an old federal-style ancestral home. This structure has a 15-degree, four-slope roof with two chimneys, and the traditional four-room layout on the first and second floors. Unfortunately, as the economics of farming declined, house maintenance suffered and eventually this farmhouse became a ruin.

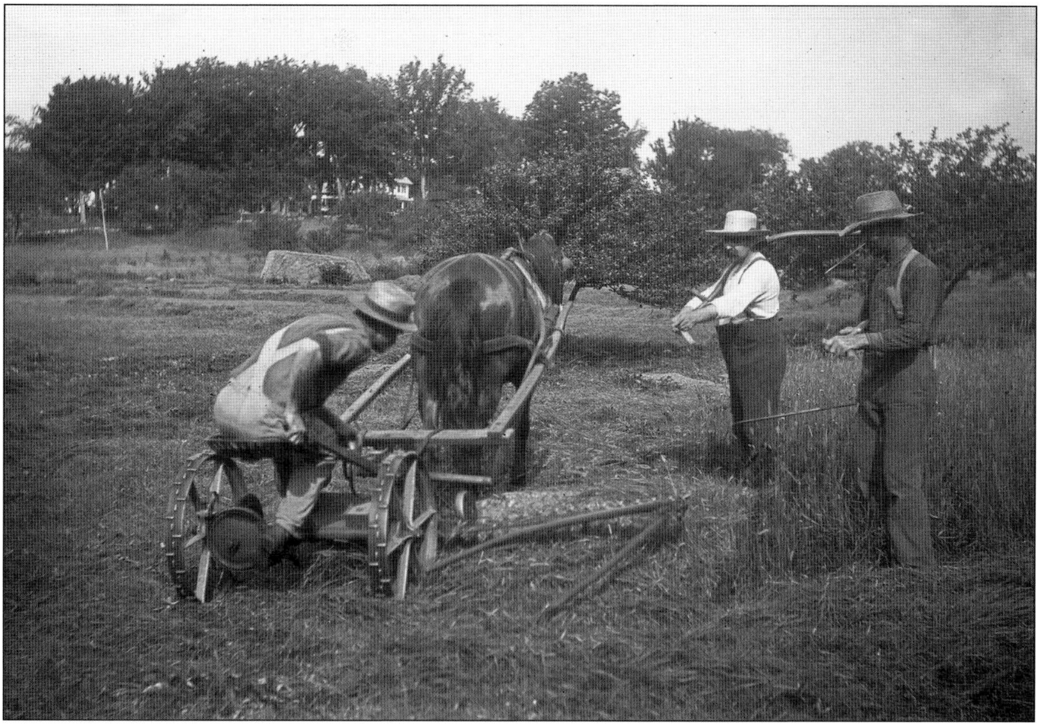

Hay was a critical commodity, and the 1,500-acre farm at Rosewald on Center Road was ideal for haying. In this picture, there is a farmer operating a horse-powered cutter bar, with two men with scythes watching the effort. William Neidner, the owner of Rosewald Farm, planted rose bushes along the sides of the road that gave the farm its name.

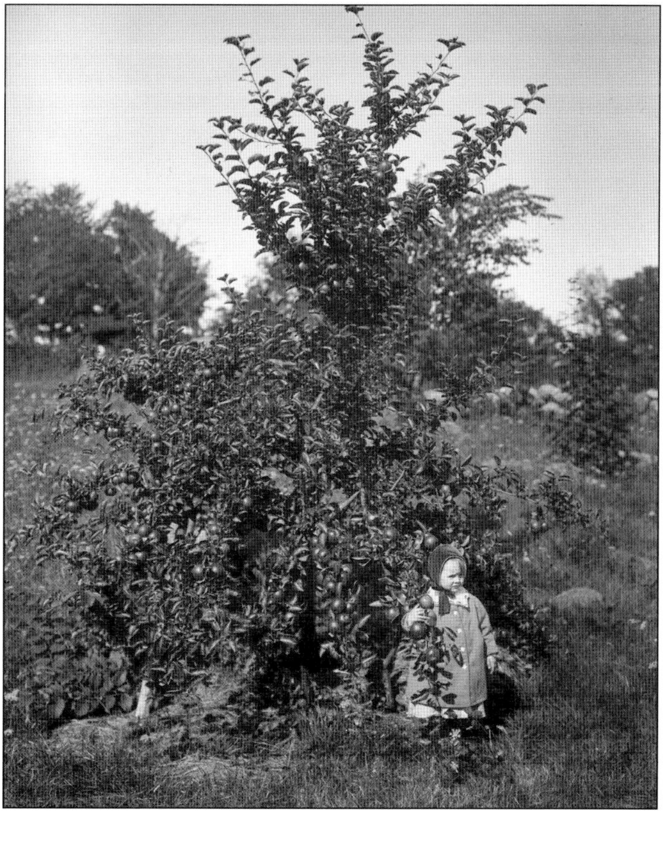

Hay, apples, corn, and potatoes were the most significant crops grown in Hillsborough. John Shedd, a Bunker Hill veteran, established his potato patch in 1780. Apple orchards were prevalent on most farms and homesteads. A fine example of a Hillsborough apple tree is photographed here with a little girl awaiting permission to pick. Forty pounds of apples from one tree was the norm.

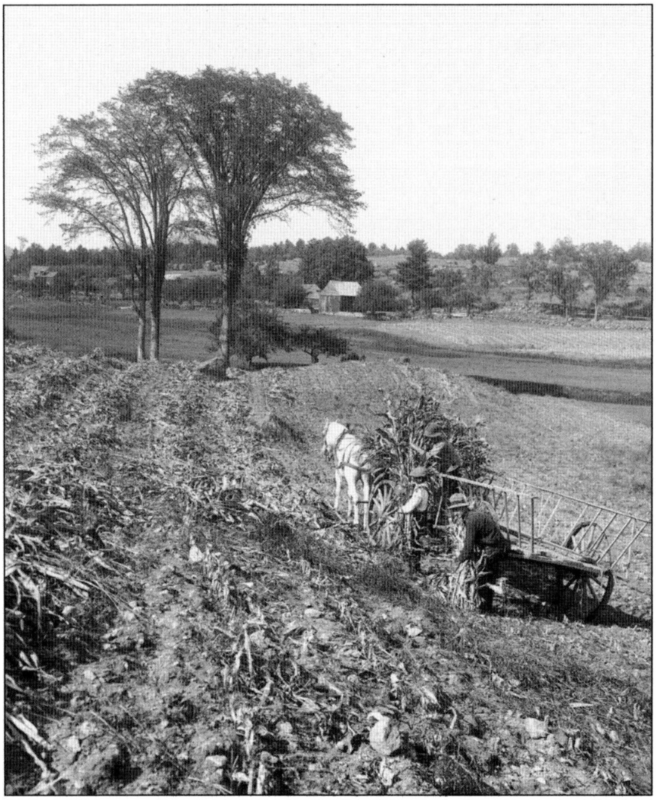

Harvesting corn was a major effort in the fall, with horsepower and rudimentary mechanical devices used in support. As seen at left, loading corn was essentially a manual process. Unloading the corn from a wagon with a team of horses into the chopper and up into the barn for storage was somewhat more automated, as seen below. Corn was normally the winter feed for the herds of dairy cows. Hillsborough had a number of dairy farms, with H.G Martin's Hillsborough Dairy Company being the largest producer of pasteurized milk and creams.

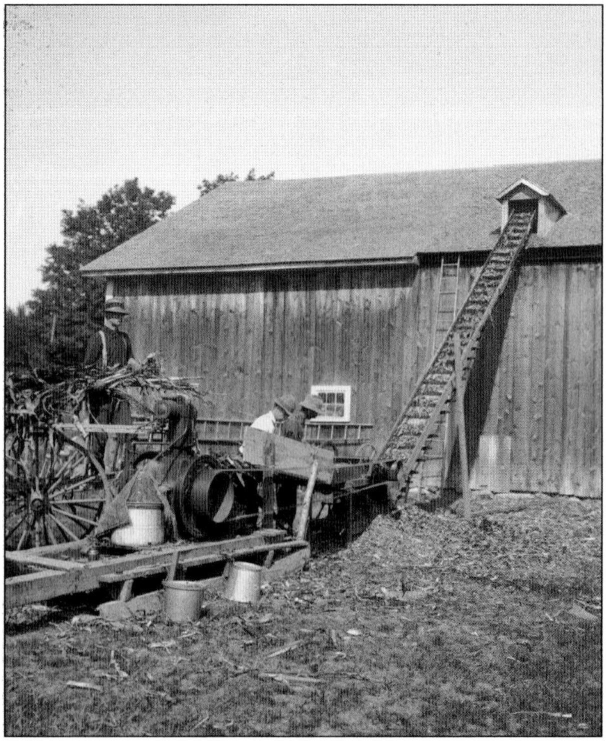

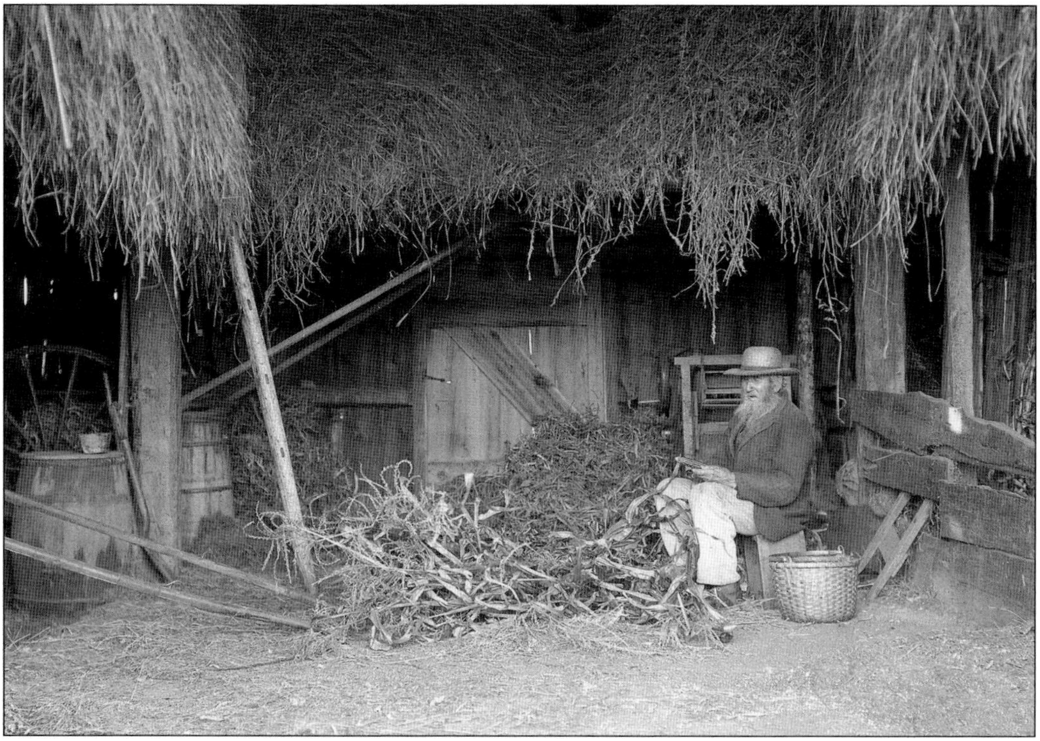

This early photograph of an old-timer shucking corn seems to suggest a slow summer day. Farming in Hillsborough reached an apex around the outbreak of the Civil War. The farmer at that time was nearly self-sufficient. He was a feller of trees, tiller of the soil, and blacksmith, as well as his own doctor, lawyer, and manufacturer. This old timer deserves a quiet day every once in a while.

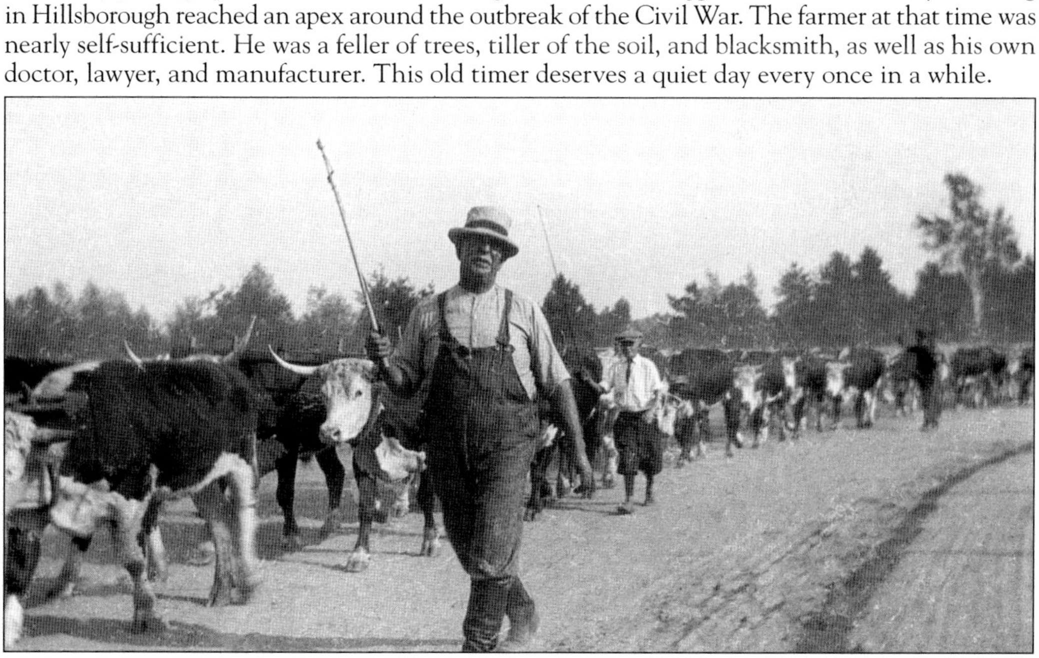

There were many herds of dairy cows in Hillsborough, including the fine herd of Guernsey cattle at Rosewald Farm. Cattle drives were common to and from town, either to summer feeding areas around Washington, New Hampshire, or even, before the advent of the railroad, to the slaughterhouses in Brighton, Massachusetts. In this picture, Frank Gay is leading the herd.

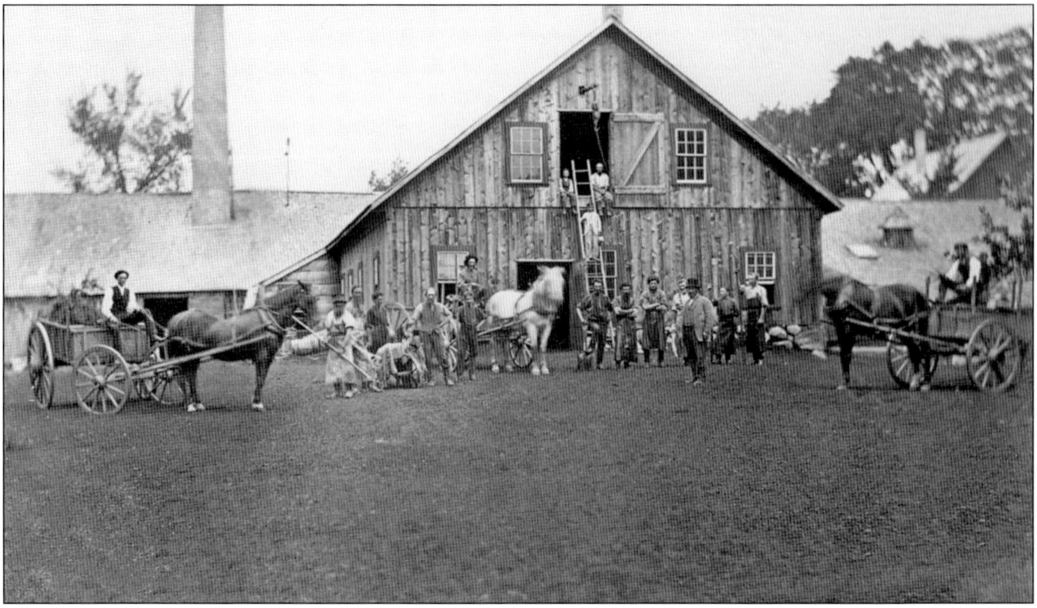

At one time, there were several tanneries in town, predominately in Hillsborough Lower Village, as represented in this photograph. Leather was used in many ways in an agricultural economy. Samuel Kimball started one of the first tanneries in the 1830s. The Westcott and Fuller Tannery became nationally noted as the producer of "Westcott Calf." The gentleman in the top hat is J.G. Fuller.

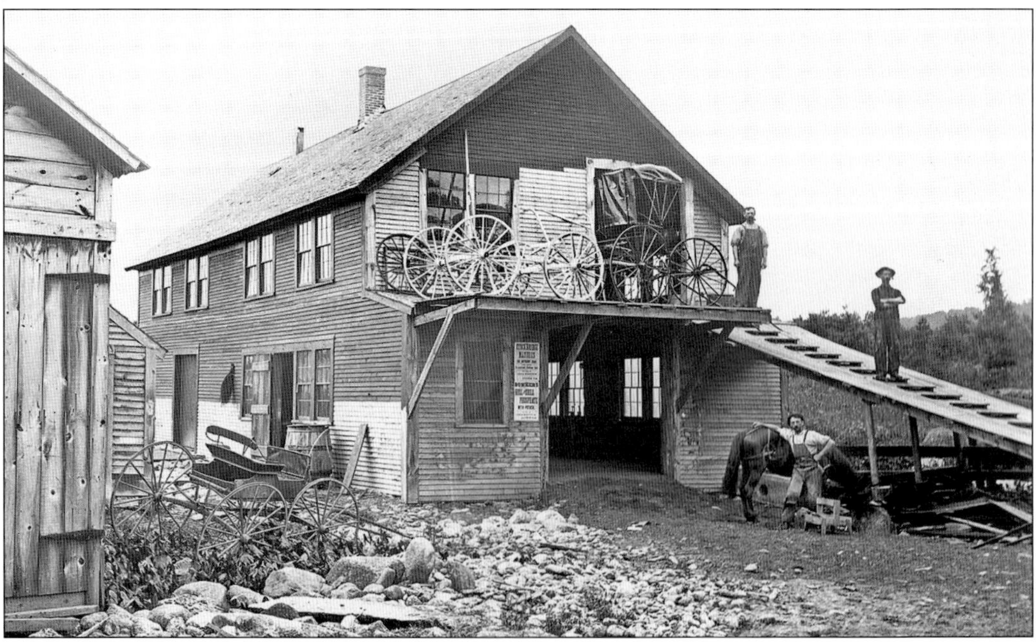

Hillsborough had a significant number of manufacturers processing raw materials from its water-powered mills. A flourishing business was that of the Jackman Brothers, who operated a sawmill plant for wooden manufacturing of furniture, chair legs, shovel handles, H.M. Bartlett's rackets, and carriages. The Lower Village carriage shop shown here has a unique production system with finished product rolling off from the top floor.

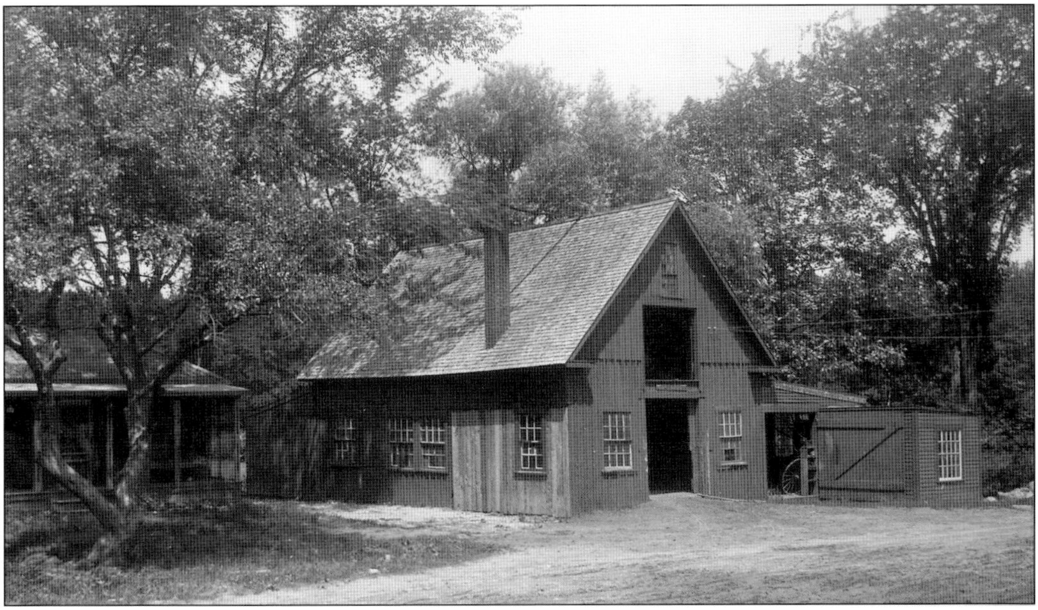

This blacksmith shop in the Lower Village was one of several scattered around the town. Shoeing a horse in 1896 was only $1. Later, Jimmy Oski occupied this shop for his boat-building business. It was later used as a cabinet and furniture shop. In 1860, a foundry and machine shop was established in Lower Village as a natural outgrowth of the blacksmithing tradition.

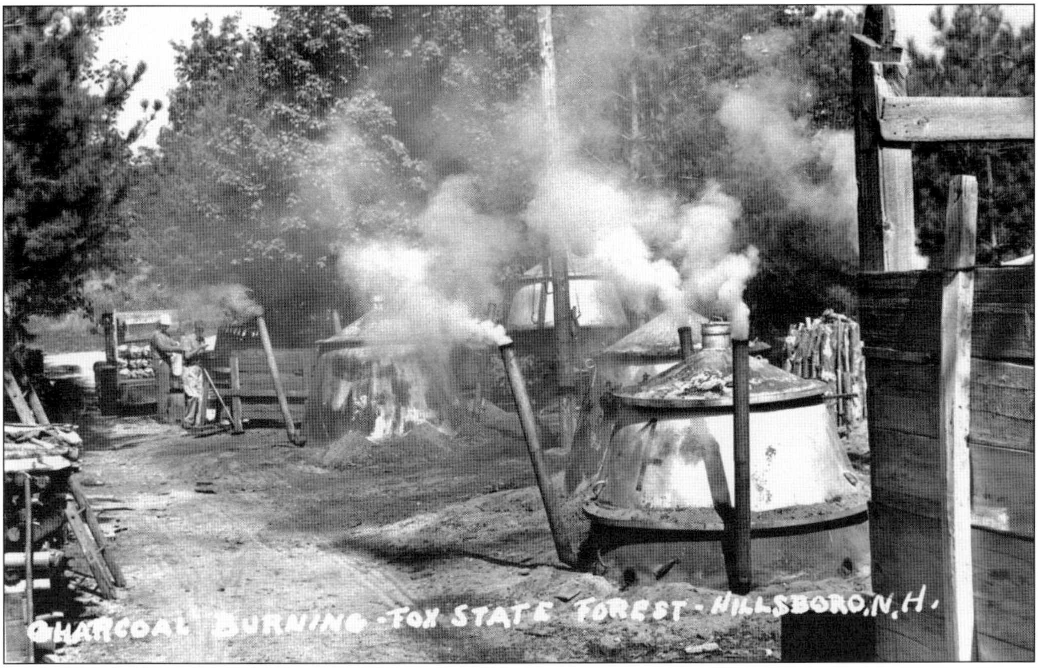

The Fox State Forest occupies an area on either side of Center Road, and is bounded by Bog Road on the east and Bible Hill Road on the west. The original forest consisted of both conifers and hardwoods, including large pine, basswood, ash, oak, chestnut, and maple trees. It is an endowed research forest with many long-term programs. To make use of wood unsuitable for the sawmill, an ancillary business of charcoal making was established at Fox State Forest.

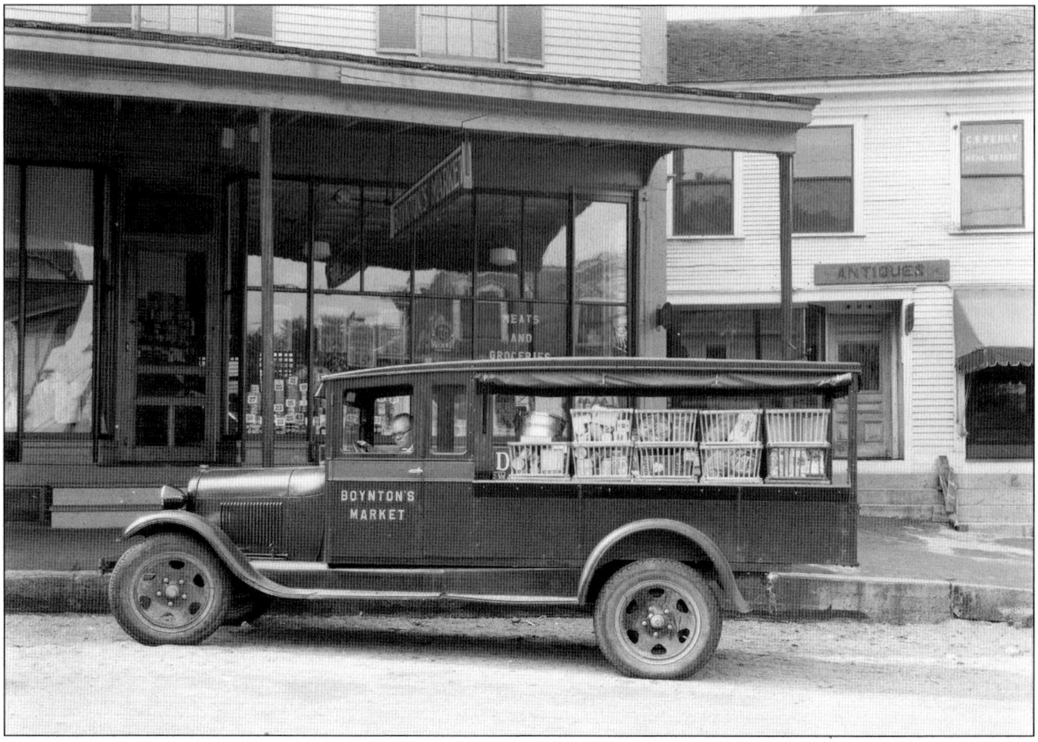

George W. Boynton was a purveyor of groceries, meats, and provisions, as well as fruits, vegetables, and farmers' produce. Boynton was the dean of Hillsborough grocers, having started his company in 1912 on the basement floor of the Marcy Block and lasting in business until 1952. A typical grocery bill in the 1920s was two pounds of sugar for 22¢, a box of berries for 12¢, tea for 35¢, and pot roast for 75¢. The c. 1923 picture above gives a view of Boynton's storefront and delivery truck. The picture below is an interior snapshot of his store.

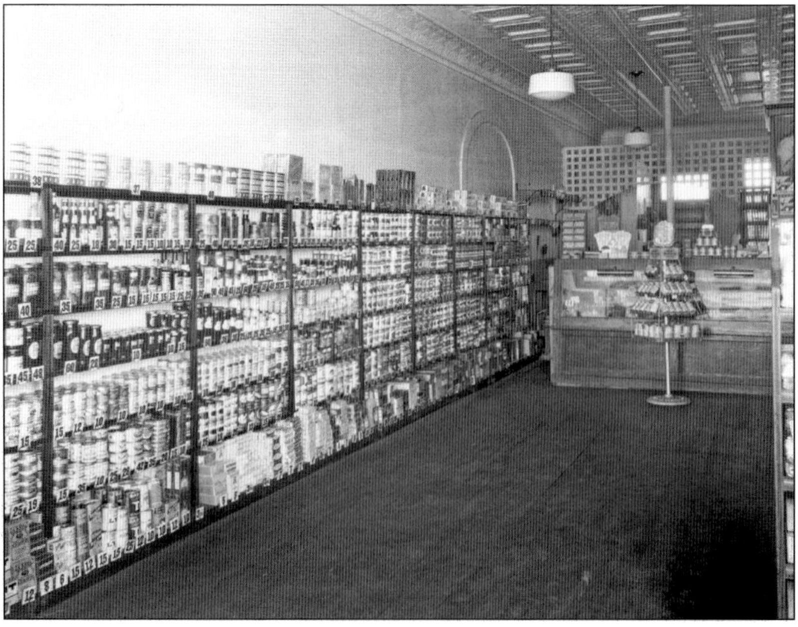

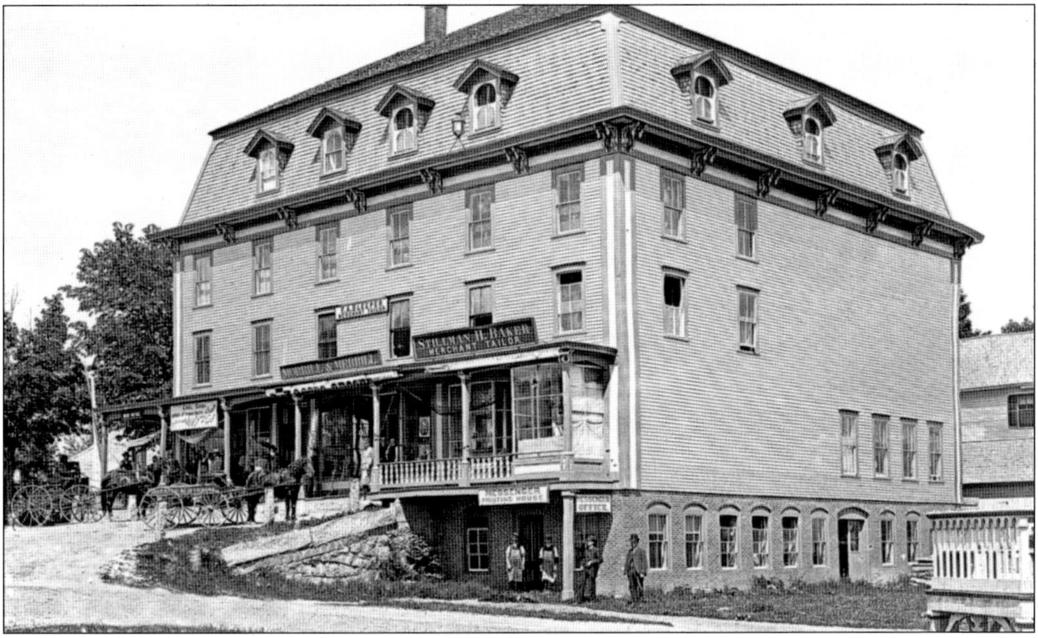

The Child's Opera Block, currently called the Withington Block, has been home to several merchants. The centerpiece in 1887 was Morrill and Merrill, a dealer in dry goods, small wares, boots, and shoes. Back then, a pair of boots retailed at $3. The Hillsborough *Messenger* occupied the basement floor and was owned by publisher L.P. Lincoln. Another notable tenant was Kimball Dry Goods, which advertised in 1906, "Sebasticook skirts and Tomson's glove fitting corsets with the habit hip."

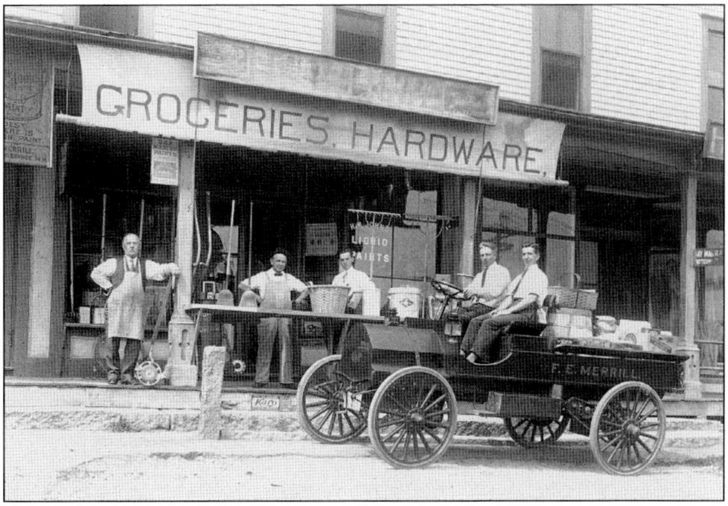

By 1905, Frank Merrill owned the dry goods store outright, and specialized in groceries and hardware. However, his real passion was not necessarily retailing. Music was his avocation, playing in the Wahneta Orchestra and leading his own, Merrill's Orchestra. Bernard Annis, a Sunday school teacher, is the passenger in the delivery truck.

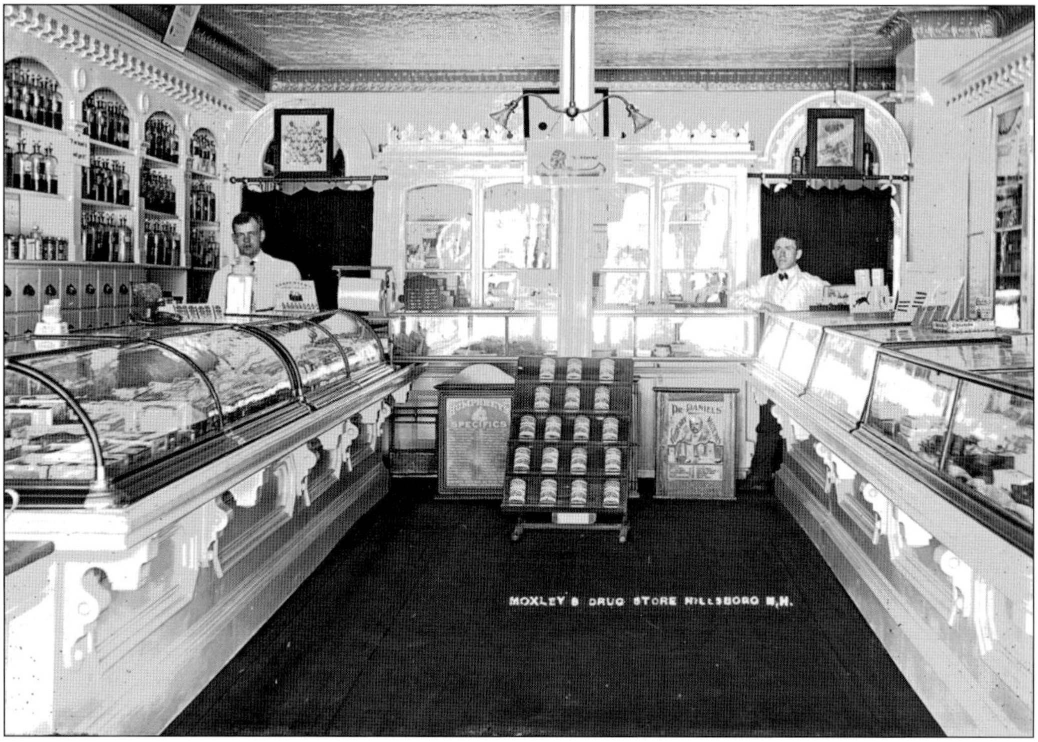

R.W. Moxley's drug store and soda fountain was situated in the Whittemore Block in Central Square. It competed with Charles S. Perry's drug store and soda fountain located around the street in a brick structure, the Butler Block. The soda business was new in 1900, with "first class apparatus using pure fruit juices and pulps with plenty of ice," according to a sign inside.

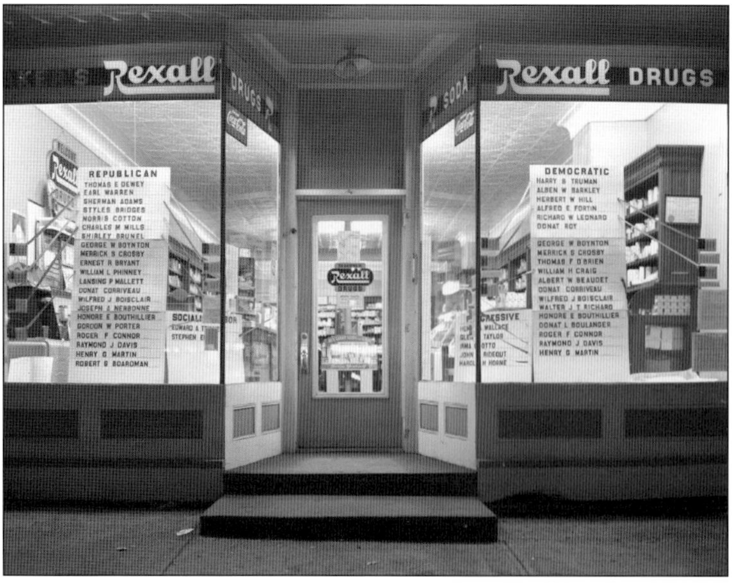

By 1906, the Rexall chain store, owned by the Morrison brothers and later by Perry, replaced Moxley's store. In this photograph, the Hillsborough League of Women Voters placed election posters in the storefront windows. Unfortunately, this limited window-shopping somewhat so one could not see the inventory of Bloodline Liver Pills or 93 hair tonic, which restores gray hair, cures dandruff, and stops baldness.

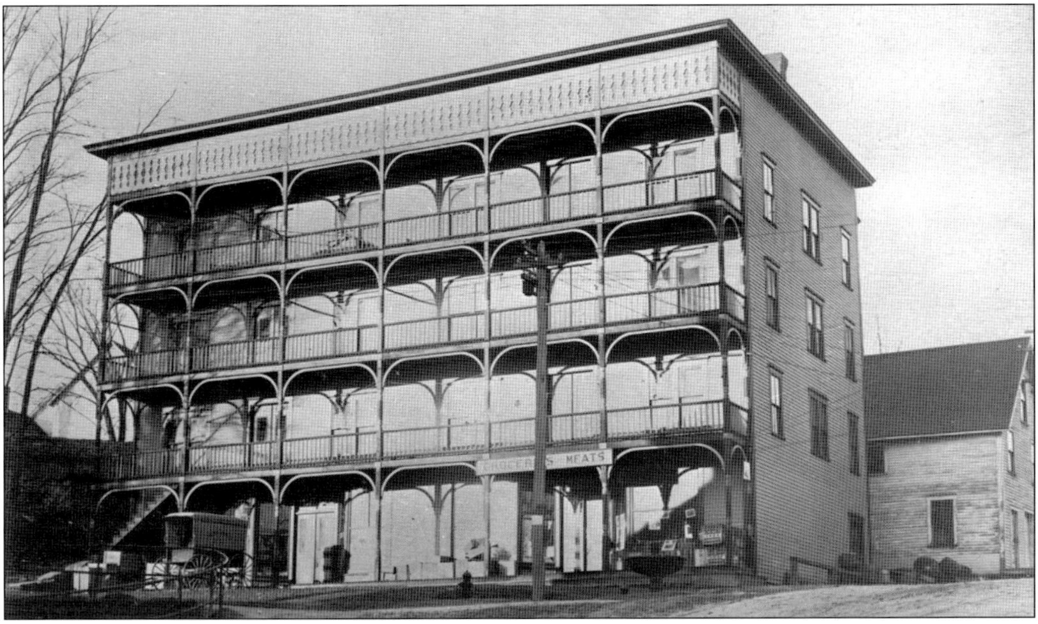

Victor Moseley was another popular dealer in meats, groceries, and provisions. He established his store on the first floor of this high-rise structure, located across the bridge and adjacent to the mills. The store was later acquired by Henry Gerini, whose son Ennio continued to run the store for many years. Ennio recently celebrated his 90th birthday.

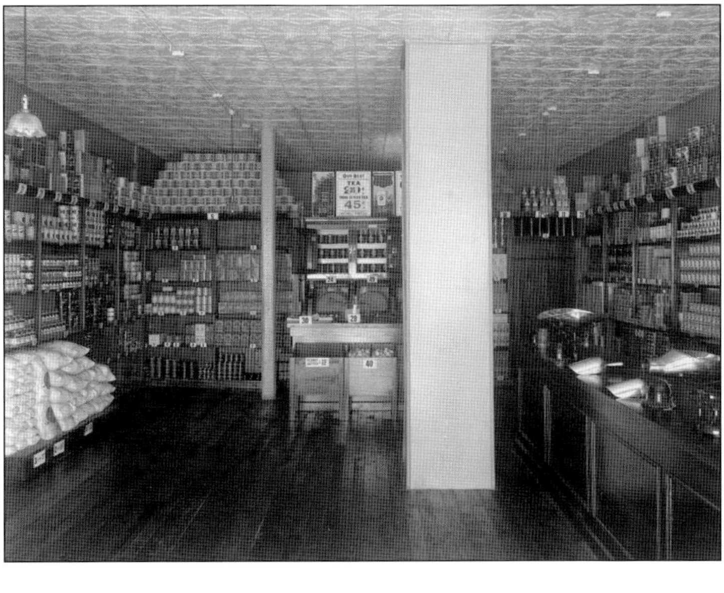

The Great Atlantic and Pacific Tea Company (A&P) established a store at the Colby Block, also the location of William Newman's Plumbing Shop, the Manahan Studio, and the Spiritualist Society. Today, Colby Block is the site of the Congregational church's parking lot. The A&P paid particular attention to the display of its products, as shown in this interior photograph.

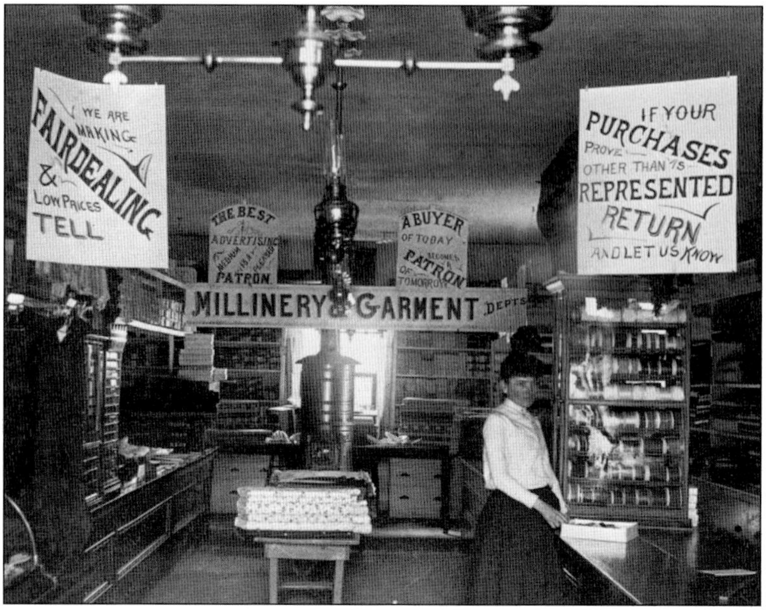

This is an early photograph of a millinery and garment department store. Farrar Sisters' 1880s millinery store focused on customer service, as its several display signs suggest. The Farrar Sisters had competition from the Bruce and Rumrill's millinery store.

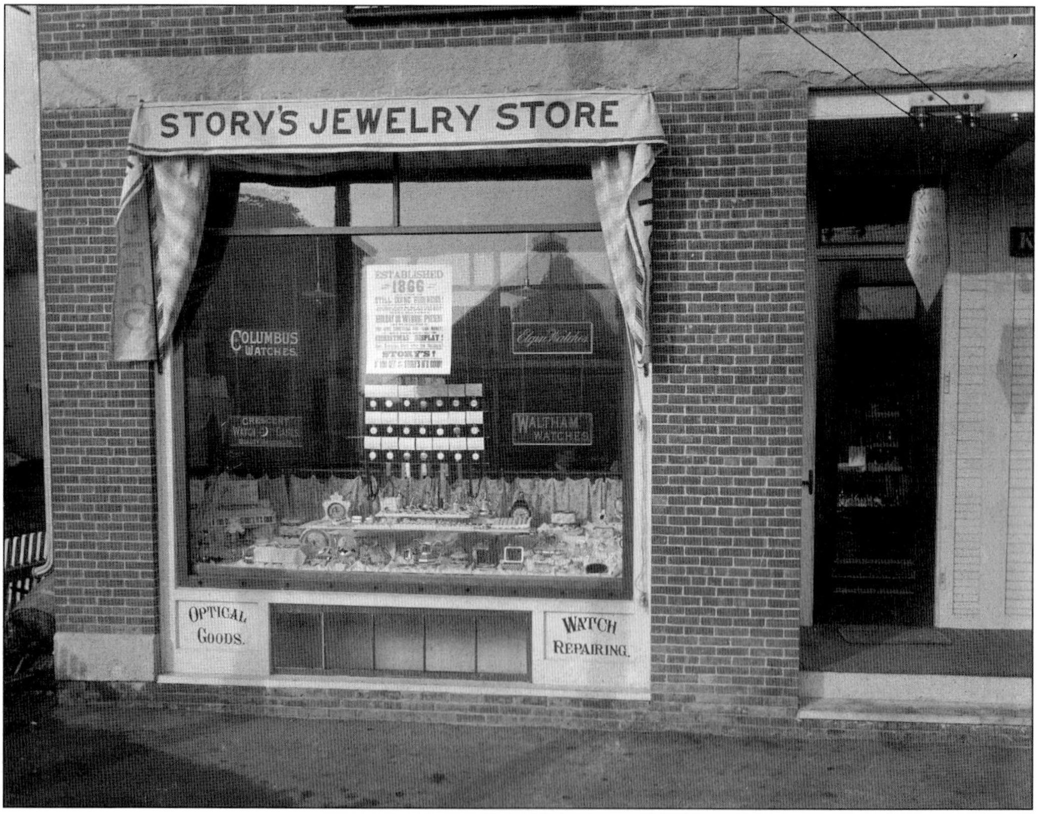

Located on the ground floor of the 1894 Rumrill Block was William H. Story's jewelry store. His show windows were the largest in Hillsborough. The show window normally displayed samples of watches, clocks, jewelry, plated ware, and eyeglasses. The right half of the Rumrill Block was occupied by Kimball and Roach, proprietors of the Boston Store.

Six

Public Institutions and Public Works

Just like any quintessential New Hampshire town, public institutions played a vital role in the social growth of Hillsborough. Churches, schools, and government buildings have always been the central focus and meeting place for the townspeople.

Religion was always in the forefront of the early settlers' minds. At the first town meeting, at the house of Capt. Samuel Bradford on November 24, 1772, the townspeople decided to build a meetinghouse and called Jonathan Barnes to be the first settled minister of the town. It took nearly seven years to raise funds and construct the building, but in 1779, the first meetinghouse was completed. Due to the town's growth, a larger new meetinghouse was built in 1794. However, on March 8, 1814, the church and state essentially separated in the town. From that time on, different religious groups were allowed to use the meetinghouse but were no longer funded by the town. Several denominations flourished over the years in Hillsborough including Baptist, Methodist, Congregationalist, Catholic, Universalist, and Spiritualist congregations.

Schools were also an integral part of the social fabric of the town. Prior to 1775, teachers were supported by private donations and schools functioned independently. In 1785, the town voted to start allocating money for schools, and in 1788, it started dividing the town into school districts. It did not, however, appropriate money until several years later. Hillsborough Academy was built in the Lower Village in 1821, and its first professor was Dr. Simeon Bard. The academy was moved to the center of town in 1840. In 1861, the two school districts in Bridge Village combined and built one school with a primary and higher grade. Eventually Hillsborough Academy merged with this new school in 1864, and the Valley Academy was created. The name of this school was eventually changed to the Union School in 1876, which essentially became Hillsborough's high school. By 1920, the six rural school districts in Hillsborough had 101 pupils. Eventually, with educational reforms by both the state and federal governments, the Hillsborough school system evolved into its present state. By the 1950s, all the one-room schoolhouses were closed and replaced by a central grade school.

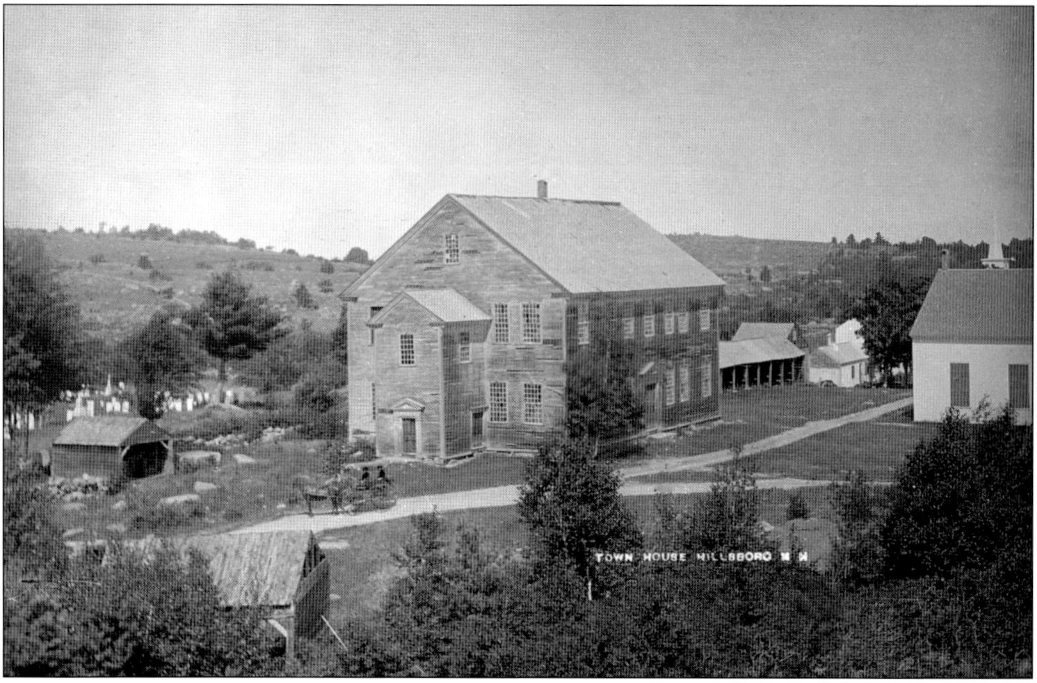

The old meetinghouse was actually known during its initial construction in 1789 as the "New Meeting House," the third of its kind in Hillsborough and second structure in the Center. For many years, it was used both as town hall and for religious services. After it was no longer used for religious purposes, it continued to be used for town meetings but the town offices were relocated to Hillsborough Bridge. In 1874, it was abandoned for town meetings as the population continued to shift from the center to Hillsborough Bridge.

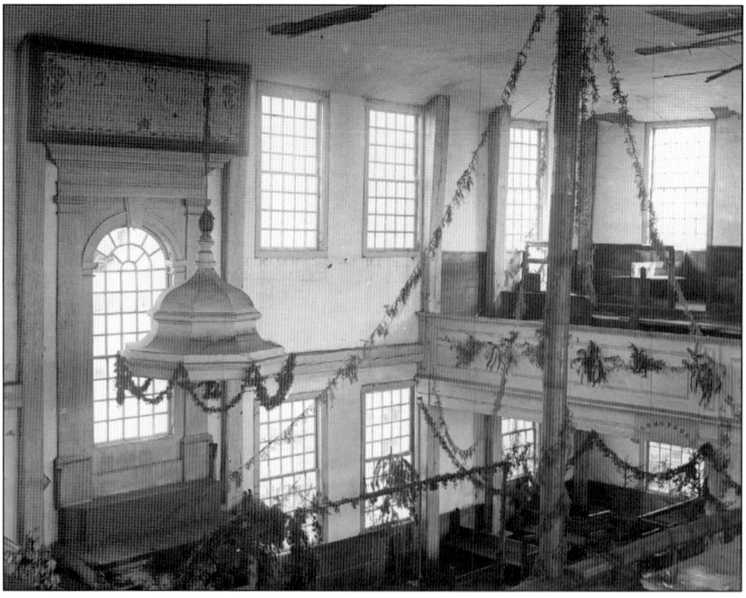

The interior of the meetinghouse, pictured here with Christmas decorations in the mid-1800s, was very elegant. The ground floor contained 54 pews, which sold for between £8 and £13 in 1788, plus four pews reserved in front of the pulpit for aged persons. The pews in the galley were sold in 1794. Above the pulpit was a tablet commemorating Samuel Symonds, the major benefactor.

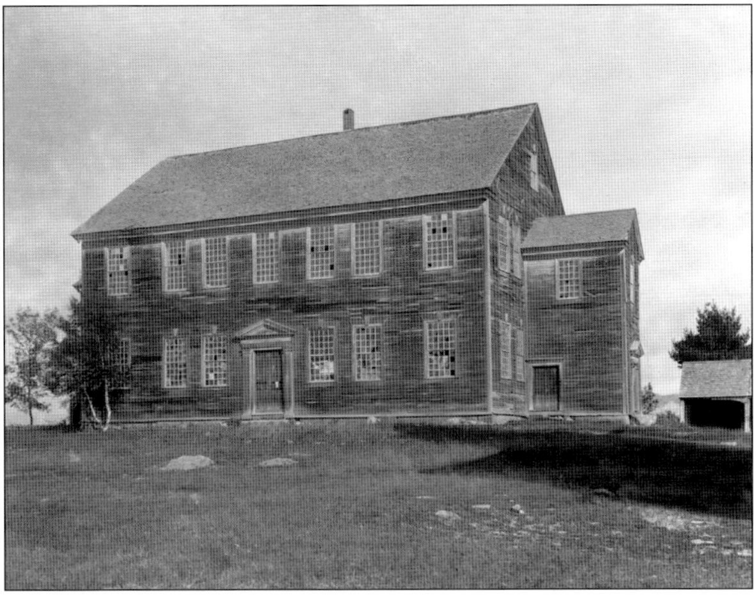

After abandonment for town purposes, the old meetinghouse was subject to vandalism and townspeople who used every opportunity to carry off relics. In 1890, the town appropriated money for the restoration of the landmark. However, on the morning of June 19, 1892, the structure was in flames, perhaps subject to a tax revolt. The horse sheds on the right remain to this day.

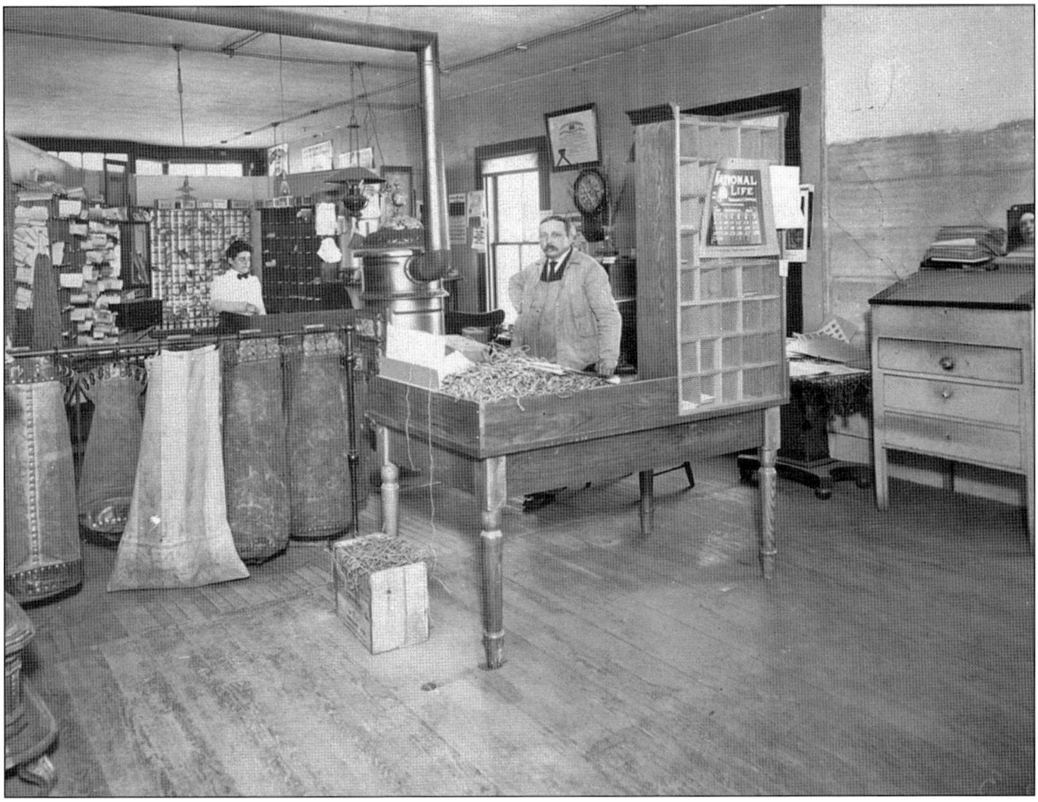

In 1803, the first post office was established in the Lower Village. The post office in Hillsborough Bridge was established in 1827 and operations changed little over the years. Many prominent men in town held the position of postmaster over the years, including Benjamin Pierce, Ephraim Dutton, William Whittemore, William Story, De Witt Clinton Newman, Charles Kimball, James Butler, and Frank Merrill.

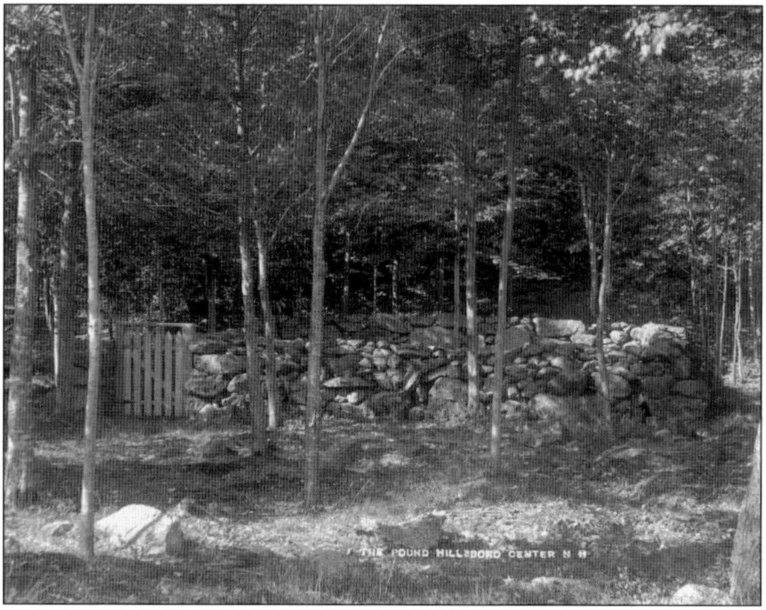

The town pound was built in 1774 with Elijah Fuller as the first pound keeper. Tradition has it that the newest-married male was put in charge of the pound. Eunice Baldwin of the Daughters of the American Revolution carefully restored the pound to its original appearance, and it remains so to this day.

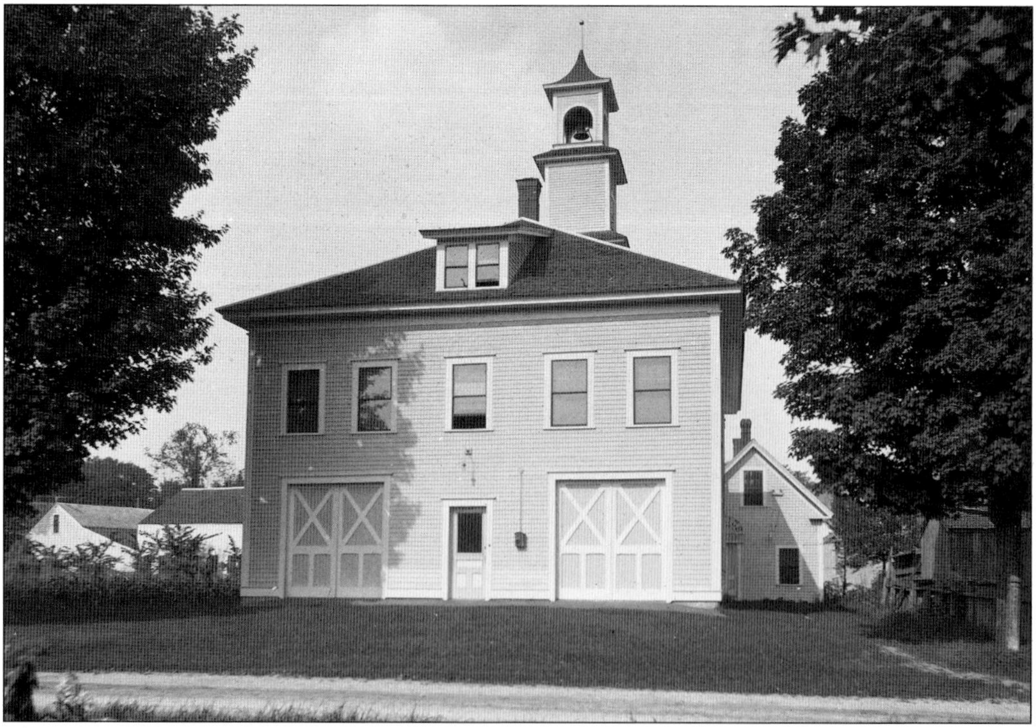

This large structure was the town firehouse. The first floor contained two stalls for fire equipment, the second floor had an office and meeting room, and the third floor was the captain's office. The small structure to the right was the town jail. The firehouse has been fully restored as a town museum operated by the Hillsborough Historical Society.

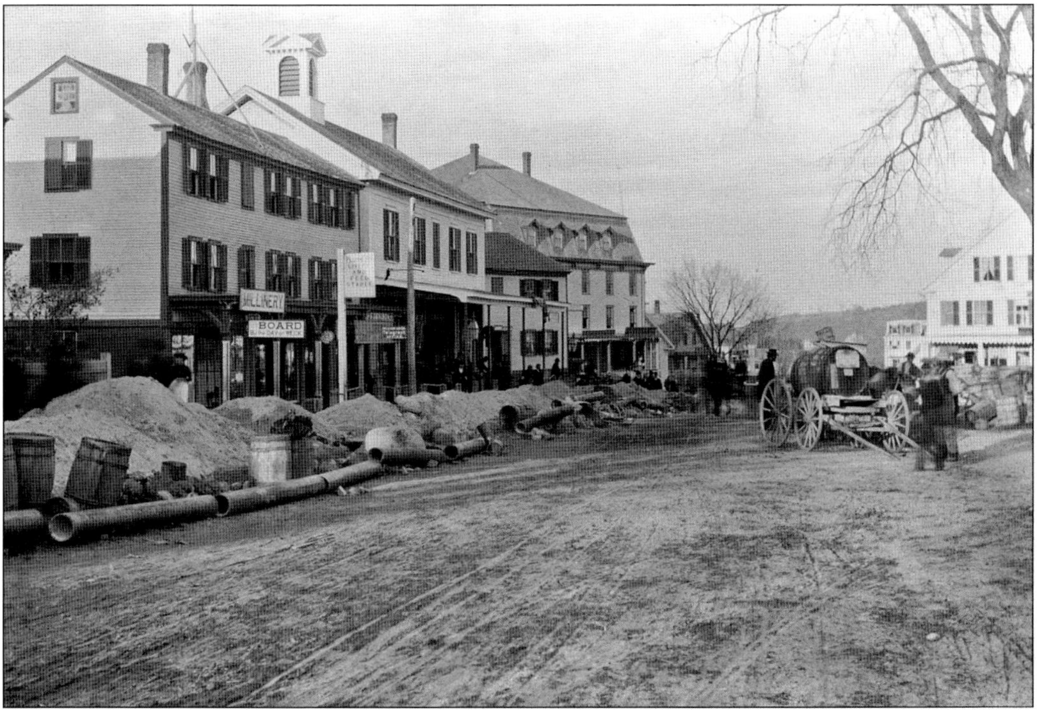

The first water system was constructed in 1887 using cement-lined iron pipes. The main line was re-laid in 1910, as shown in this West Main Street picture, at a cost of $26,000. The pipes were 16 inches in diameter, and men worked without earth-moving equipment.

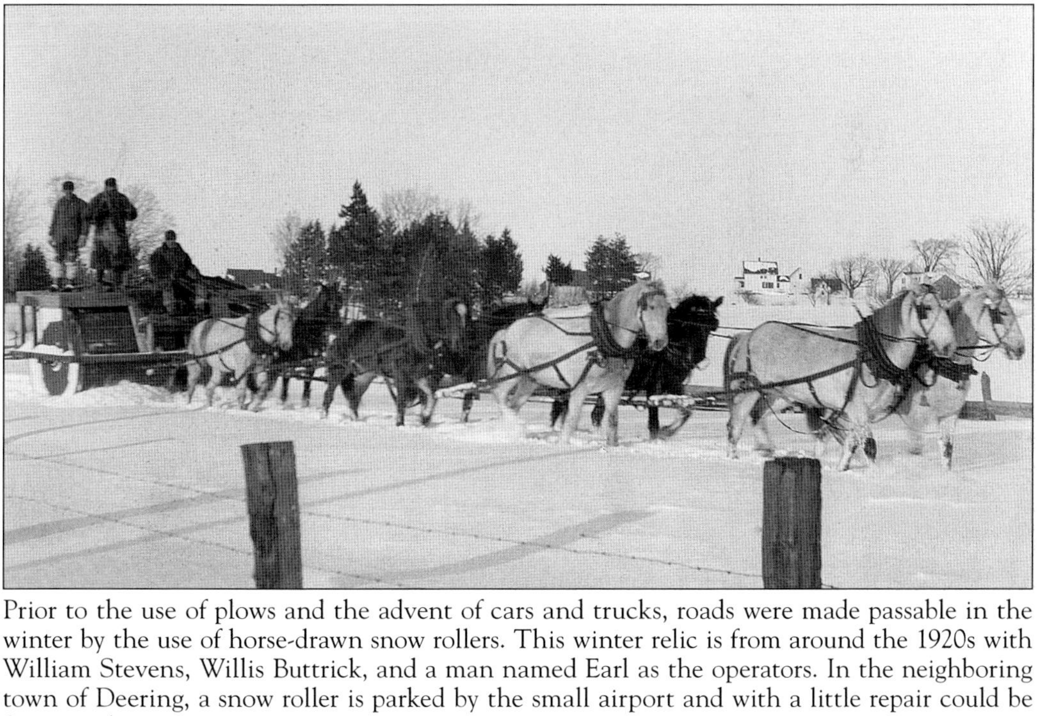

Prior to the use of plows and the advent of cars and trucks, roads were made passable in the winter by the use of horse-drawn snow rollers. This winter relic is from around the 1920s with William Stevens, Willis Buttrick, and a man named Earl as the operators. In the neighboring town of Deering, a snow roller is parked by the small airport and with a little repair could be functional again.

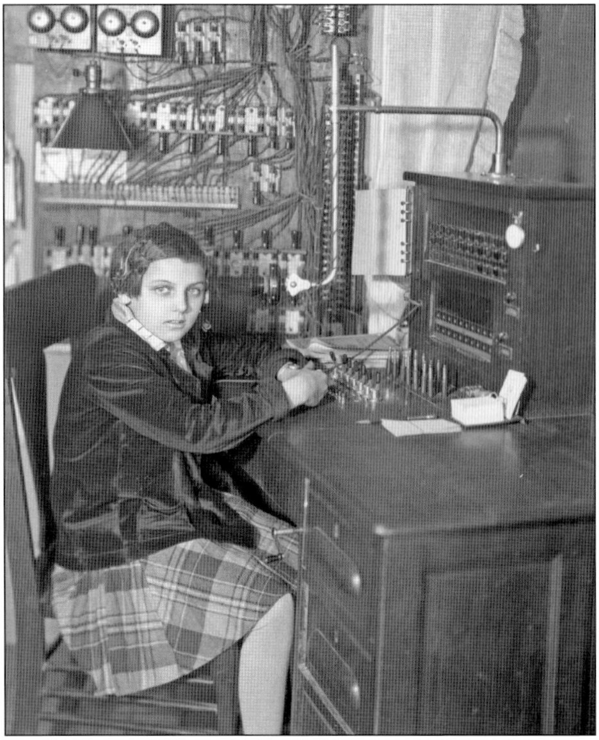

The telephone was first introduced to Hillsborough in 1891 with the advent of two telephone companies. George W. Lincoln established the Triangle Telephone Company in the Upper Village. The Contoocook Valley Telephone Company served the rest of the town. By 1908, there were 167 telephones in the area. Telephone operator Jane Clement, pictured here in 1932, probably knew most numbers by heart. For example, Hillsborough Dairy was 37-4 connecting to Kimball's Goods at 7-6.

Dirt roads were the norm in Hillsborough and still represent a significant part of the town's infrastructure. Municipal water wagons were used in the summer dry season to curtail dust. One such wagon is shown here in Hillsborough's Central Square. Note the early kerosene lamp for street lighting.

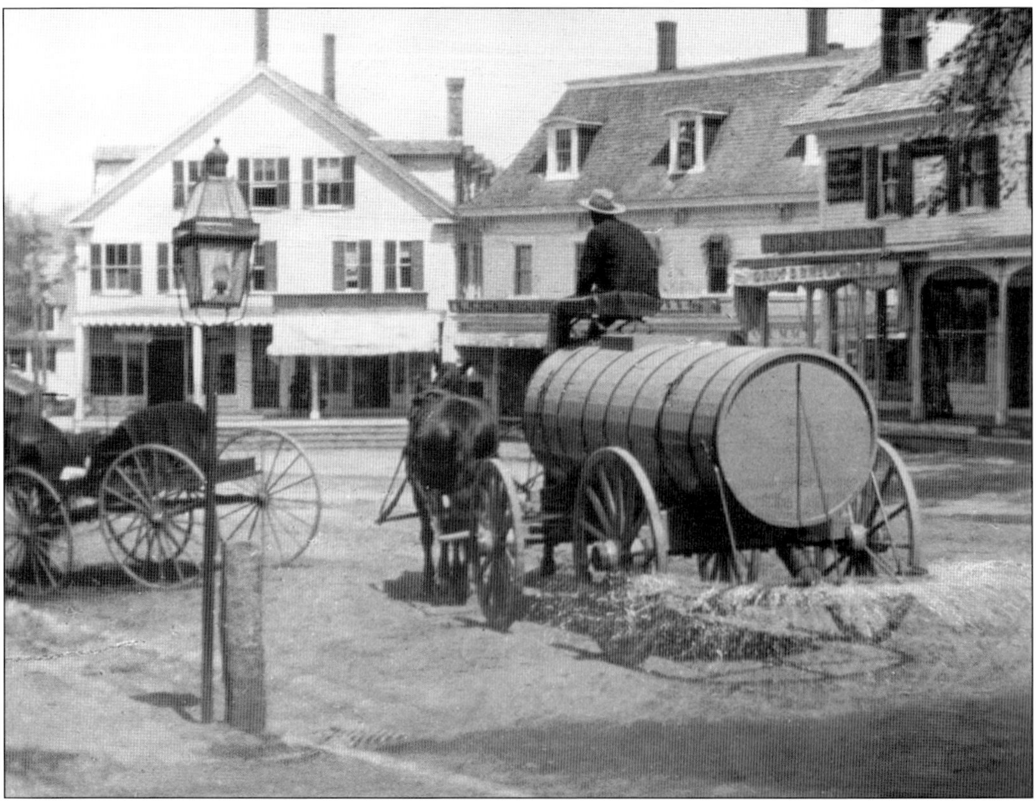

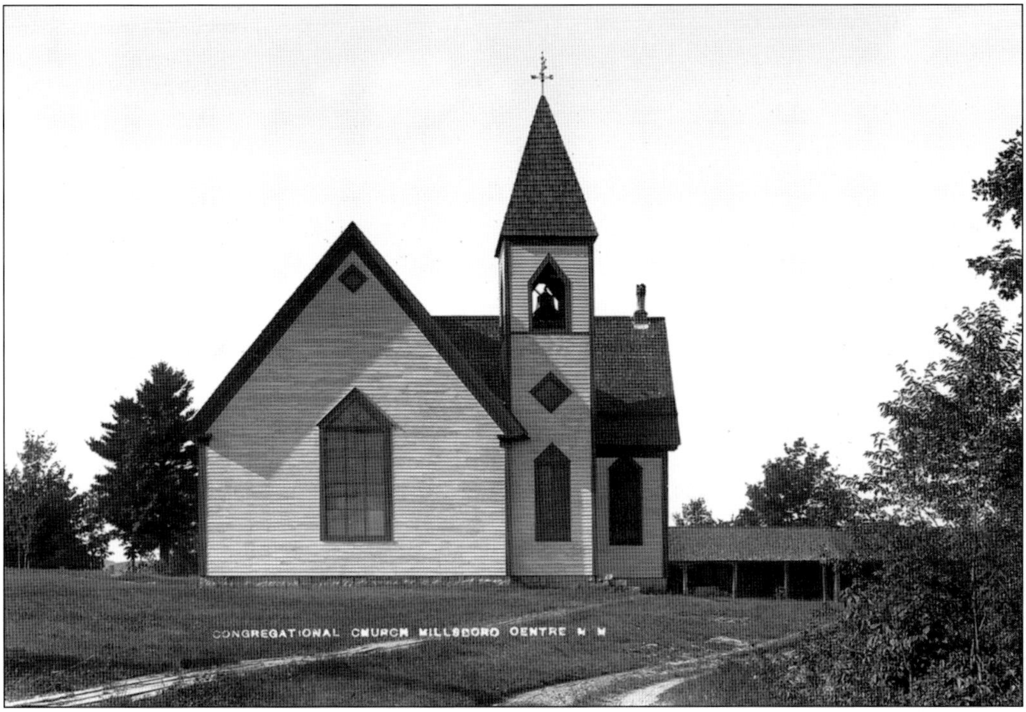

Soon after the old meetinghouse and Congregational church burned in 1892, a new Congregational church was built by Lyman Dinsmore, pictured above. During its time, it has seen numerous weddings, community club meetings, and concerts. Church services are still held in the summer accompanied by organist and artist extraordinaire Sissi Shattuck.

The Old Baptist Church was built on land purchased from Lt. John McNeil in 1821, situated at the midpoint between Upper and Lower Villages. The church had a magnificent belfry with a bell of 1,500 pounds. Over the years, the church had problems unifying the Upper and Lower Village parishioners. Both factions had separate services on the Sabbath until 1893, when it was torn down and auctioned off piecemeal.

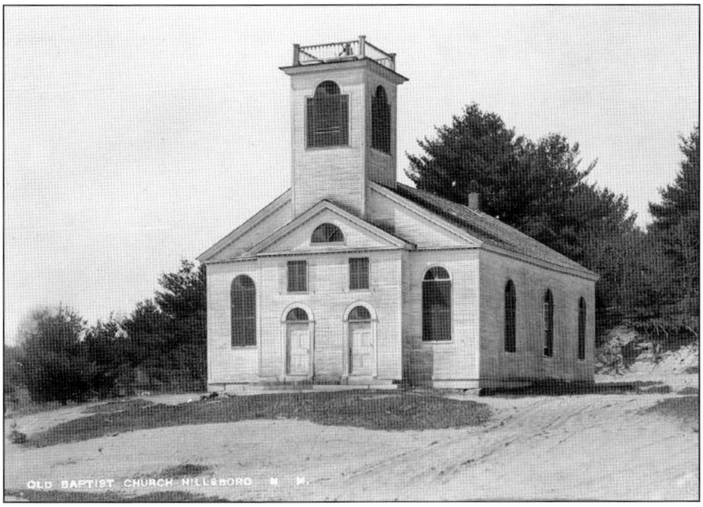

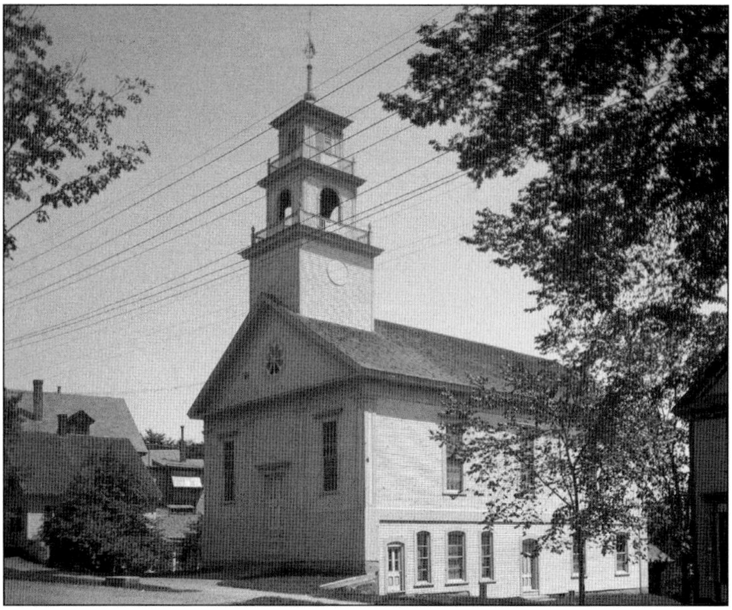

The Congregational church in Hillsborough Bridge was first located on Church Street, opposite the site of Saint Mary's Catholic Church. In 1860, the church was moved to its present location on West Main Street. Gov. John Smith contributed $50,000 for alterations and a larger steeple; ever since then, it has been known as the Smith Memorial Congregational Church.

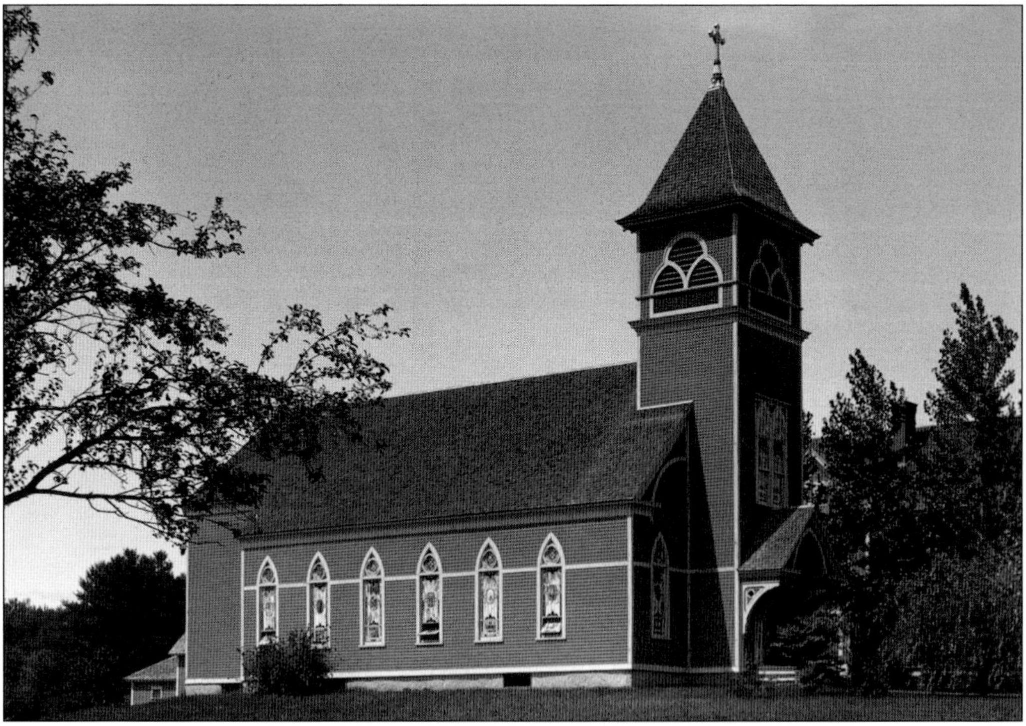

The first Catholic mass was celebrated in Hillsborough in 1881. Two years later, Fr. Daniel Fitzgerald built Saint Mary's Church honoring both Saint Mary and Mary Pierce, the wife of Hon. Kirk D. Pierce. Fr. Charles Leddy served as pastor from 1919 until 1945. During his tenure the church expanded greatly in membership.

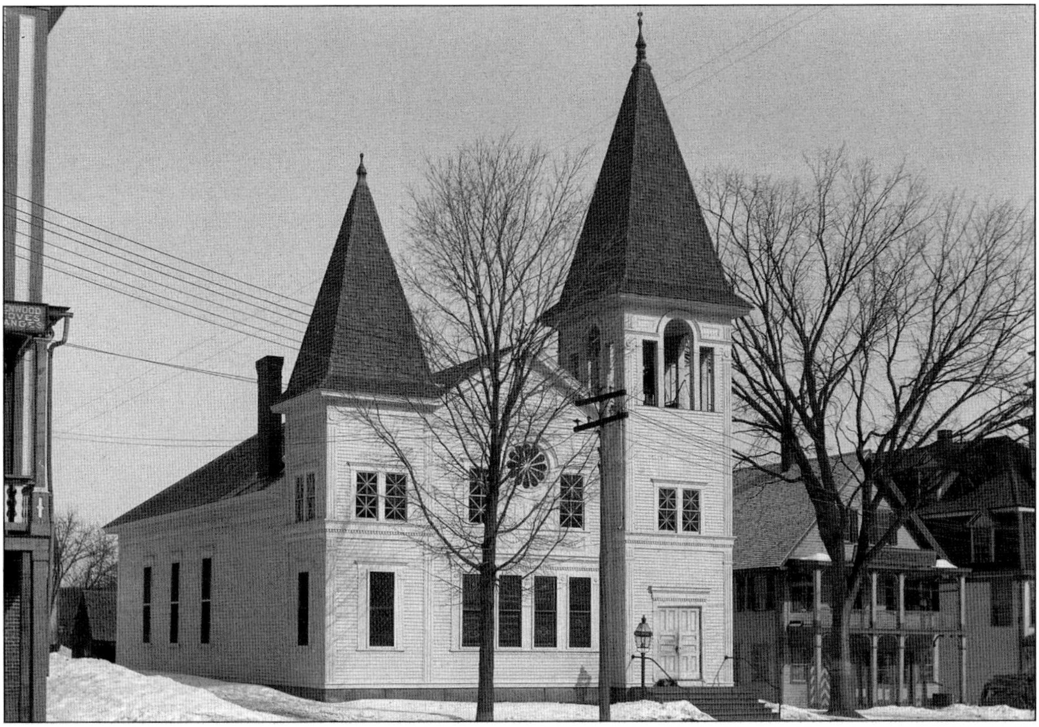

In 1840, the first Methodist church was erected on School Street. This picture shows the old church after it was moved to Henniker Street in 1865 and enlarged; it was further enlarged in 1894. Note the buildings on the right, one had a bowling alley inside, and the far pagoda-style structure was the Grand Army of the Republic meetinghouse.

The citizens of Lower Village always dreamed of having their own church with the end of the Baptist church; the Ladies Aid Society made that dream a reality. On May 17, 1883, the society was formed with 12 original charter members paying 25¢ annual dues each. These women were able to raise enough money to construct the chapel, breaking ground in May 1886 on land donated by S. Wescott and Sons. The Union Chapel was completed on March 9, 1887, at a cost of $2,081.38.

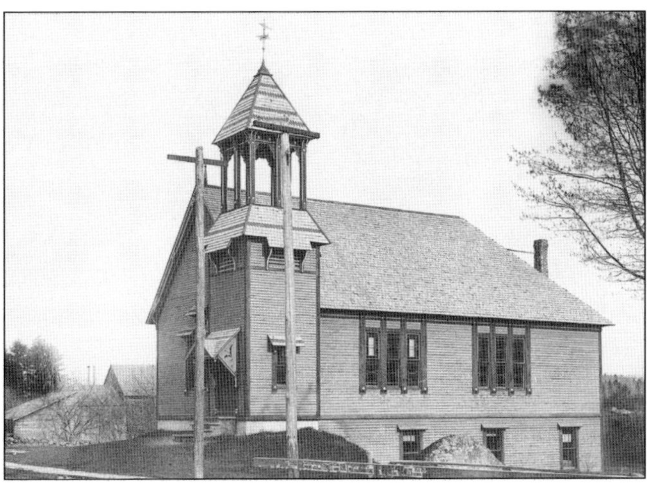

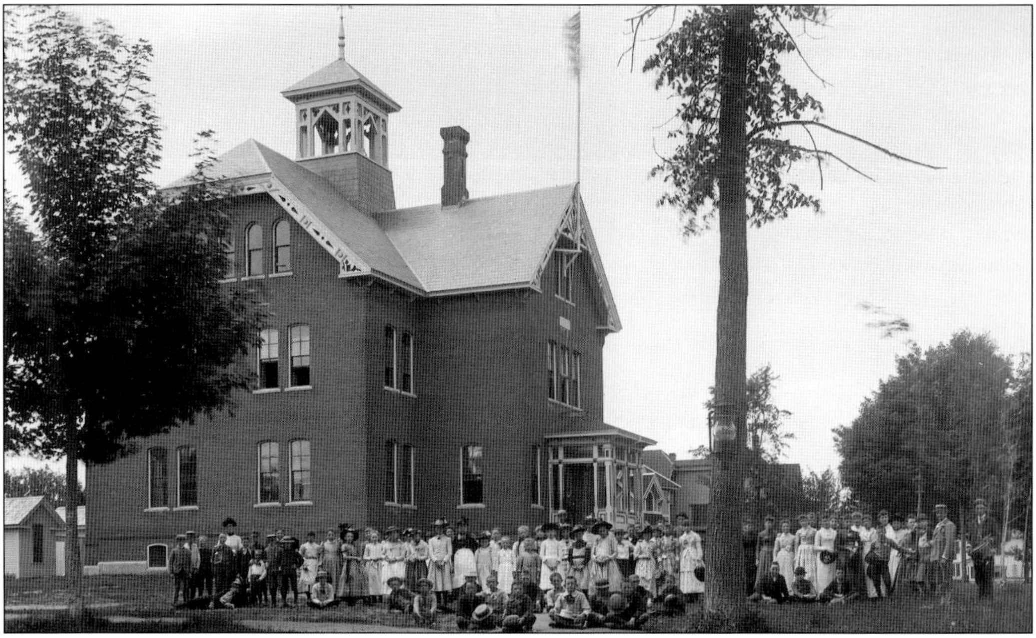

This three-story brick school replaced the Valley Academy in 1883 because school enrollment had sharply increased. This school picture was taken shortly after the school opened. Teachers were well paid at $40 a month, when $1 a day was the average wage. In 1890, three new rooms were added to the structure, as shown below, for a cost of $5,000. In 1900, there were nine teachers and 300 pupils. By 1920, the school enrollment leveled off at 60 high school students, with Robert Anderson as their headmaster, and 239 students in grades one through eight. The staff included 13 female teachers, with Cora Scruton being responsible for 67 first and second graders. The high school had a 10-to-1 student ratio and was considered a high-performing institution by the state.

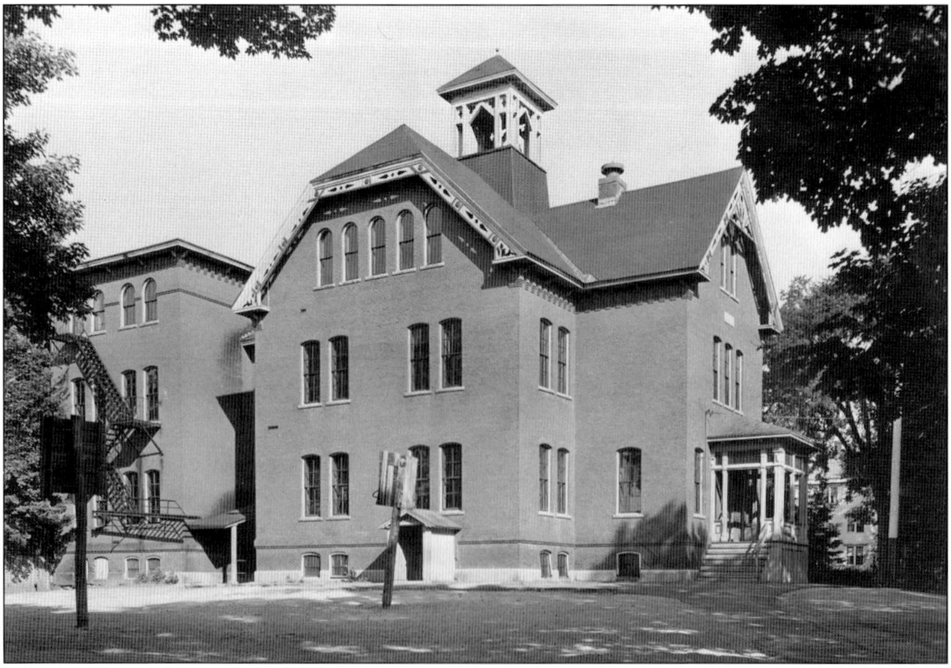

In the early years, the children of Hillsborough went to class in one-room schoolhouses. In all, there were 18 wooden structures and one brick. The old brick schoolhouse at right was located on Gleason Falls Road. It was the only brick schoolhouse in town. It was also said to be the school Franklin Pierce attended.

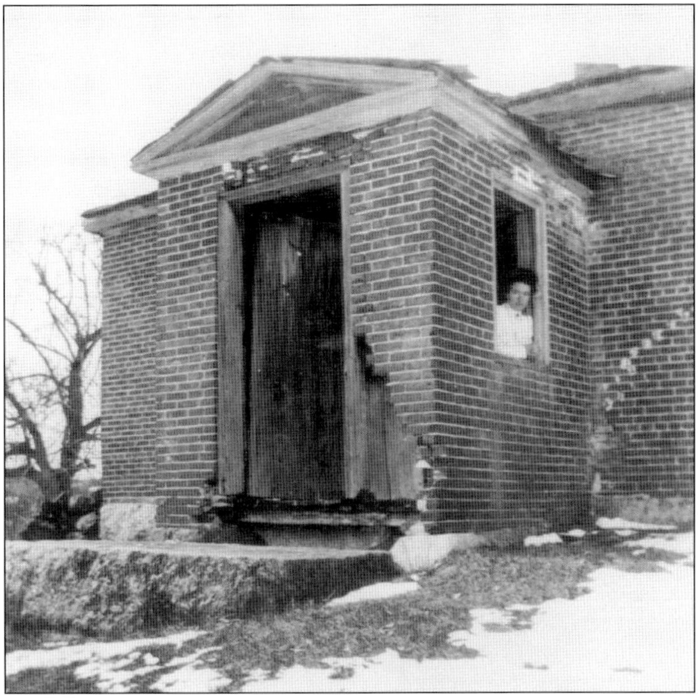

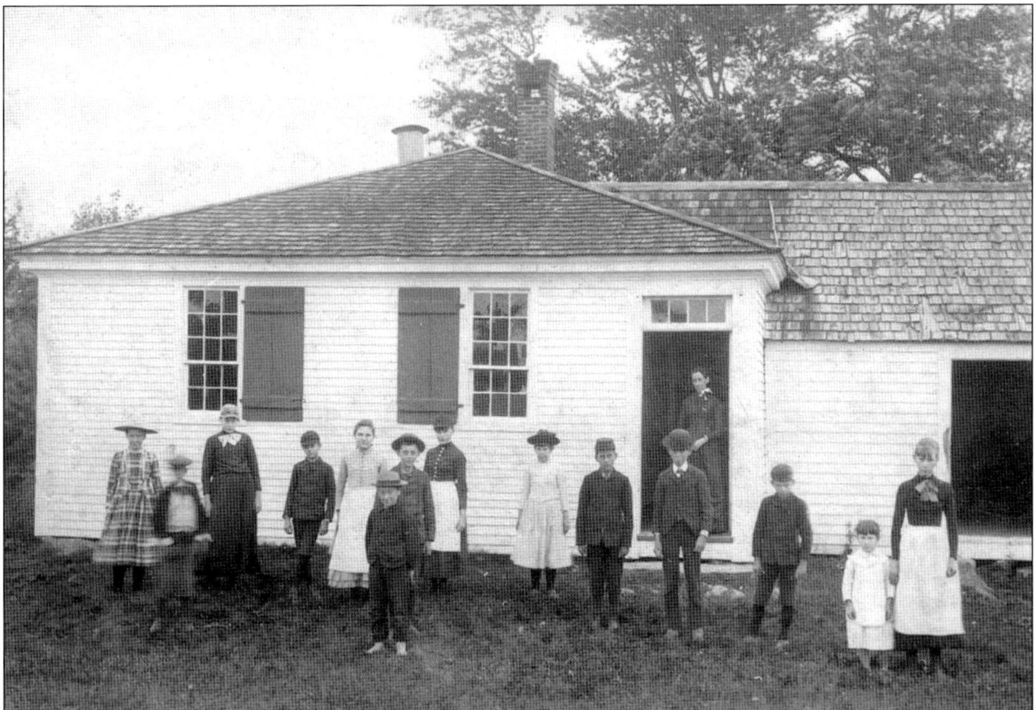

The Center Schoolhouse was active until 1951. This 1920s picture shows typical students. Standing in the doorway is Lisabel Gay, a longtime teacher and local historian. The Center Schoolhouse still stands today, fully equipped with desks and chalkboards.

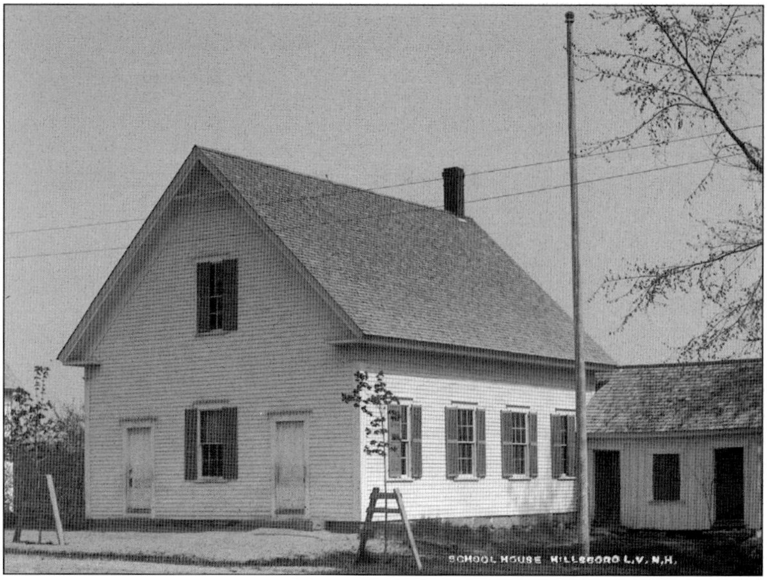

The Lower Village Schoolhouse was one of the last active one-room schoolhouses in town, ending its service in 1951. When this picture was taken, the schoolhouse had the largest enrollment in Hillsborough, with 31 pupils in 1920 under the supervision of teacher Deborah Brown.

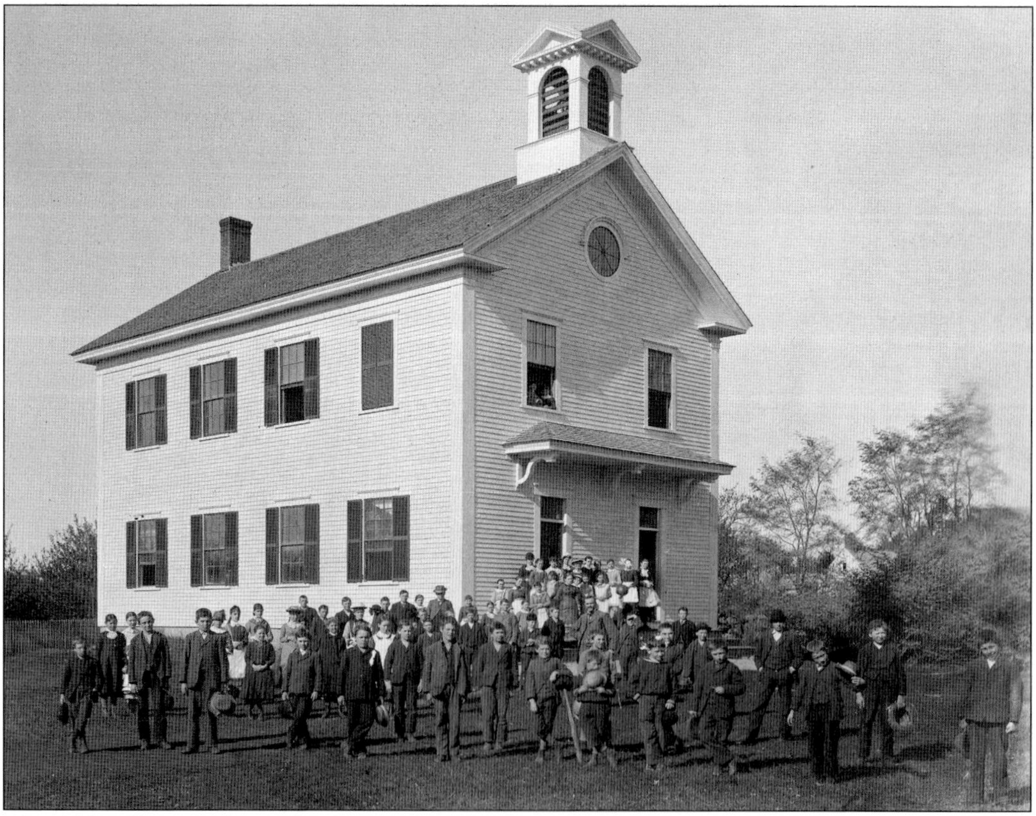

The Old Valley Academy, the first grade school in Hillsborough, was built in 1861. The primary grade for those under the age of 12 was assigned to the ground floor, while the older pupils occupied the second floor. In 1876, it was renamed Union School and became the high school. Replaced by the new brick school in 1883, it was moved to West Main Street and became the Butler Block with stores on the first floor and the Grange Hall on the second floor.

The Flat School was another one-room schoolhouse located on West Main Street. At the time this picture was taken in the 1920s, Elizabeth Thompson was the teacher and the student population never exceeded a dozen. Mary Pierce was also a teacher there for many years. It was remodeled several times and now is the location of Dunkin Donuts and Yanni's Pizza.

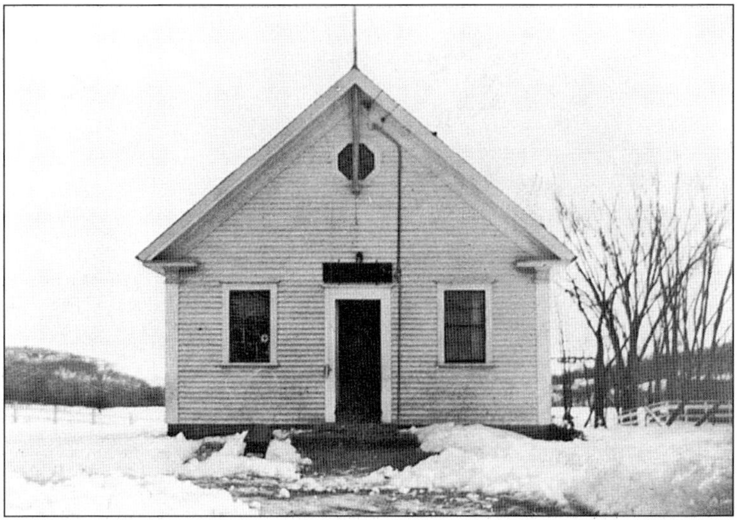

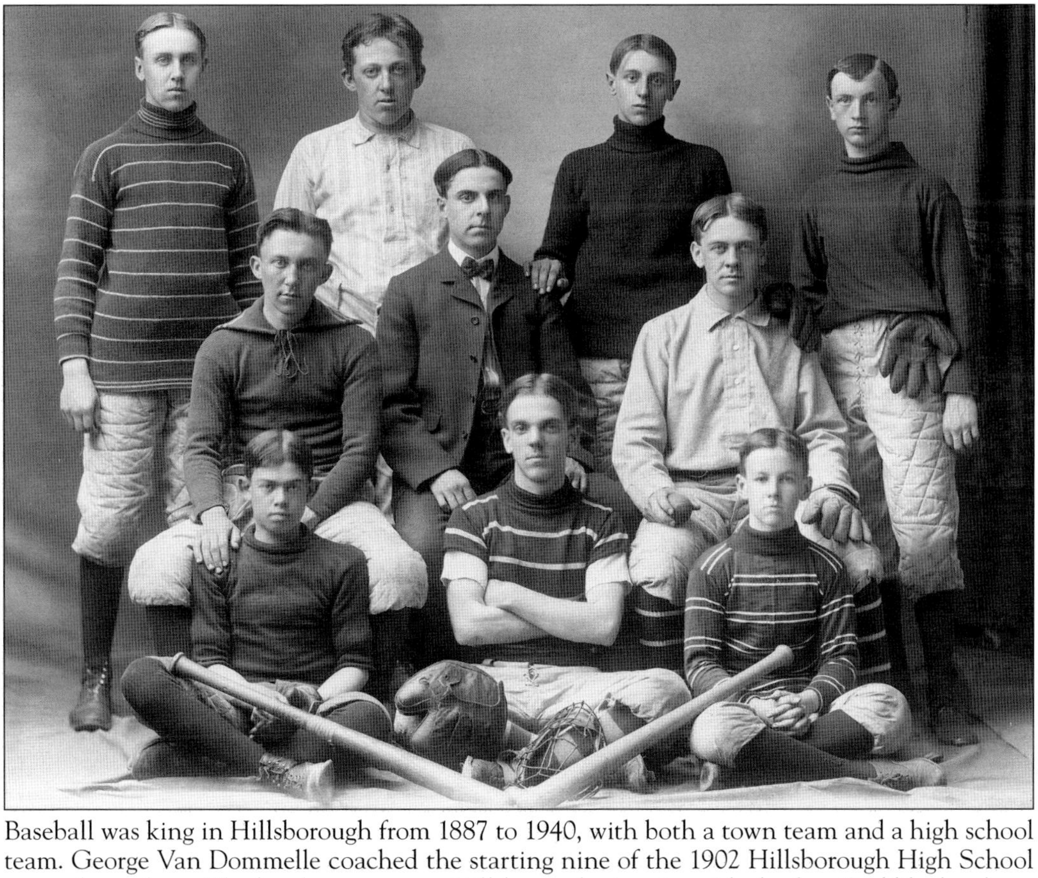

Baseball was king in Hillsborough from 1887 to 1940, with both a town team and a high school team. George Van Dommelle coached the starting nine of the 1902 Hillsborough High School team, shown here. The local powers were Hillsborough, Antrim with the four Cuddihy brothers, and Henniker. Perhaps the best Hillsborough ball player was Merritt Crosby.

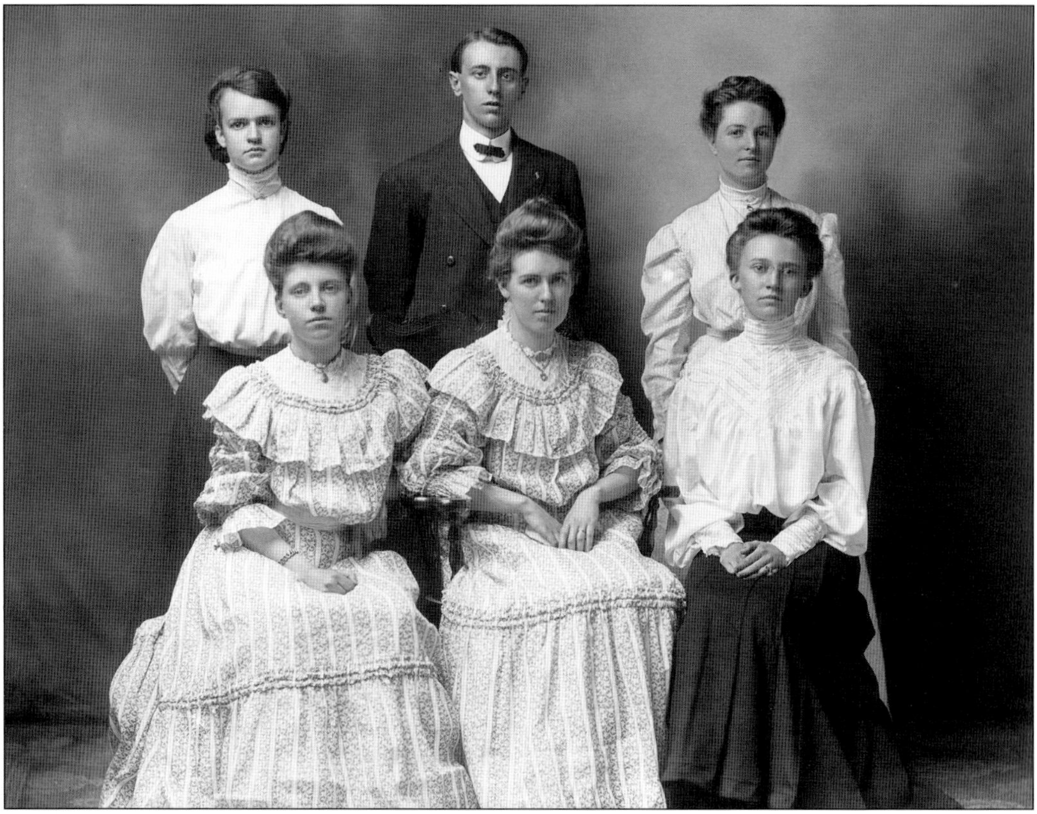

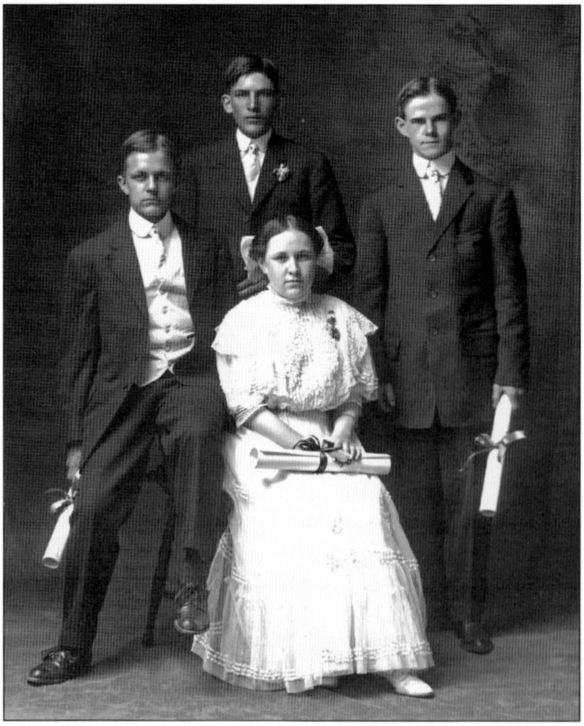

Graduation was normally a formal affair, with boys in fashionable suits with bow ties and girls in fancy dresses with no ankles showing. At the turn of the 20th century, high school graduation classes in Hillsborough were often quite small, which led to interesting student bodies. The exception was the class of 1902, which graduated 20 students. Seen above is the 1905 class, with one lucky boy, and, at left, the 1908 class, with only one girl, Marion Colby. Colby graduated from Tufts University and taught for many years, indicating that a first-rate education was possible in a small school. Marion also lived to the age of 92. Her childhood portrait can be found in the Manahan collection.

Seven

Recreation and Celebration

Celebrations and recreational activities have always been among the few ways townspeople and summer visitors could all come together to socialize and enjoy each other's company. If there was ever a reason to celebrate in the town, usually there would be a parade. Fourth of July celebrations, Old Home Days, Veterans Day, Memorial Day, and any other holiday would be celebrated with a parade down School, West Main, and Henniker Streets. Bill Dumais was the organizer of many of these parades during his lifetime.

Music has always played a role in Hillsborough's history. In 1825, the Hillsborough Brass Band was incorporated by an act of legislature, and they would perform in the bandstand at Grimes field. The Wahneta Orchestra was started in 1889, and played at nearly every high school graduation in Hillsborough. In 1905, the Hillsborough Music Club was formed.

Starting in 1907, the circus would come to town via the railroad at least two to three times a summer. Barnum and Bailey, Buffalo Bill's Wild West, and Ringling Brothers visited regularly for many years, setting up tents, rides, and sideshows on the old fairgrounds.

Since the early 19th century, fraternal and social societies have formed in Hillsborough. The Masons, Daughters of the American Revolution, Grand Army of the Republic, American Legion, Woman's Club, Fortnightly Club, and the Sons of Veterans, to name a few, would meet regularly in town.

No matter the season, Hillsborough has always been home to some sort of sports or recreation. Baseball was one of the town's favorite pastimes. From 1887 to 1940, Hillsborough actually had its own baseball team that played at Grimes field. The serene outdoors was one of the main attractions for tourists. People could enjoy one of the many 35 lakes and ponds in town, like Contention or Loon Ponds, or enjoy a boat ride on the Contoocook River. Hillsborough has been home to many fine outdoorsmen as well. The lakes and woods have proven to be great sources of wildlife for hunting and fishing. No matter your pleasure, the great outdoors in Hillsborough offer something for everyone.

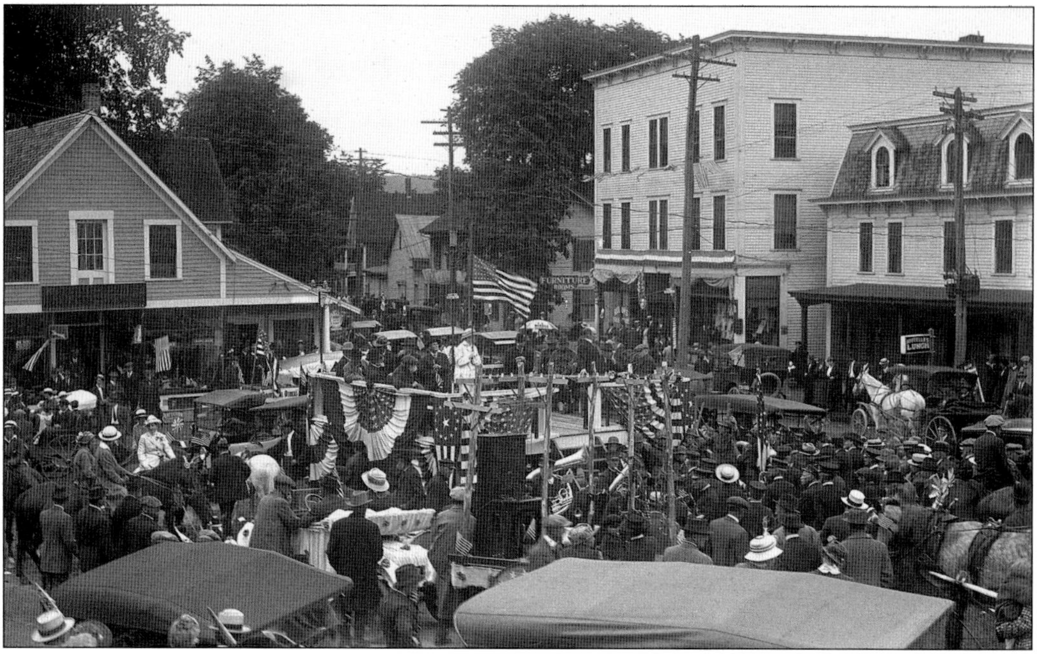

During this Fourth of July celebration in 1916, K.D. Pierce, a nephew of Pres. Franklin Pierce and a prominent local attorney, was the keynote speaker. Hundreds have gathered around the bandstand on Depot Street to hear him speak. The crowd was so large that it stretched past the Dreamland movie theater and the McGreevy-Connor Block.

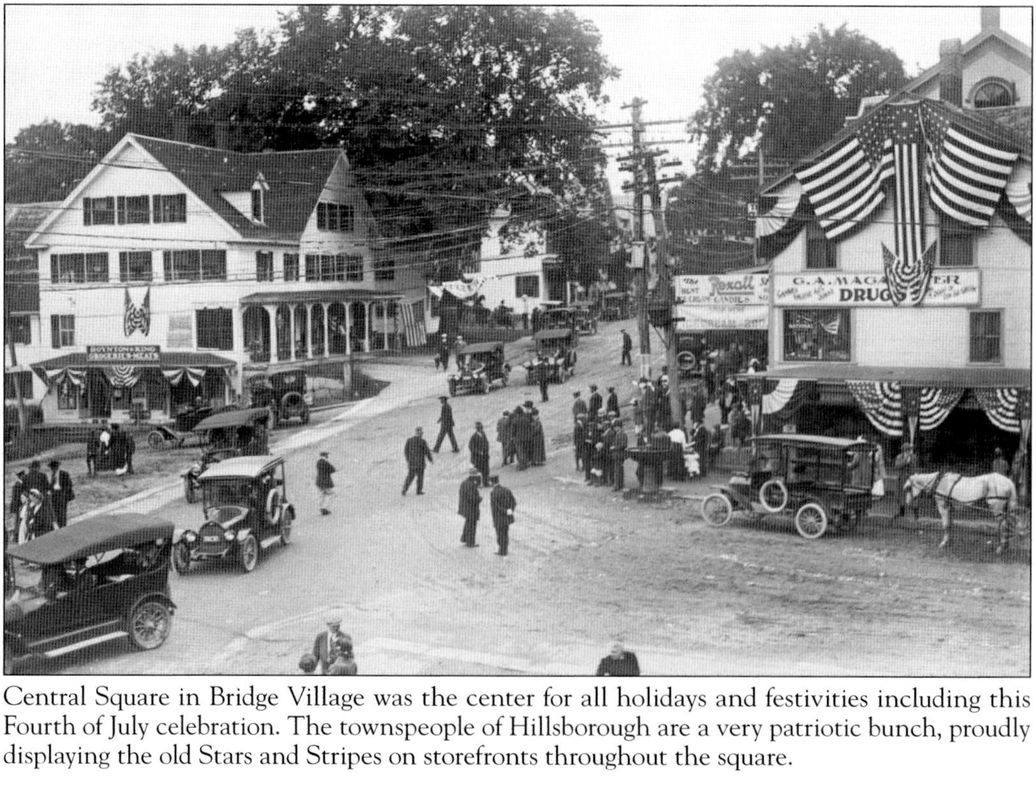

Central Square in Bridge Village was the center for all holidays and festivities including this Fourth of July celebration. The townspeople of Hillsborough are a very patriotic bunch, proudly displaying the old Stars and Stripes on storefronts throughout the square.

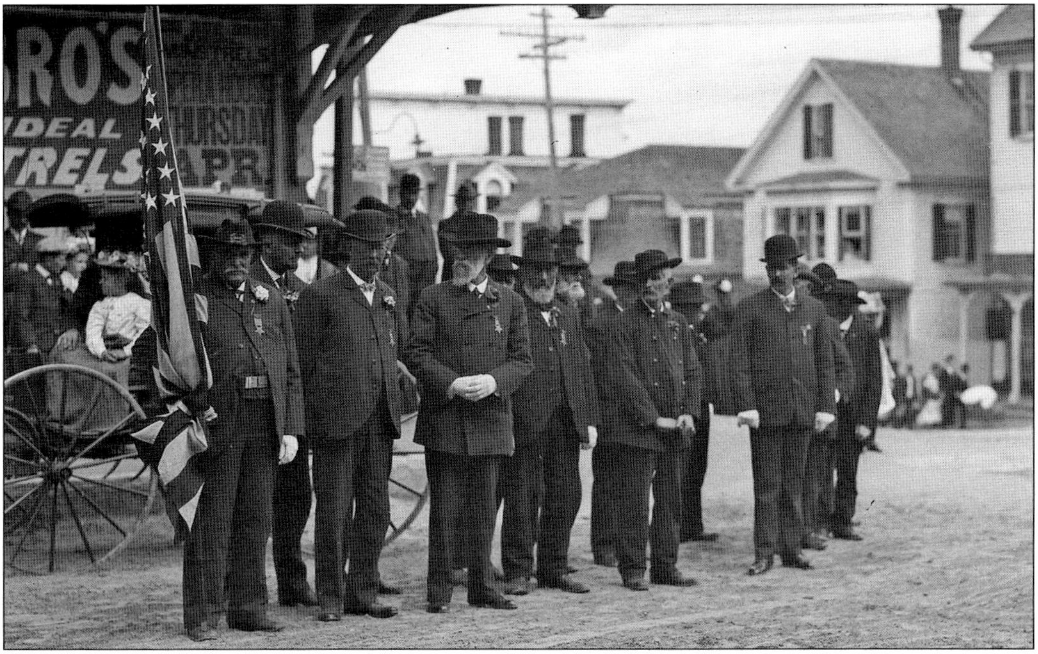

A dozen Civil War veterans organized the Grand Army of the Republic's Hillsborough post in 1876. With over 200 Hillsborough soldiers participating in the Civil War, a strong post was established. During the first year of its existence, GAR members found all the graves of veterans within the town and decorated them with flowers and flags. This 1907 photograph was taken on Memorial Day in front of Child's Opera House.

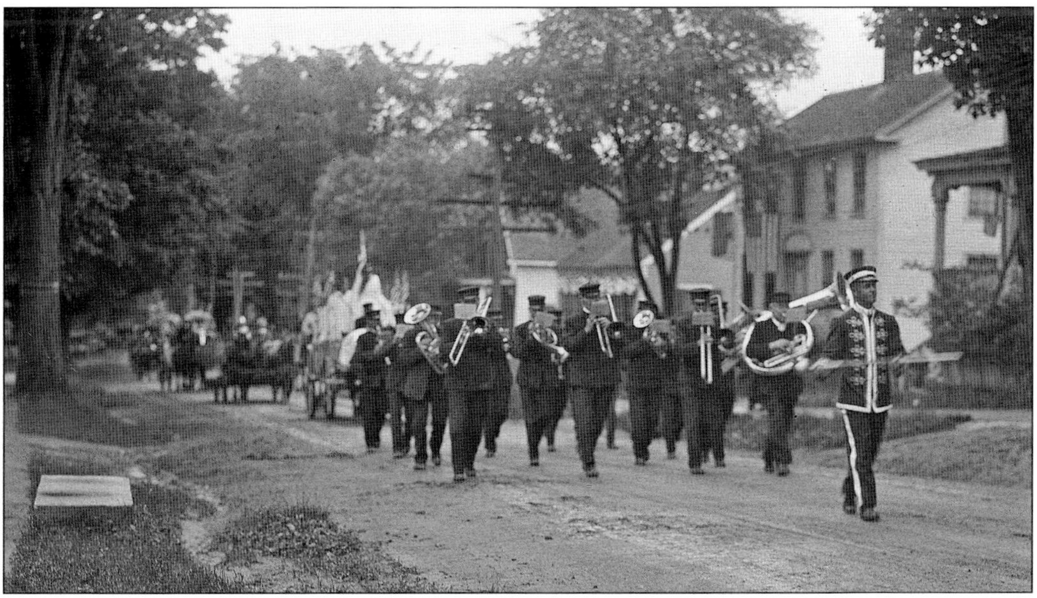

Music has always played a vital role in celebrations in town. Whether playing in the bandstand at Depot Street or Grimes field or marching down Henniker Street in a parade, as pictured here on the Fourth of July in 1916, the sound of music could be heard all day long. Note the impressive uniform of the bandmaster and the stone on the left by the Congregational church, which was used for ladies to step on to their carriages.

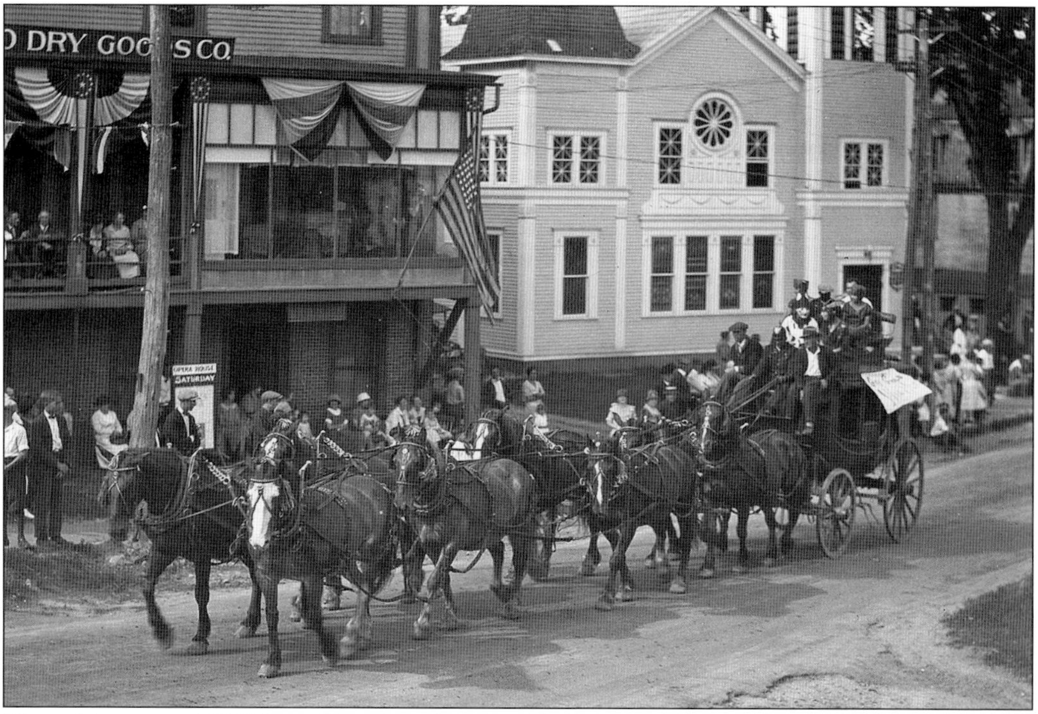

The celebration of Old Home Days was the idea of New Hampshire governor Frank Rollins. The state experienced a population explosion in the 1830s; however, several decades later, many left for the more fertile farmlands of the Midwest. In order to encourage more tourism and bring back former residents to visit their old farms, Rollins came up with the idea for towns to celebrate their heritage and homes. This picture was taken at the Old Home Days parade in Hillsborough on August 15, 1925.

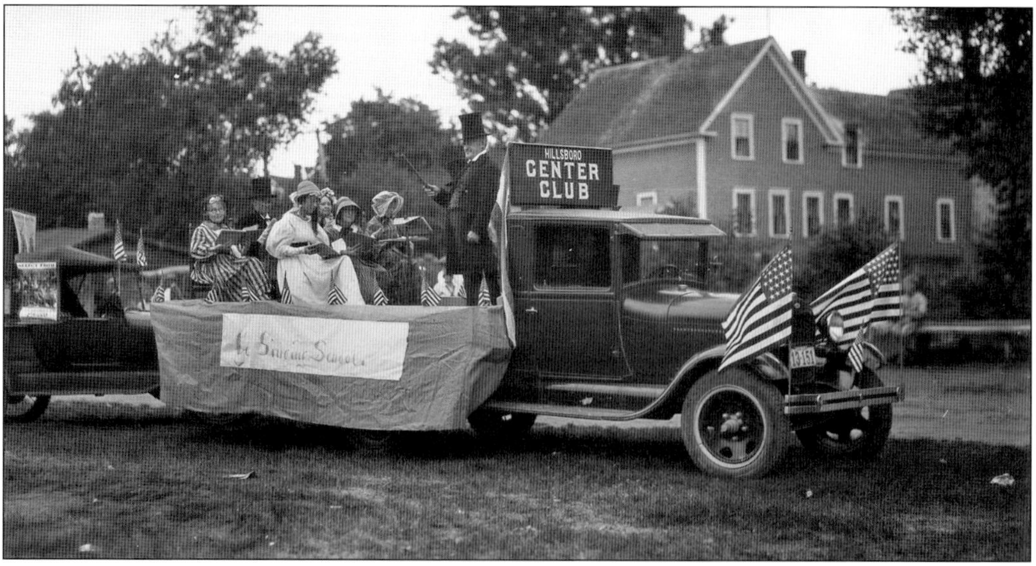

One of the unique floats of the 1929 Old Home Days celebration was that of the Center Club Singing School. It was told that the group could be heard all along the parade route. Music—whether singing or playing in one of several orchestras—has been a key avocation in Hillsborough.

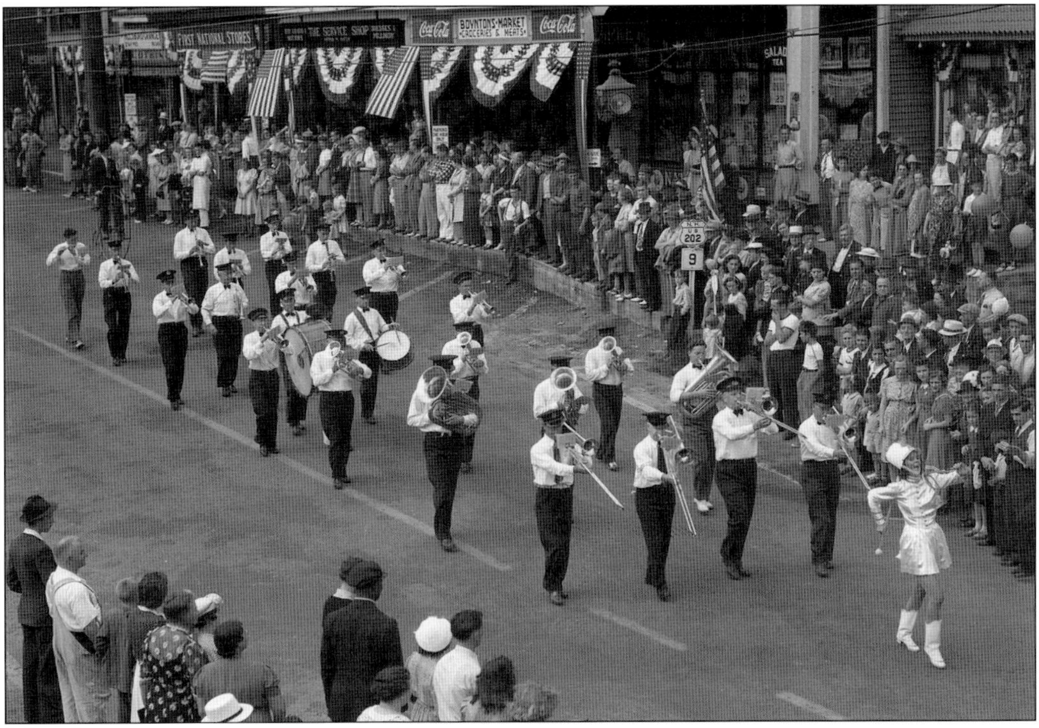

In 1940, hundreds came back to participate in the Old Home Days celebration. Here, a majorette leads the marching band down Main Street. Old Home Days celebrations were held annually for many decades in Hillsborough, but it is no longer celebrated today. Instead, the annual Hillsborough Balloon Festival has replaced it.

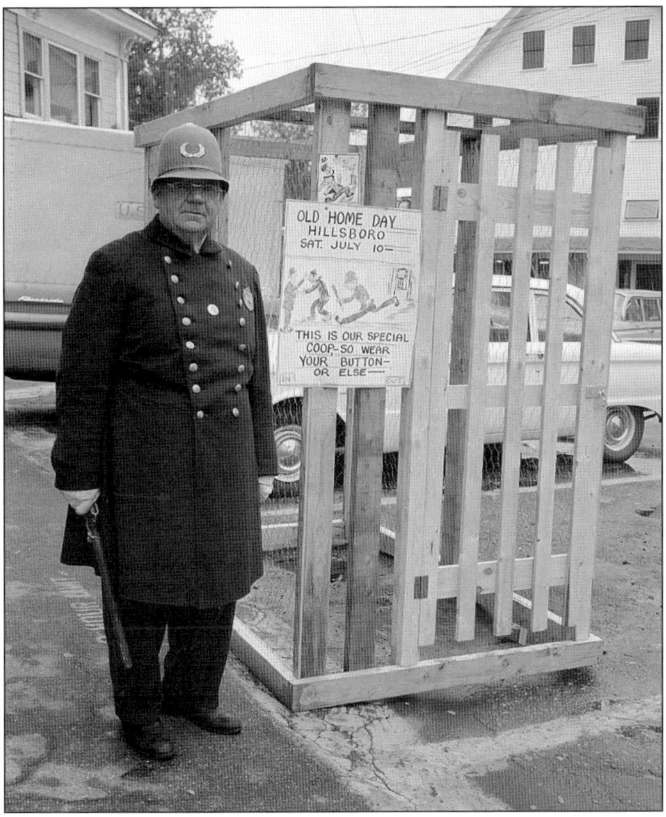

Bill Dumais, pictured here in his old-fashioned police uniform with his "coop," was the mastermind behind many of the parades in town. Through his unusual promotion tactics, he was able to encourage most citizens to take part in the festivities. For this Old Home Days parade on July 3, 1965, he encouraged everyone to wear their buttons, or else!

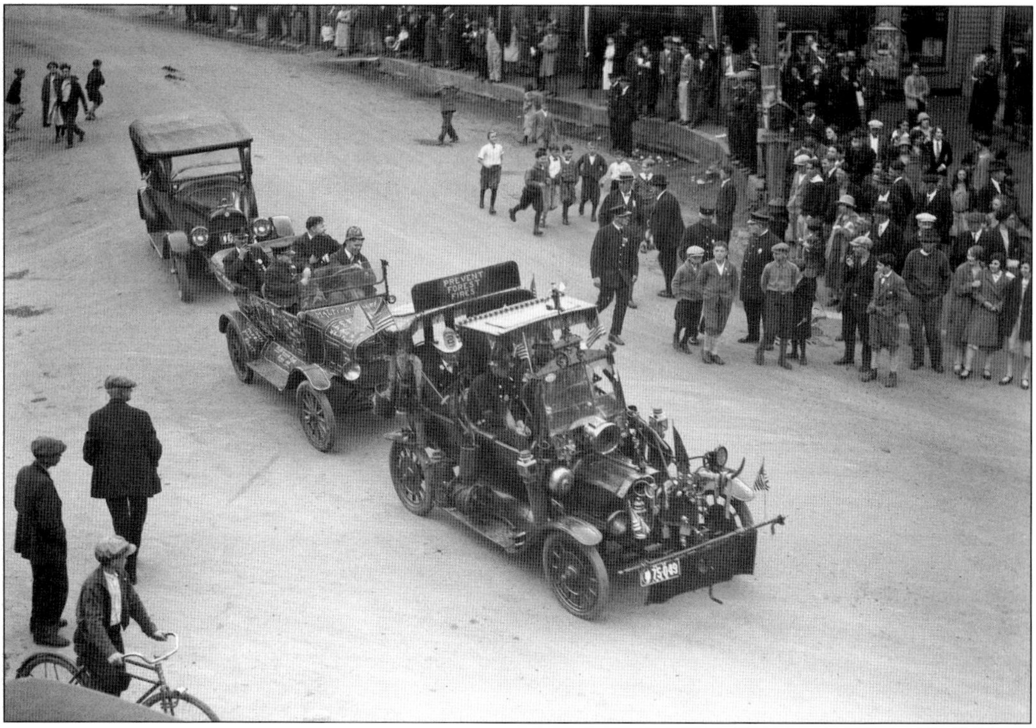

Both of these pictures were taken at the firemen's convention parade on September 24, 1926. Above are examples of fire trucks and apparatus of the time period. That year Hillsborough purchased a brand new Maxim ladder truck, which in 1959 was sold to Storyland amusement park upstate. Pictured below are the firemen from Hillsborough, led by Chief W.E. Newman, along with surrounding area fire departments marching in uniform down Main Street. Every year the firemen organized a major weekend in town, which along with a parade included a ball, banquet, matinee amusement rides and arcade, and Sunday evening fireworks. The tradition continues today during the Hillsborough Balloon Festival.

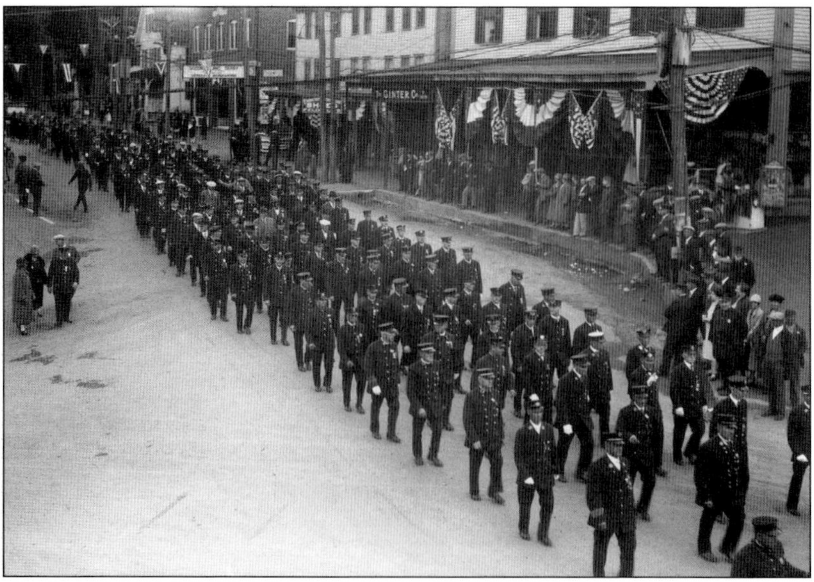

The grandest celebration of them all was the Hillsborough bicentennial celebration. The honor guard, followed by a horse-drawn cannon, marked the start of the parade. The artillery company started the celebration by firing a 14-shot salute on the fairgrounds at noon. They used an old six-pounder brass cannon, cast in 1847, to fire one-pound charges of black powder, a great thrill to the children of town.

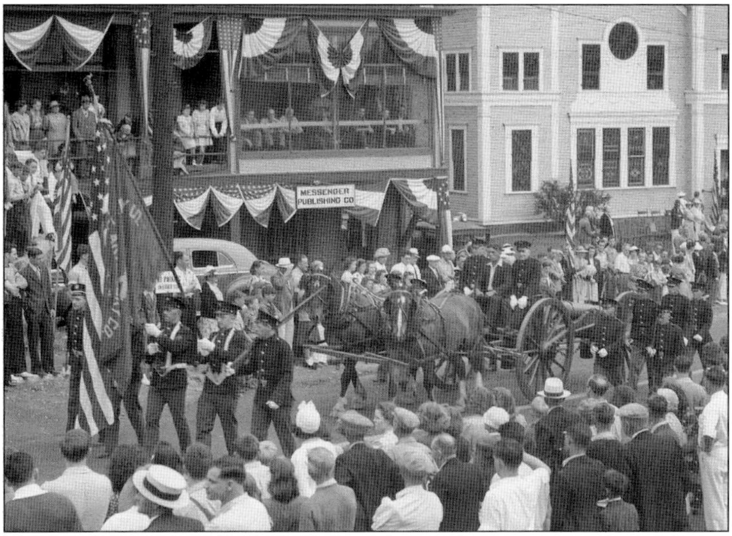

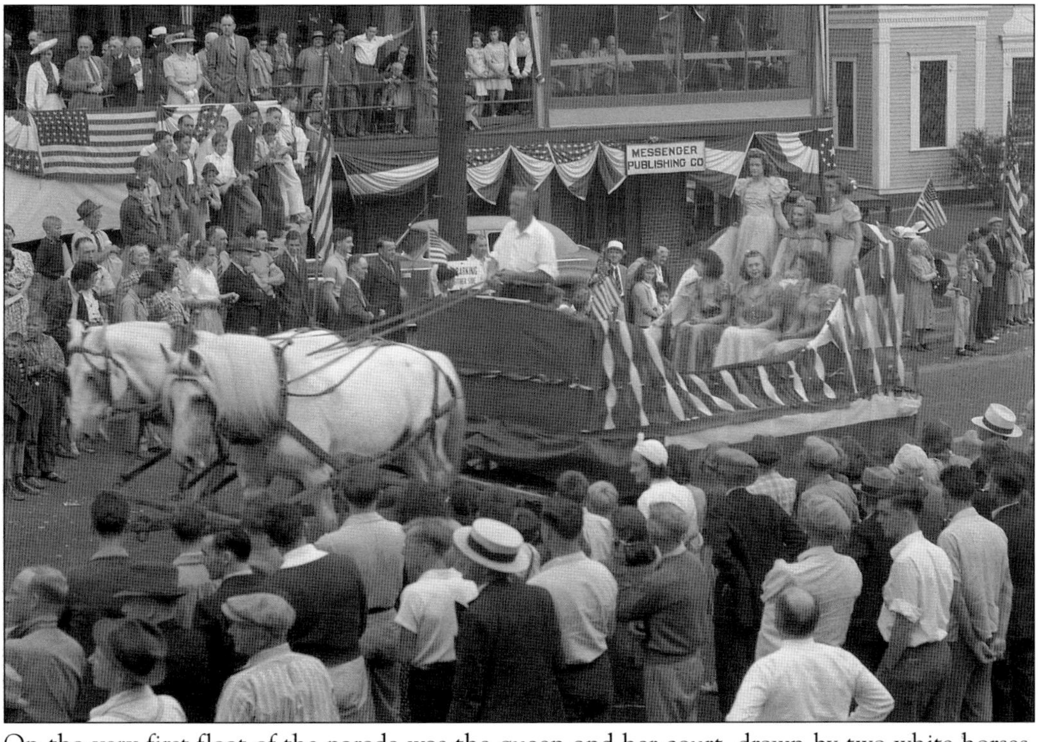

On the very first float of the parade was the queen and her court, drawn by two white horses. Jean Beard, daughter of Earl and Vanessa Beard, was selected as "Miss Independence Day" from 16 of the town's girls. Along the entire route, the group was given a great ovation.

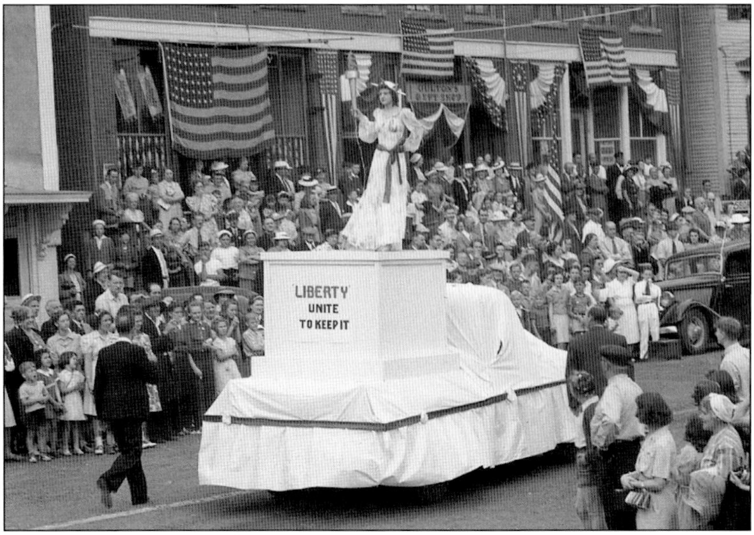

The bicentennial parade was more than a mile long and contained more than 60 floats. Of special note was the Pineland Poultry Farm float, which had a young girl portraying the Statue of Liberty with a sign reading "Liberty: Unite to Keep It." The parade was travelling along School Street, passing the center building, which housed the first town library on the second floor.

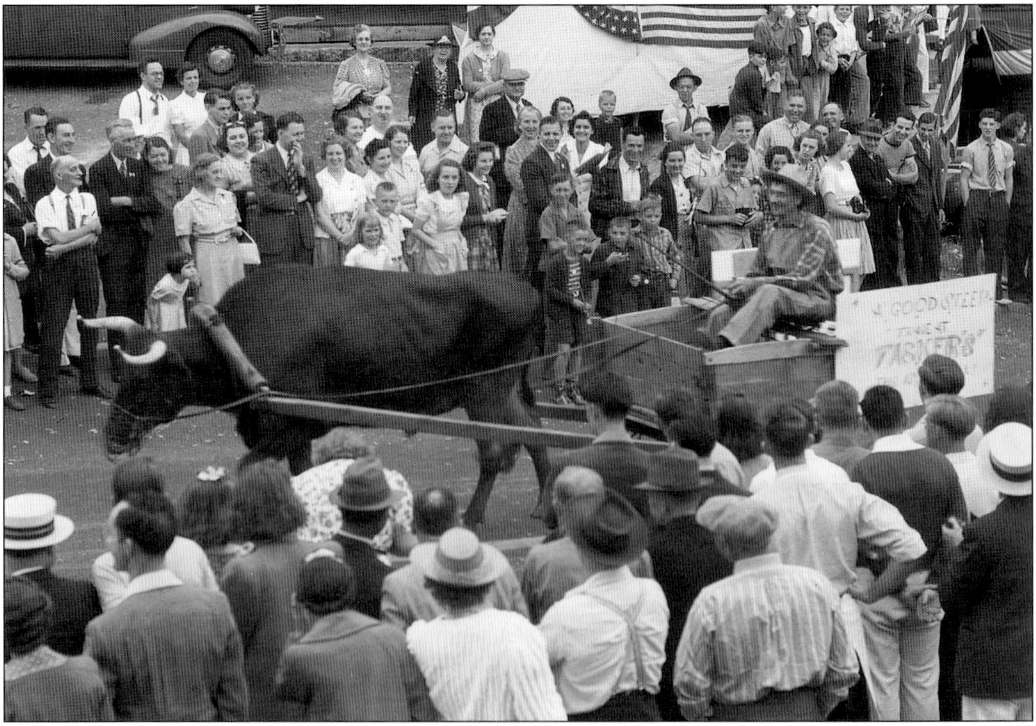

Even though it was the simplest float, the Tasker's Store float was the only one to have its picture in the *Boston Herald*. It was a big steer driven like a horse by a man on a cart. The only thing on the side of the cart was a sign that read "A good steer, trade at Tasker's. This is no bull."

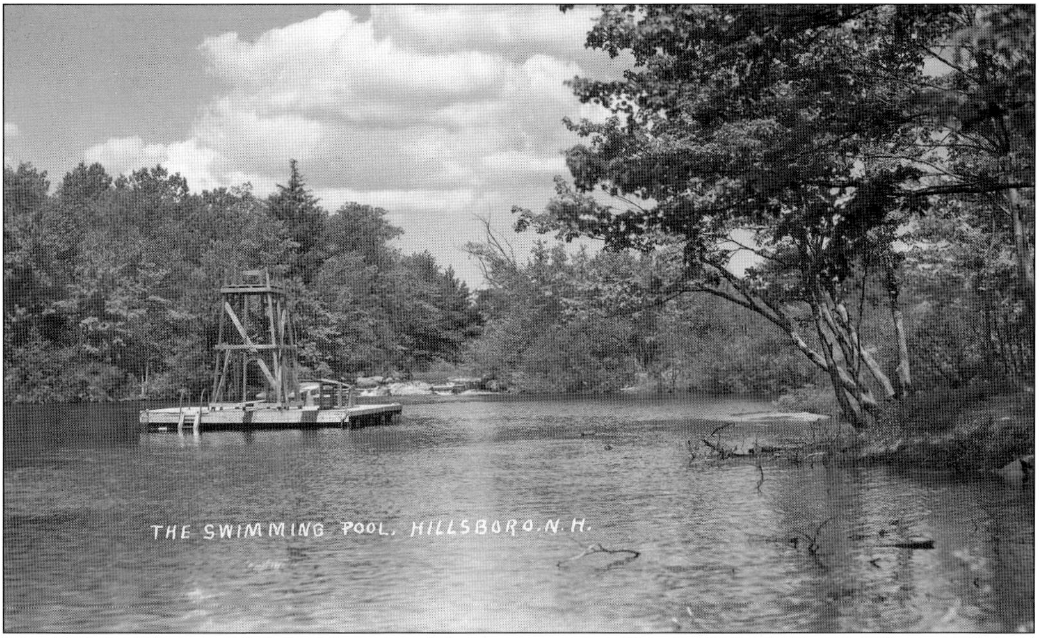

Commonly referred to as Hillsborough's "swimming hole," Beard Brook was the favorite spot for locals and tourists alike to enjoy a refreshing dip from the summer heat before Manahan Park opened in the early 1960s. In 1935, a Works Progress Administration crew led by Frank Glading built bathhouses, a diving board, and swimming float.

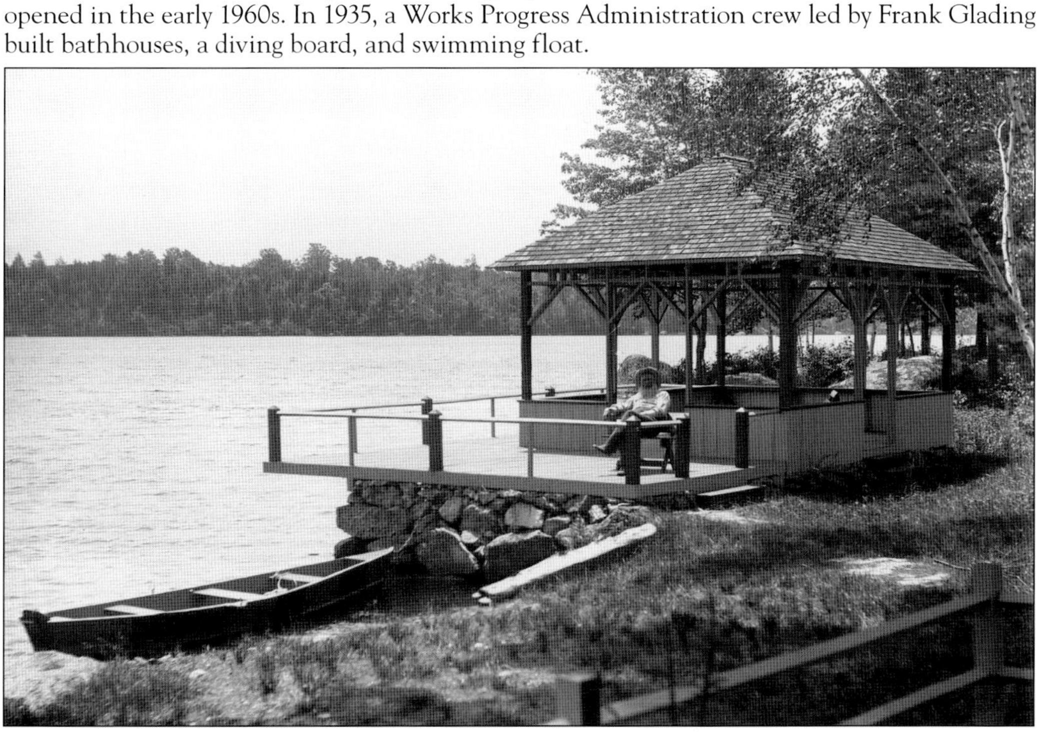

The summer cottage of William H. Manahan, known as the Birches, was situated on Loon Pond. On the water's edge, he had a gazebo constructed where one could enjoy the view of Lovell Mountain across the pond. Today Loon Pond serves as the town's water supply and remains clear and refreshing.

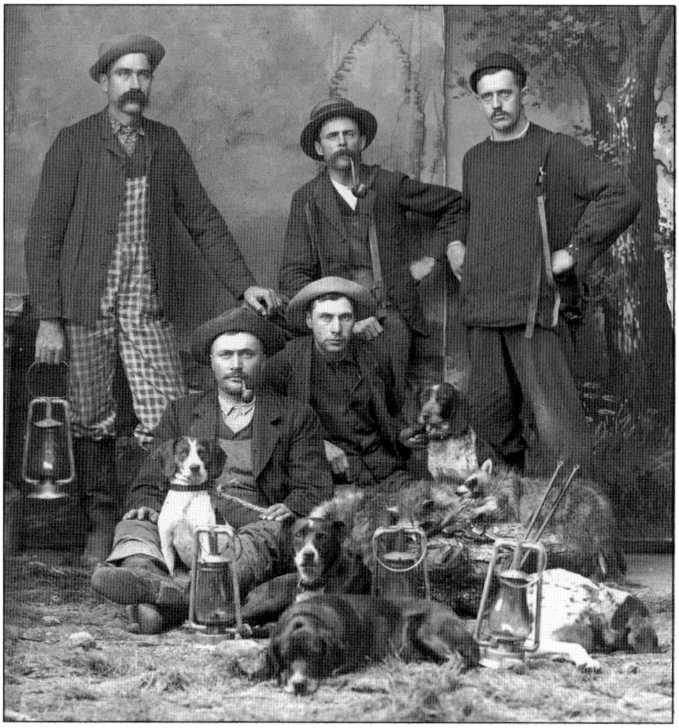

The woods of Hillsborough are home to many types of wild game. The group of men pictured here with their dogs have just returned from a coon-hunting trip. It appears that they had a pretty successful go at it. Well, actually, this is a staged picture in Manahan's studio with a curtain backdrop.

This picture of J.A. Rawson and his trusted hunting dog was taken on November 16, 1939. Rawson was an excellent marksman, evident by the ducks that he had shot earlier in the day lying in his boat. He now sits ready for the next opportunity, while his dog waits for a chance to retrieve his master's downed duck.

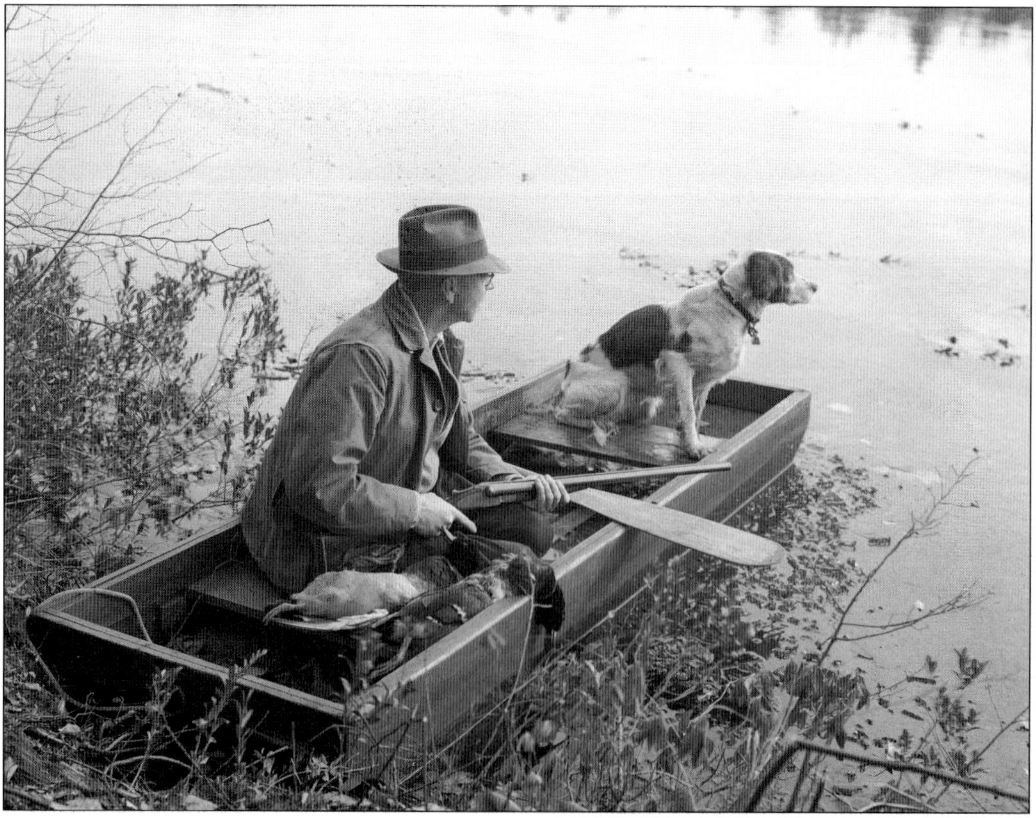

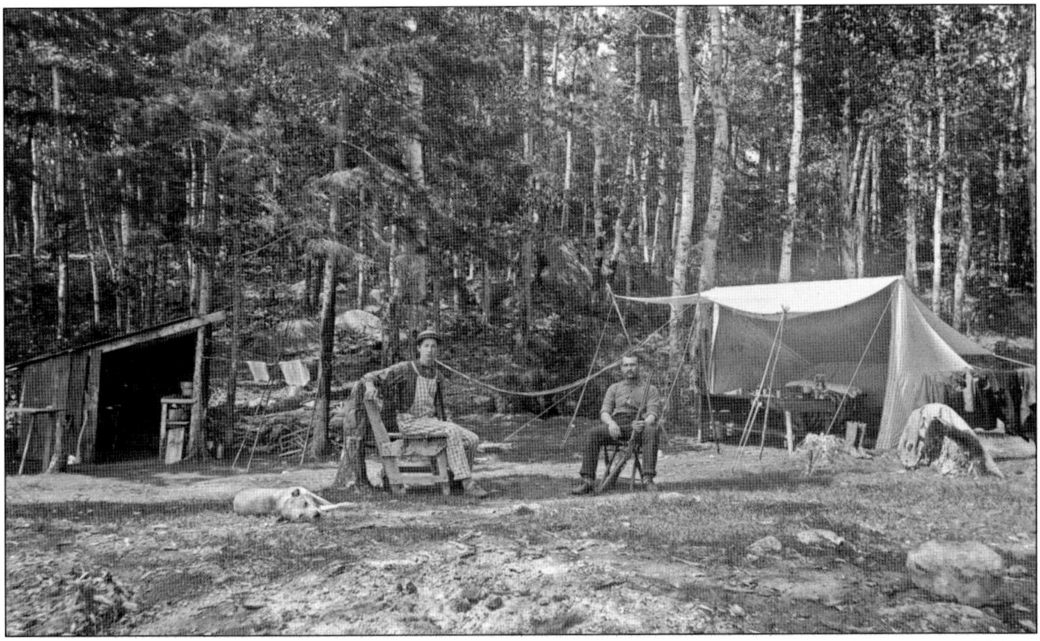

It was not uncommon for men to take hunting trips in the Hillsborough woods that would last several days. These two men have set up camp for the day, and are undoubtedly hoping for a successful hunt. Game hunting has been a major attraction, with deer, turkey, pheasant, black bear, and an occasional moose as the prize.

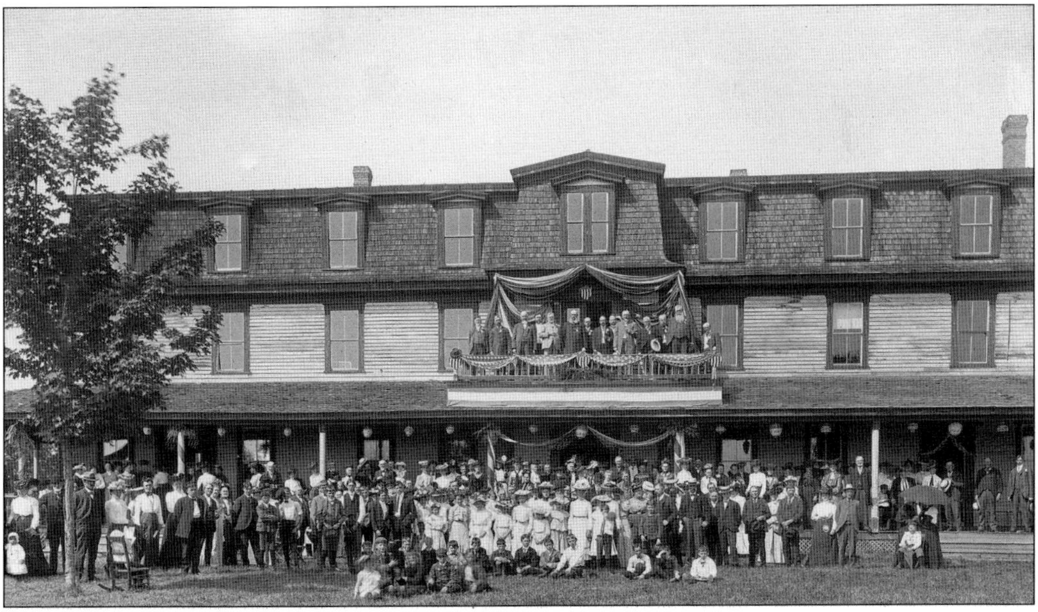

This 1903 photograph is of the Lake View House on the shores of Loon Pond. This was a popular summer vacation spot just north of Hillsborough Center. Guests and employees are posing in front of the hotel for one of the first Old Home Days. Water sports and steamboat rides made for a memorable summer.

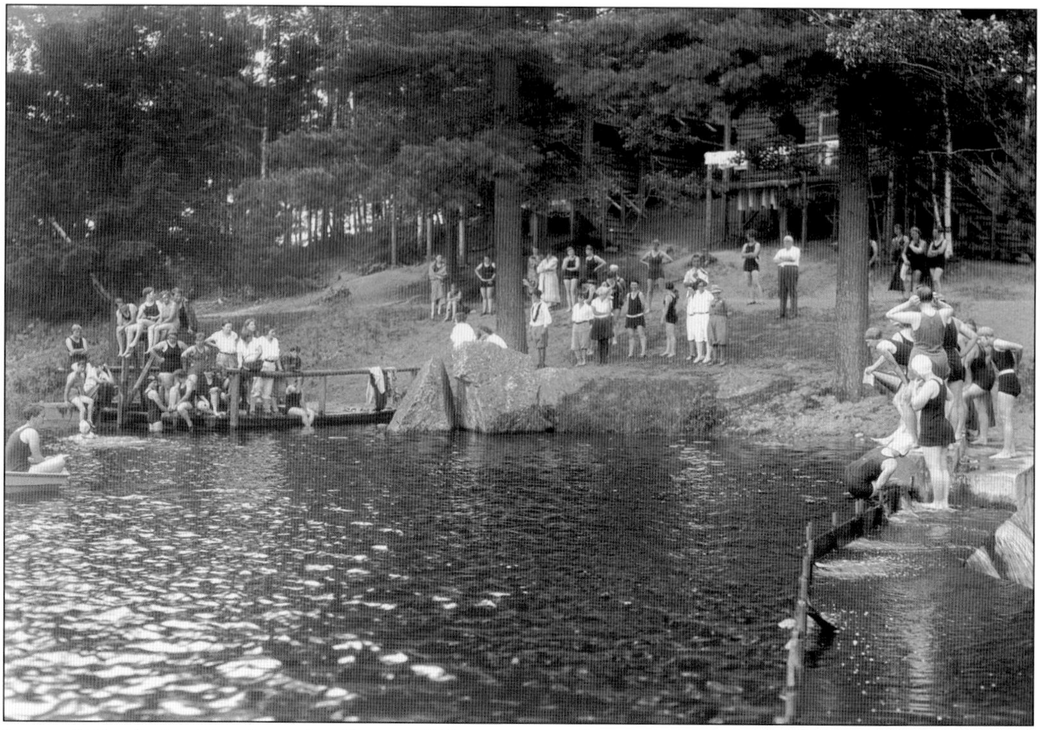

Just off Cooledge Road in the Upper Village going towards East Washington was the all-girls Posse-Nissen Camp. It was situated on approximately four acres of land and had access to its own pond. It was a place where girls could enjoy both water and land sports. The campers could go swimming, canoeing, or dive off of the large raft into the pond. Or, if dry land was more to their liking, the campers could go horseback riding, hiking, play field hockey, or learn archery. This camp was very popular from the 1930s to the 1950s.

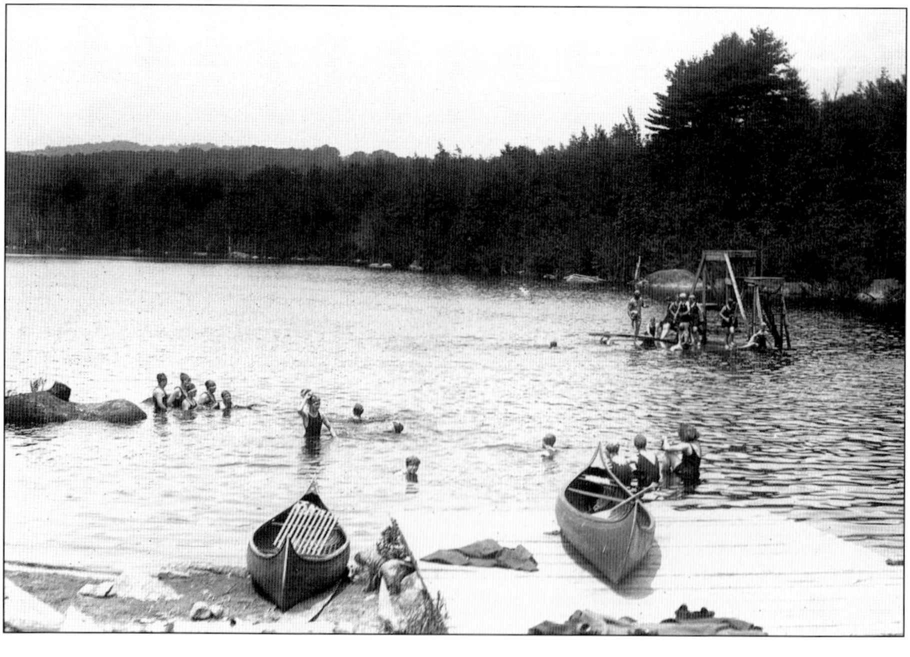

Eight

Natural Disasters

New England has always been known for its unpredictable and sometimes extreme weather. Two natural disasters will always be remembered in Hillsborough town history—the flood of 1936 and the Great New England Hurricane of 1938.

On March 11 and 12, 1936, the Contoocook River went on a rampage due to recent rains and sudden warm weather that caused a rapid snowmelt. By the first night, the water level was rising at a rate of a foot an hour, the lowlands were flooded, and bridges were being torn apart. In an effort to prevent extensive property damage, townspeople feverishly sandbagged around the mills along the river. By nightfall on the second night, the water had reached its peak and started to recede, but the damage was done. Water Street was washed out, the main highway to Antrim was flooded, some houses were swept away and destroyed, small buildings at the Woolen Mill were broken apart, and the old sawmill building collapsed. Even though the town was isolated for a day, Hillsborough fared better than many other towns and cities in the state.

Nicknamed the "Long Island Express" for its speed, the Great New England Hurricane of 1938 formed in September. It was a massive storm that was approximately 500 miles wide with an eye nearly 50 miles across. With no advanced weather notification system like those of today, the people of New England had no time to prepare for what was coming their way. On September 21, the hurricane made landfall as a category 3 in Long Island and soon struck the mainland. It took just a few hours to make its way through all of the New England states and eventually into Canada. In its wake, the hurricane caused approximately $308 million in damages and took over 700 lives. In all, over 57,000 homes and 26,000 automobiles were damaged or destroyed, and 20,000 electrical poles were downed. This Great New England Hurricane of 1938 remains the most powerful, deadliest, and costliest hurricane in the history of New England.

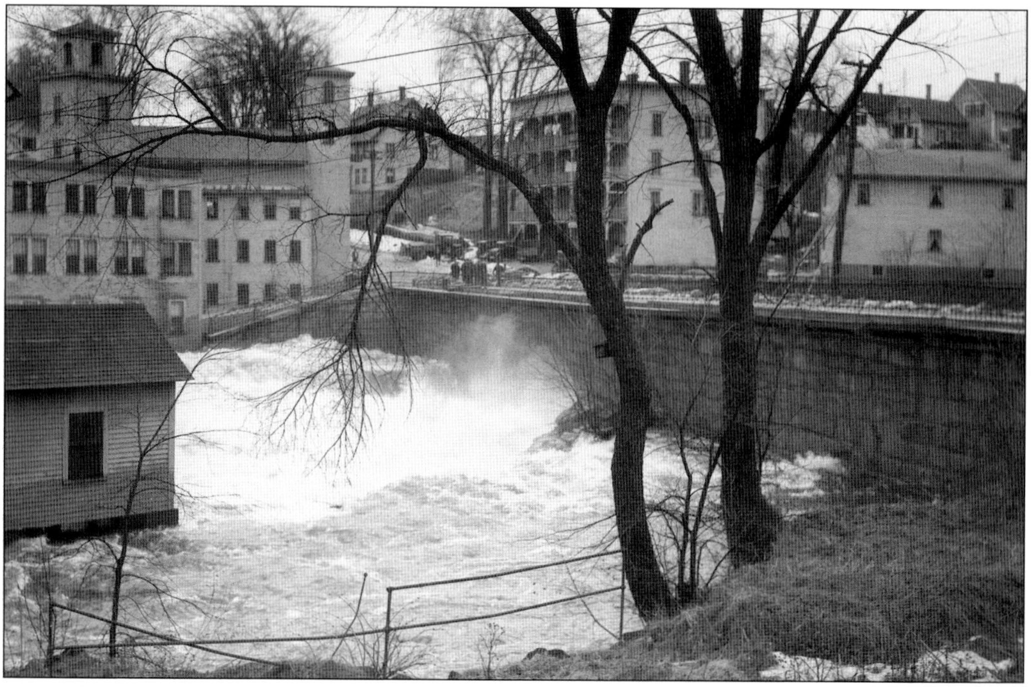

From the vantage point of River Street, one could see the fury of the Contoocook River as it rushed under the stone arch of the Bridge Street Bridge on March 11, 1936. The river was to rise even more during the evening.

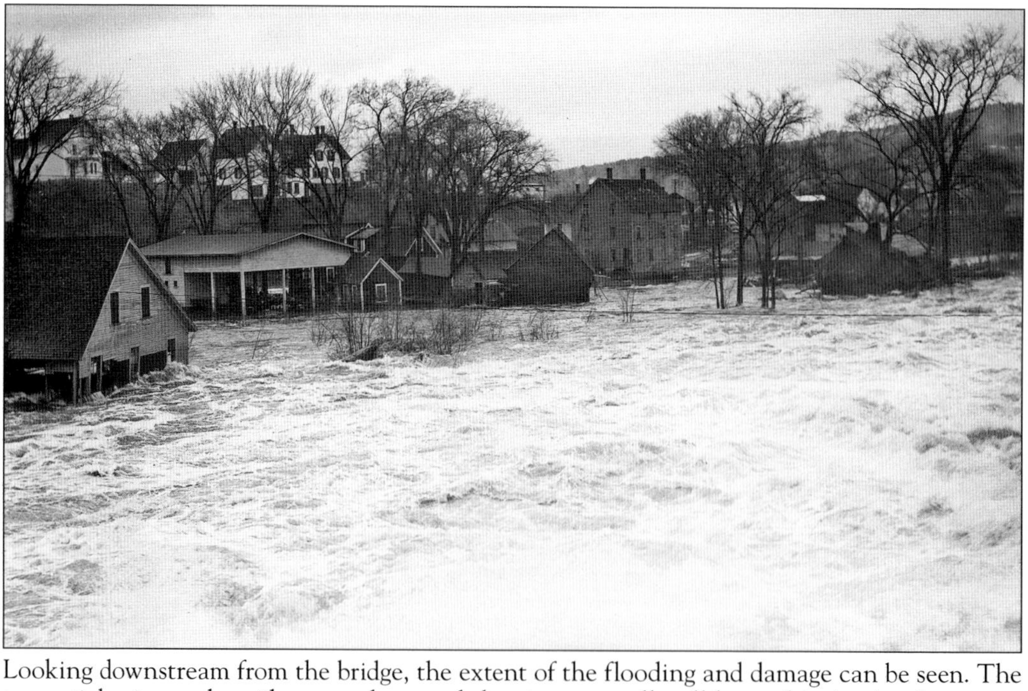

Looking downstream from the bridge, the extent of the flooding and damage can be seen. The torrential rains and rapid snowmelt caused the river to swell well beyond its banks, destroying everything in its path. Luckily, residents along the river were evacuated and no one lost their life that day.

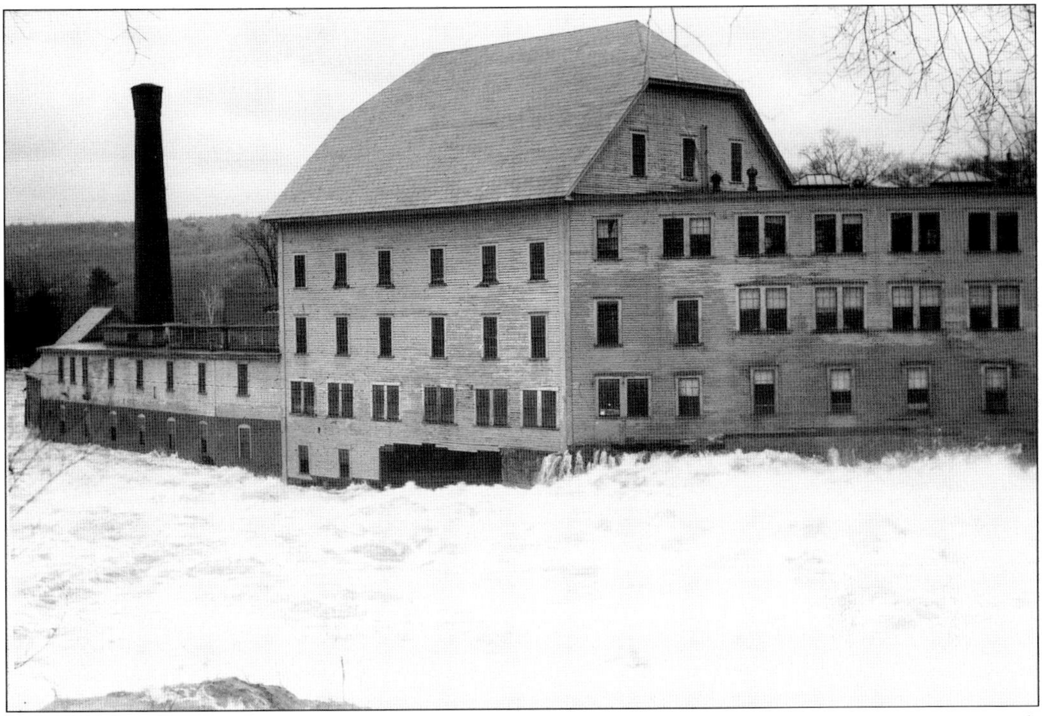

The Contoocook (Hosiery) Mill fared much better than most buildings along the Contoocook River. It only sustained minimal damage in the dye room on the bottom floor. Dedicated workers moved most equipment and valuables to higher floors before the room was flooded.

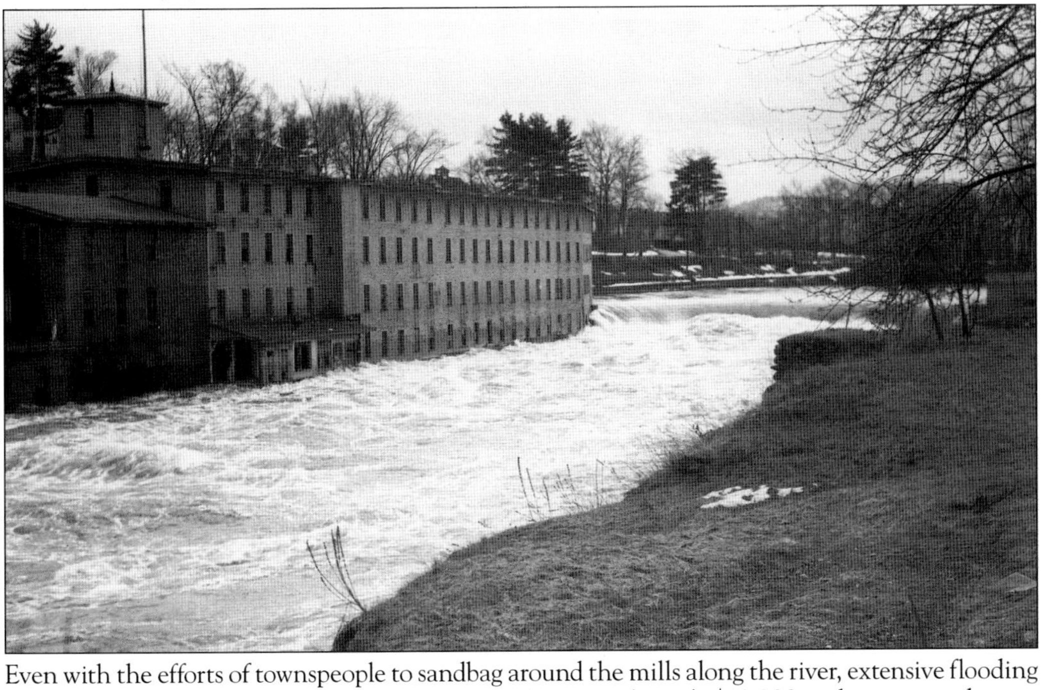

Even with the efforts of townspeople to sandbag around the mills along the river, extensive flooding and damage still did occur. The Woolen Mill itself received nearly $10,000 in damages, and many of its smaller buildings were broken apart and swept away by the rushing whitewater.

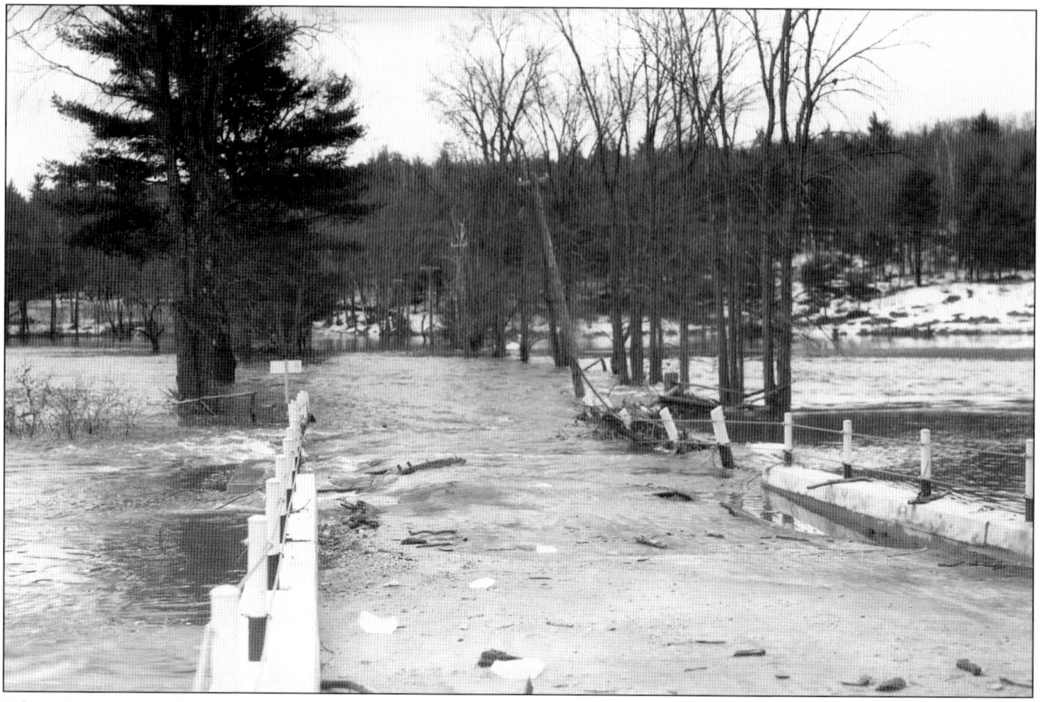

The Contoocook River rose so high that its waters flowed over the bridge on Antrim Road at West Main Street. Access between Antrim and Hillsborough was cut off for several days, until the water receded and the Antrim entrance was repaired. The stone bridge, although underwater, remained intact due to its superior construction.

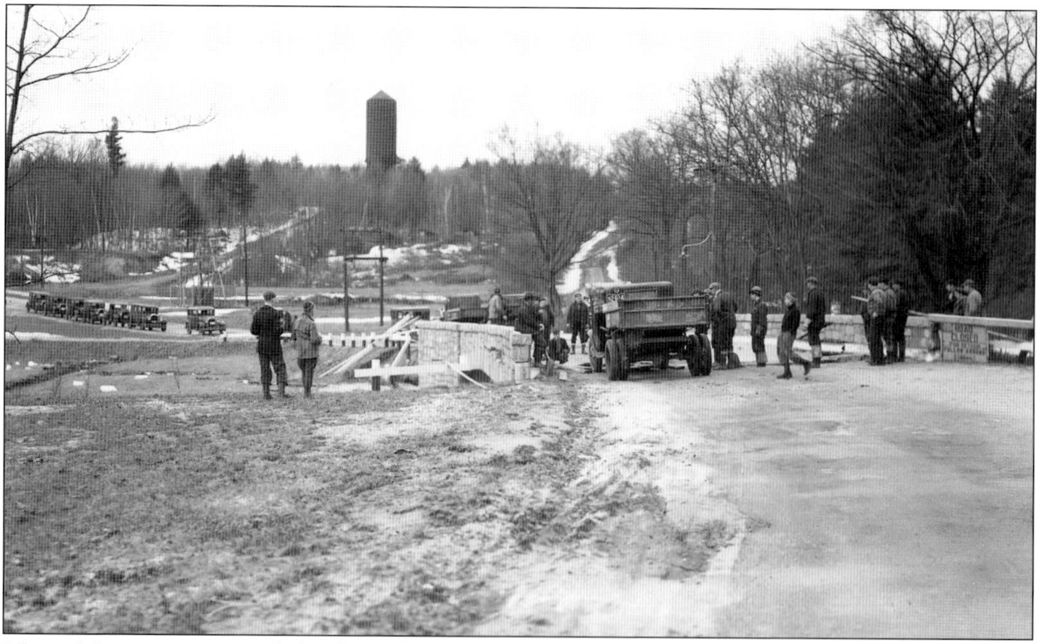

Men of the town surveyed the damage caused by the floodwaters at the bridge connecting Main Street and Sawmill Road. With repairs underway, one brave soul was picked to see if the temporary fixes would hold the weight of a car.

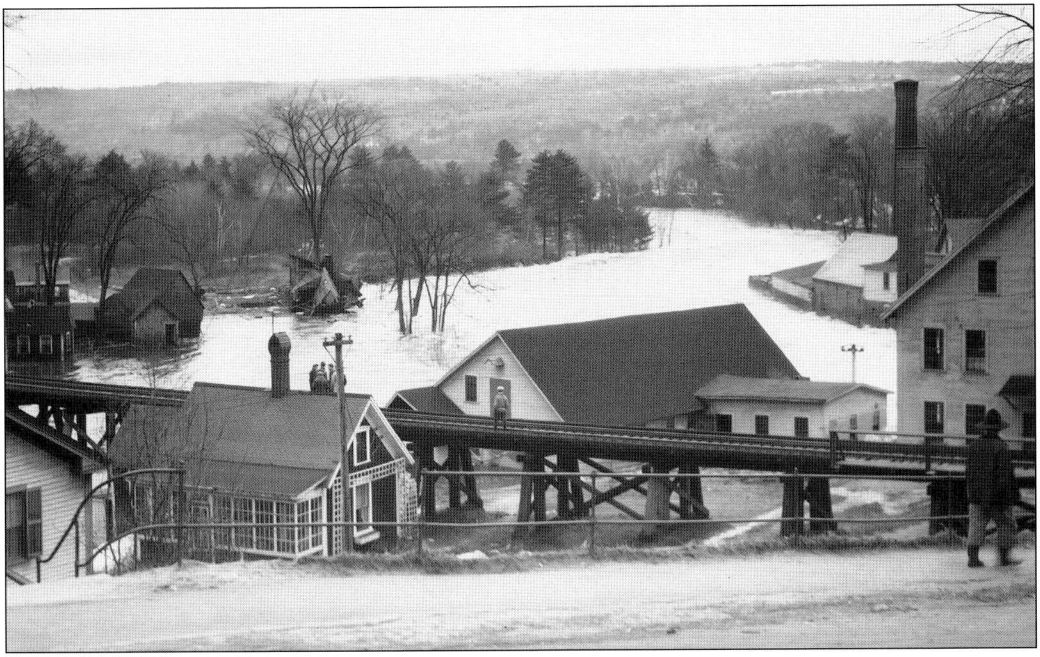

Many gathered along the railroad tracks spanning the swollen river to gain a better vantage point of the damage caused in the wake of Mother Nature's fury. The small wooden structure pictured here was no match for the unrelenting power of the floodwaters. The house next to the trestle was restored by Phil Harvey.

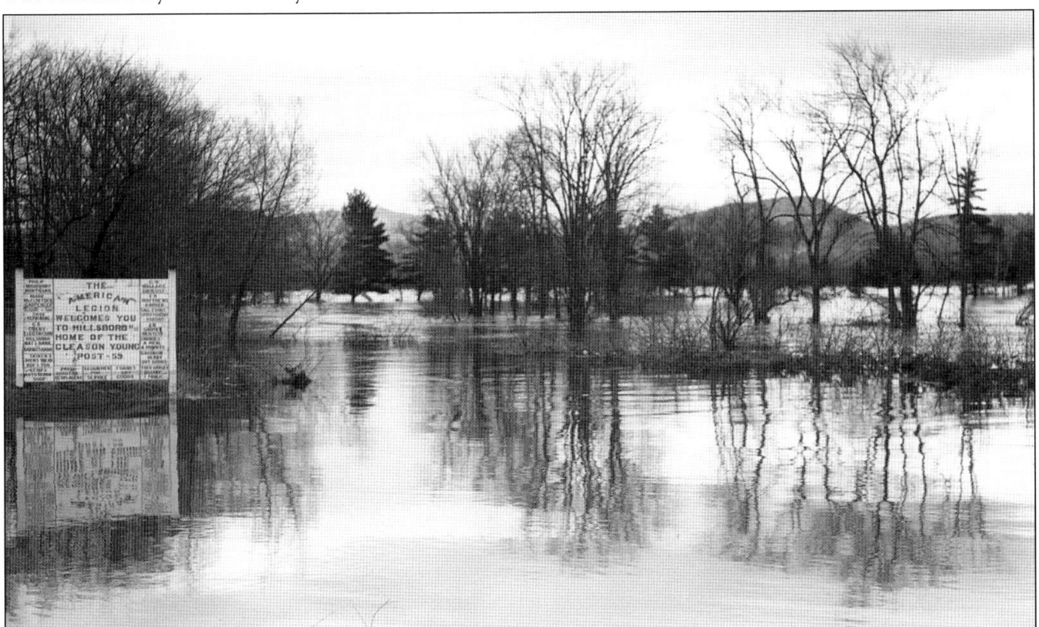

Even though this scene was not much of a warm welcome to the town unless one owned a boat, the waters eventually receded. Public Service of New Hampshire was able to keep the town supplied with light and power, the Contoocook Valley Telephone Company was able to keep communication lines open, and paper and bread trucks were able to make deliveries by the next day.

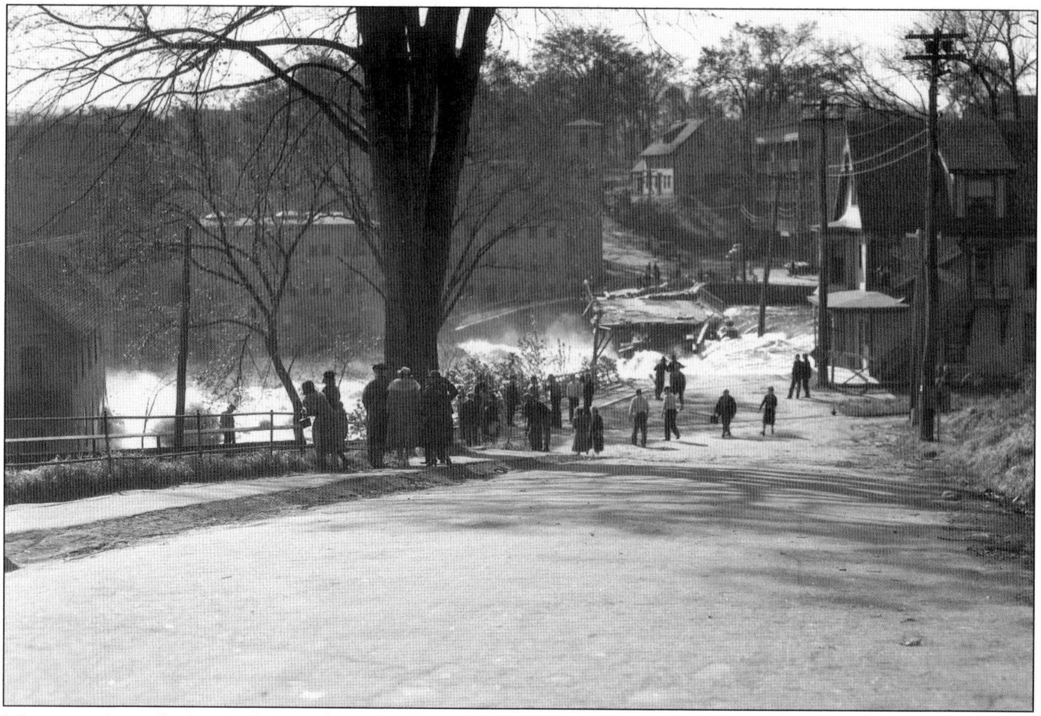

Many gathered along the roadway to watch the partial destruction of the Bridge Street Bridge after the worst hurricane to ever hit the area. The north approach to the bridge washed out, although the main arch was undamaged. The picture above was taken from the top of the hill looking down Bridge Street. It was quite a sight to see heavy stones and lumber tossed aside and torn apart like they weighed nothing. Below, William Manahan ventured dangerously close to the bridge's edge to get an up-close and personal view of the wrath of the Contoocook River.

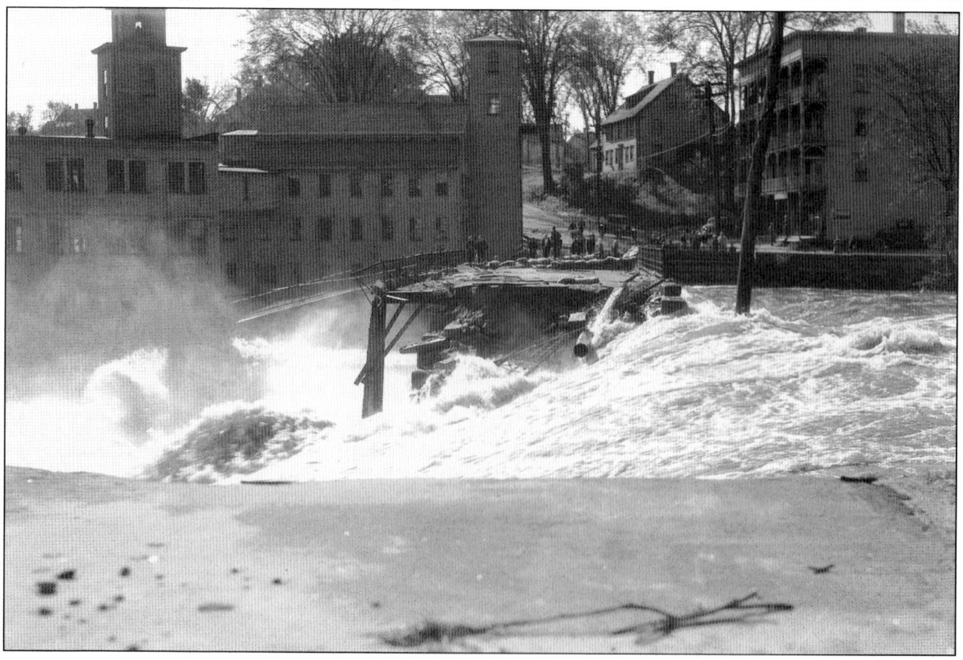

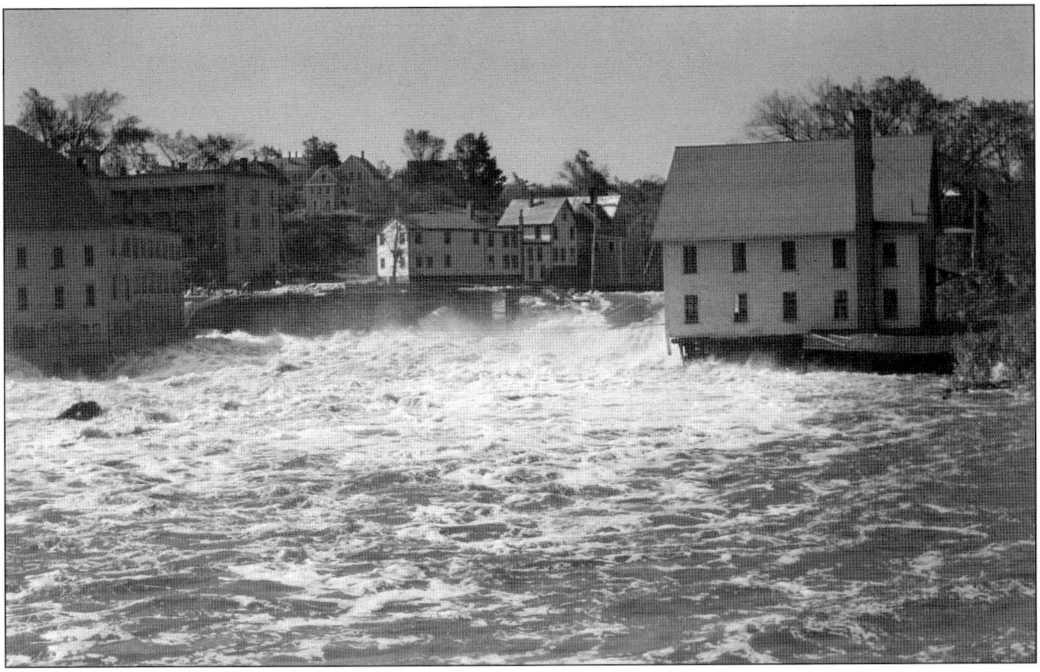

The beating the north headrace of the dam is taking is very evident in this picture. It appears that the box shop may be in eminent danger as well. Nearby, a house occupied by Dana Brown was washed down the river about 100 yards and some outbuildings of John Kemp were destroyed.

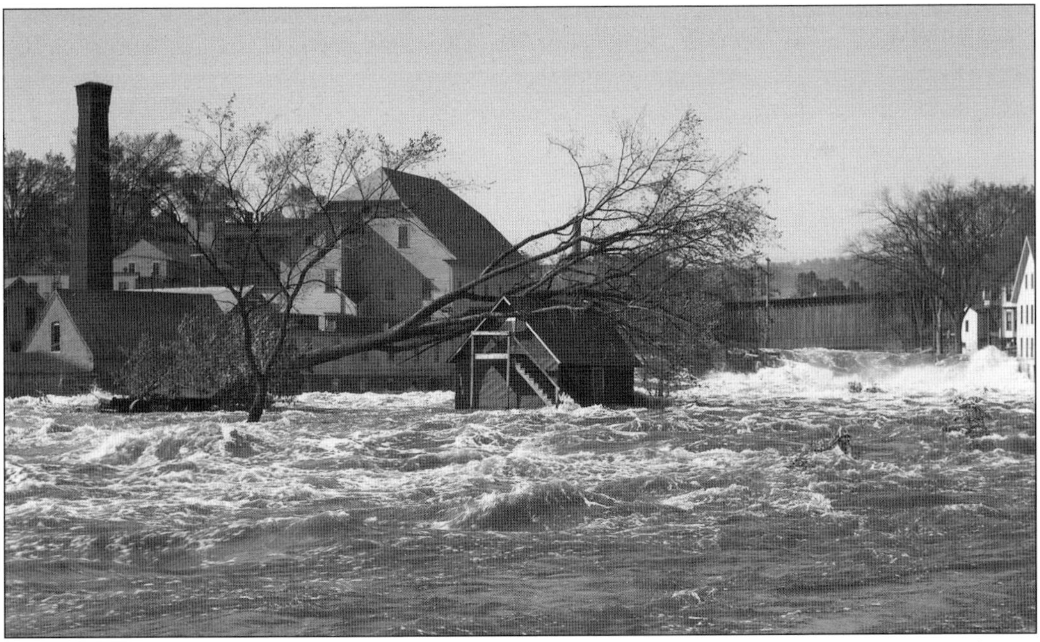

It is impressive that even under the weight of a large fallen tree and bearing the continuous brunt of the waters, this small building is still standing. The building is actually a cider mill that was eventually washed downstream and later rescued. The Kemp family kept the cider mill operational for many decades after both the flood and hurricane. From this vantage point looking upstream, one can see the water rushing through the bridge and the dam in the background.

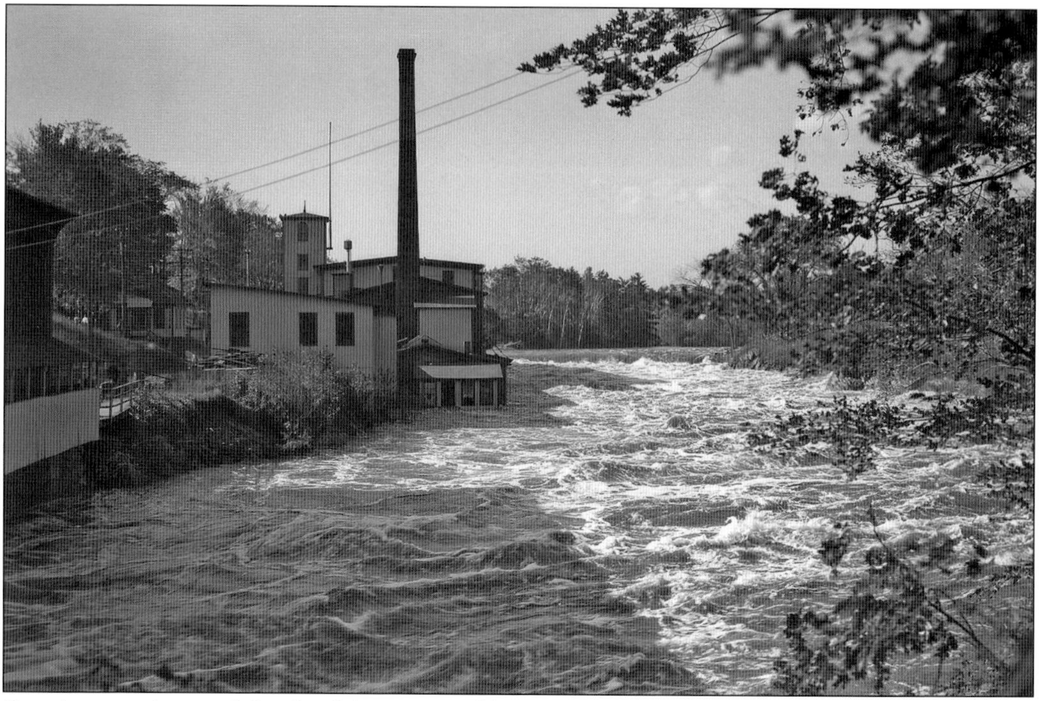

Standing on the north bank of the river and looking west, one can see that the Woolen Mill is taking another pounding from the Contoocook River, just two years after receiving extensive damage from the most recent flood. The high water mark of the 1938 hurricane was higher than the previous 1936 flood as rain, wind, and flood all converged on the mill.

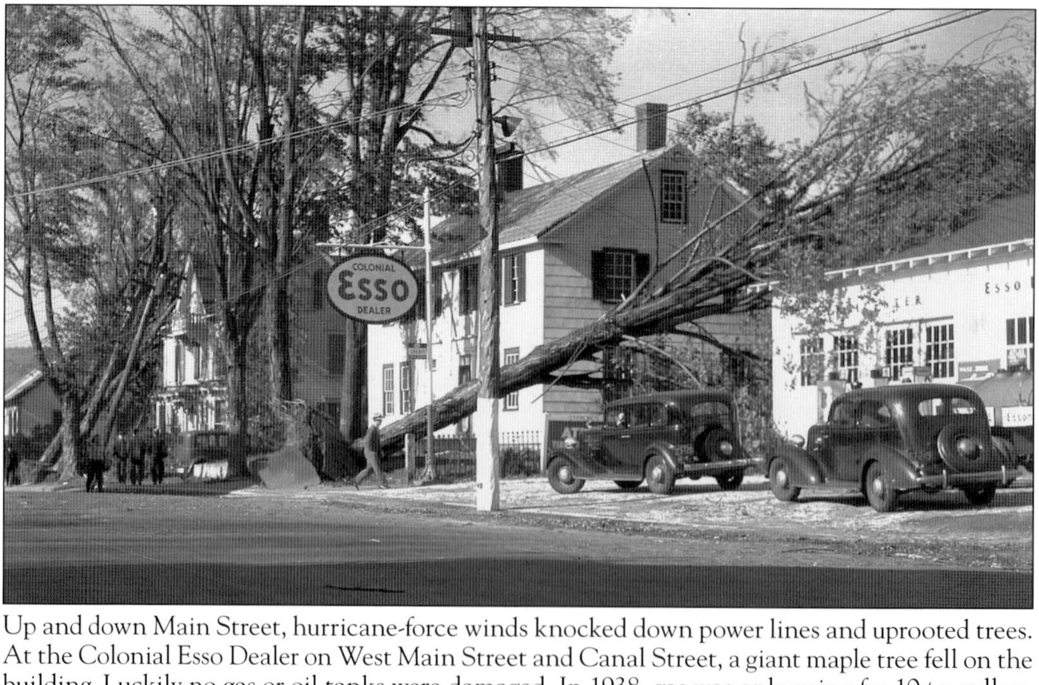

Up and down Main Street, hurricane-force winds knocked down power lines and uprooted trees. At the Colonial Esso Dealer on West Main Street and Canal Street, a giant maple tree fell on the building. Luckily no gas or oil tanks were damaged. In 1938, gas was only going for 10¢ a gallon. Walter Sterling was the owner of the gas station and also served as the town judge.

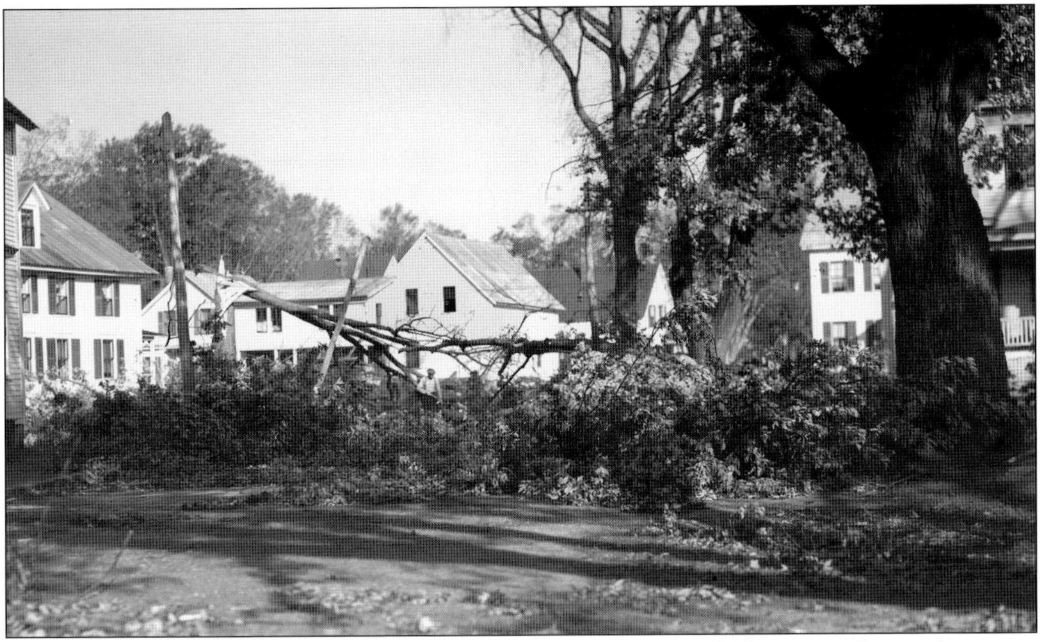

At the corner of Central and Myrtle Streets, a large tree snapped like a twig due to the strong winds. One strong-willed man, filled with the spirit of Hillsborough, has undertaken the task of clearing this tree from the road. The force of wind uprooted hundreds of shade, pine, and fruit trees, effectively closing all roads.

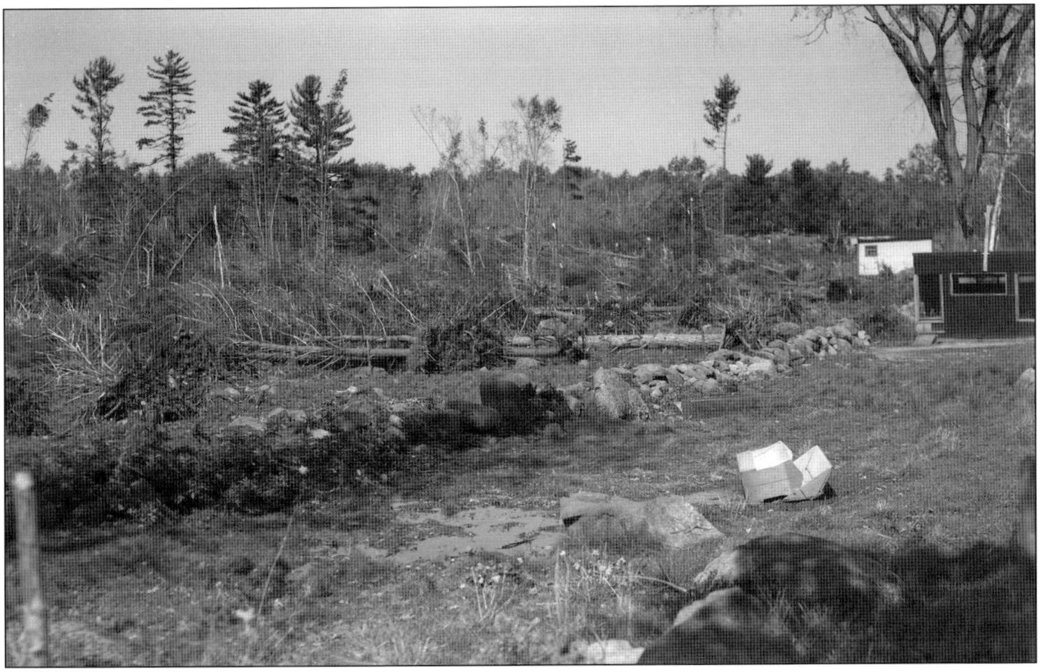

The path of destruction from the Long Island Hurricane is very clear to see. On this property, trees as far as the eyes can see were knocked over like bowling pins. Looking on the bright side, with such extensive tree damage in Hillsborough, there would at least be plenty of firewood stocked for the long winter ahead.

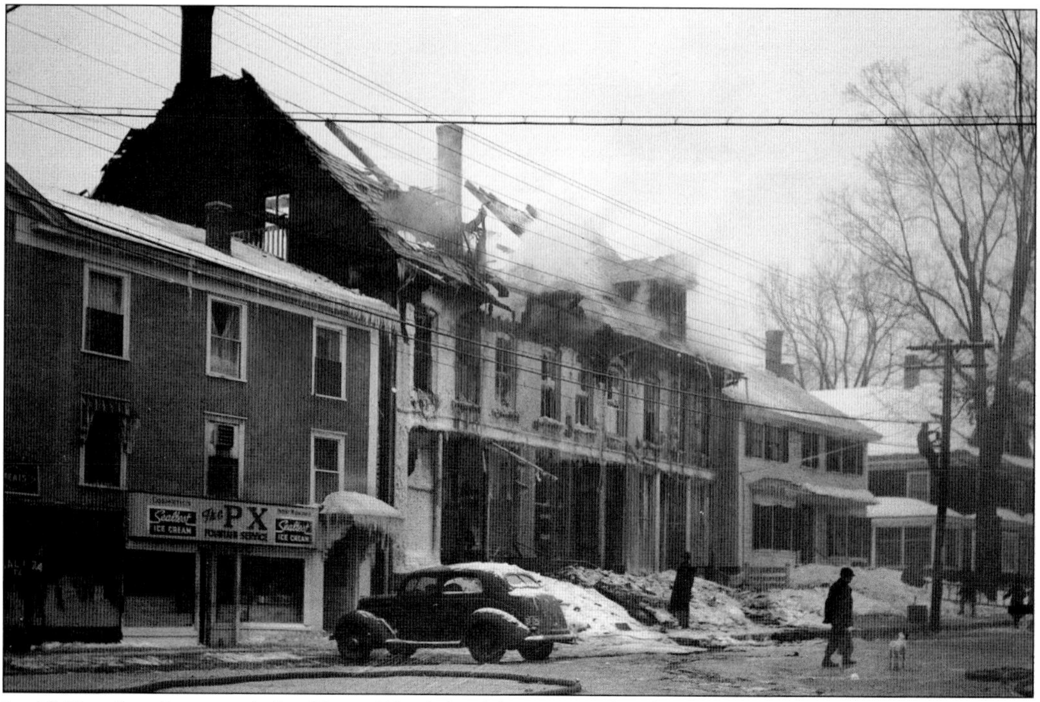

In 1947, a fire destroyed the Howe Block building on School Street. The block at one time was the home of Hillsboro Dairy and the first location of the town library. This structure was later rebuilt as the Hatfield Law office.

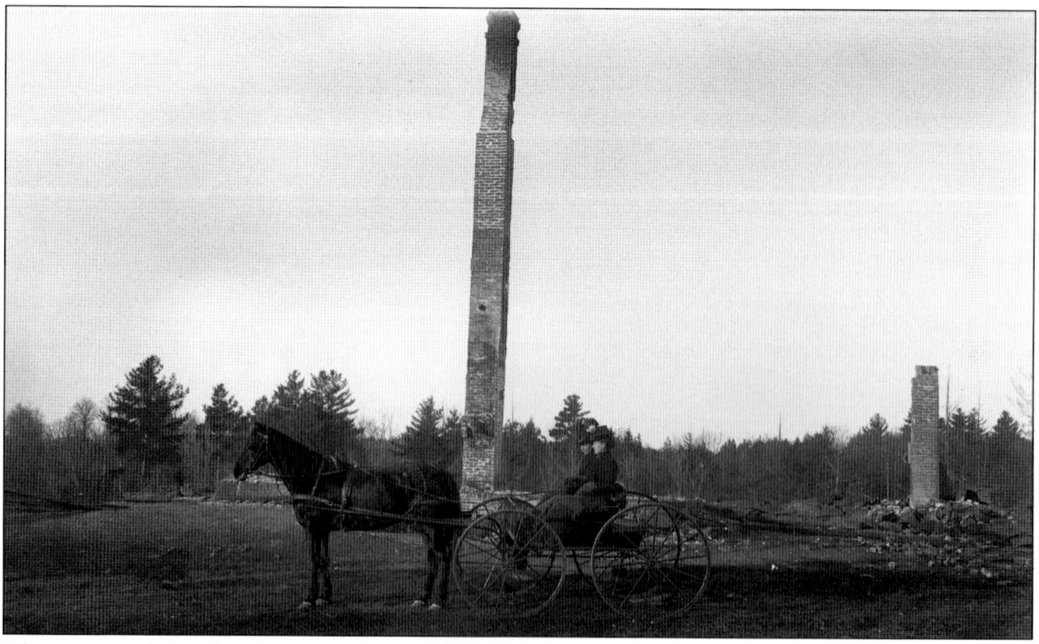

The owner of this farmhouse in Lower Village was not very fortunate after a fire engulfed his entire home. All that remains standing is the brick chimney. It appears efforts will soon begin to clear the remains of the fire and start rebuilding. Fires were quite common in Hillsborough, given the inadequacies of heating and lighting systems.

Nine

Manahan Sampler

On April 1, 1862, Col. William H. Manahan and his wife, Fannie, moved to town just one day after their marriage in Manchester. The Manahan family became one of the most well-respected and prominent families in Hillsborough. Colonel Manahan and Fannie had three children: Josephine, Frances, and William Jr. While the two daughters married and moved away, young William remained in Hillsborough and began his life's work as a photographer.

William H. Manahan Jr. was born on December 28, 1877. As a boy, he was educated at the local schools in Hillsborough and at Colby Academy in New London. As a student, he excelled as a speaker and debater, and even won the Demarest silver medal for elocution. He received his training at and graduated from the Illinois College of Photography.

In 1899, Manahan bought a local photography studio from Charles Brockway in Bridge Village. To Manahan, photography was an art form. Through his work, he documented everyday living in Hillsborough. Throughout his lifetime, he received many awards and accolades for his work. He was elected vice president of the Photographers Association of New England in 1904, and later served as president of the organization for several years. For his portrait and landscape work, Manahan received several prizes from the Photographers Association of New England and the National Photographers Association of America. In 1915, he had one of his pictures hung in the New England section of the National Salon. They also hang at the Currier Museum of Art in Manchester.

Manahan ran his photography studio for 54 years until his retirement in 1953, when it was taken over by Cyrus Phelps. In 2002, the photography studio business was sold, and over 100,000 glass plates and film negatives were donated to the Hillsborough Historical Society by Donald and Catherine (Phelps) McCulloch, the last owners. This material has become known as the Manahan-Phelps-McCulloch Collection, and a very small sampling was used in the creation of this book. In the pages to follow in this chapter, you will find what we deem "the best of Manahan."

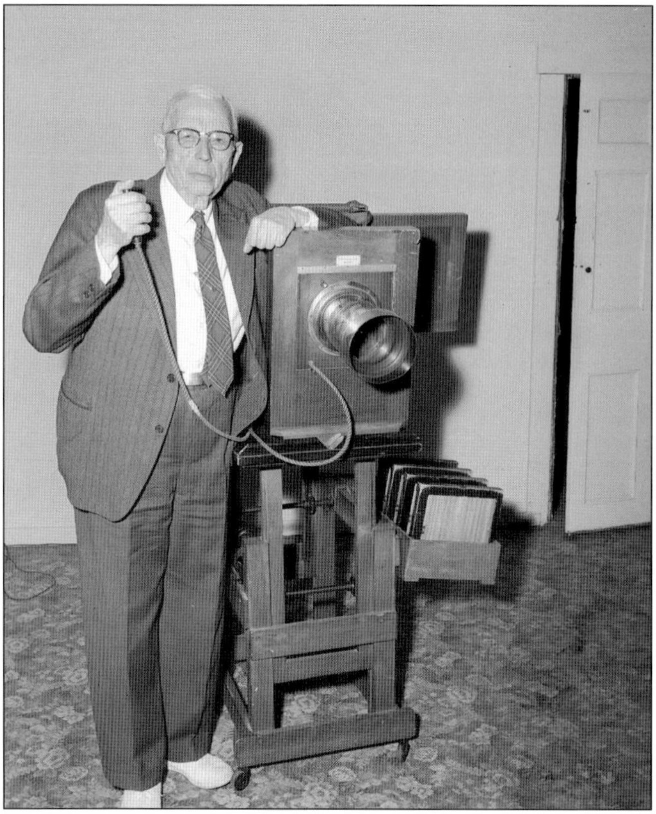

This photograph, taken in 1959 by his former assistant, Cyrus Phelps, shows William H. Manahan Jr. at the age of 81, posing with his old Anthony studio camera. This camera, along with several pieces of Manahan's photography equipment, is being preserved at the old firehouse, the current home of the Heritage Museum.

Manahan's first studio, pictured here, was located in the Lower Village on Sawmill Road in a small structure next to his home. It was in this building that he practiced his photographic techniques and mastered his trade. Sawmill Road was such a busy complex in the 1800s that it was once named Main Street.

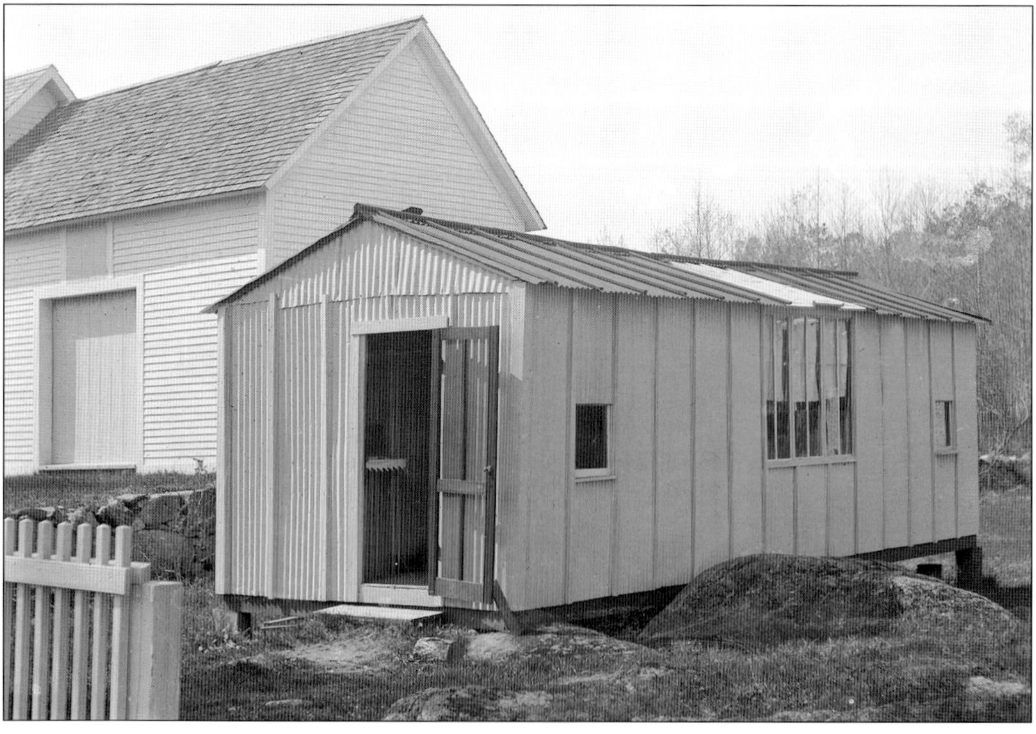

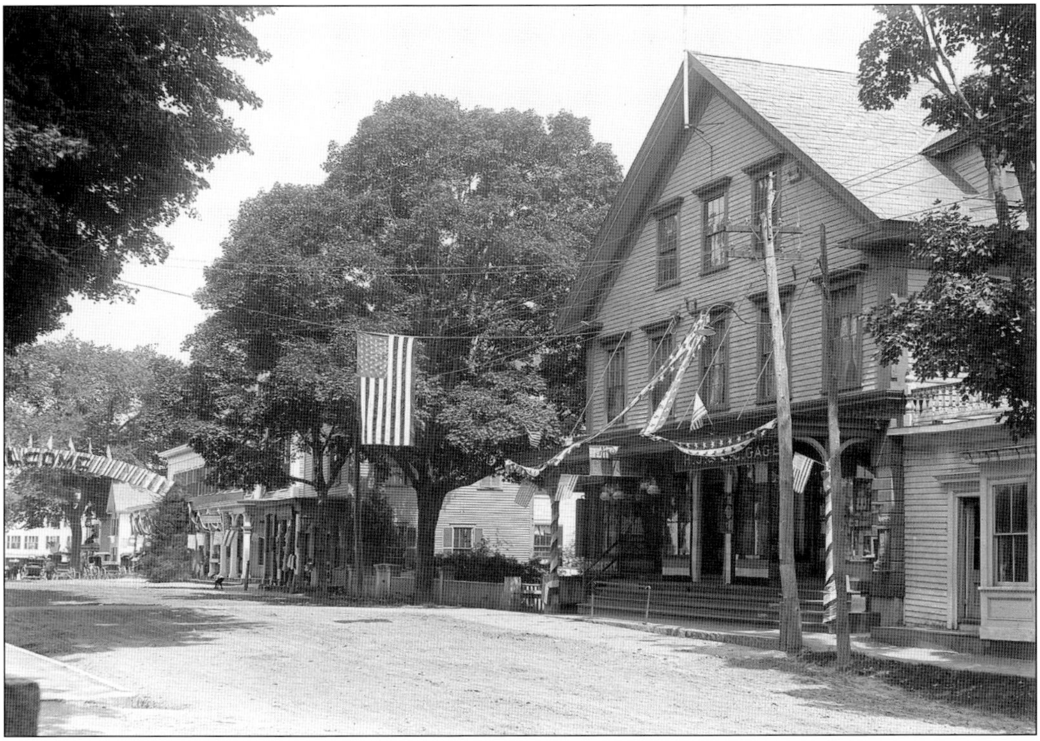

In 1899, Manahan purchased the photographic studio owned by Charles Brockway. This studio was located in the Newman-Colby Block of Hillsborough Bridge at 42 West Main Street. Manahan married Brockway's niece, Ethel, in 1902 and she eventually assisted him in the studio.

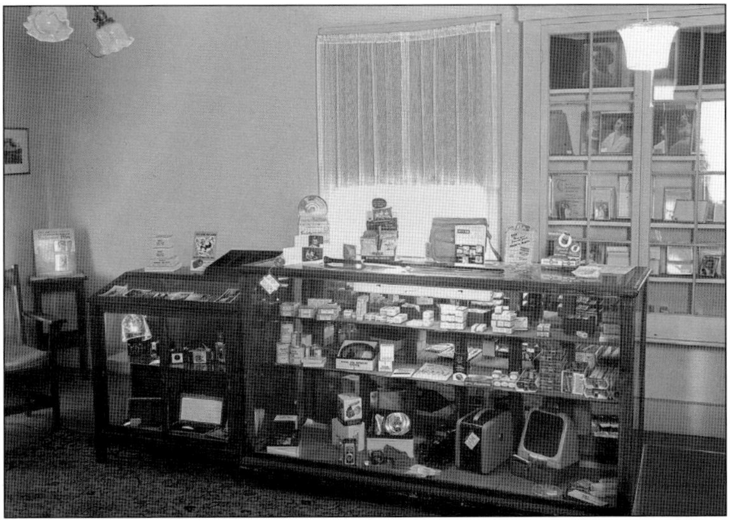

The reception room was the liveliest part of the Manahan studio, and was where his patrons waited for their portraits to be taken. The room served not only as a seating and social area for his customers, but also as an exhibit space where he proudly displayed his work. Possibly, like his friend and fellow photographer in Boston, John Garo, he may have served "bathtub gin" to his waiting clientele.

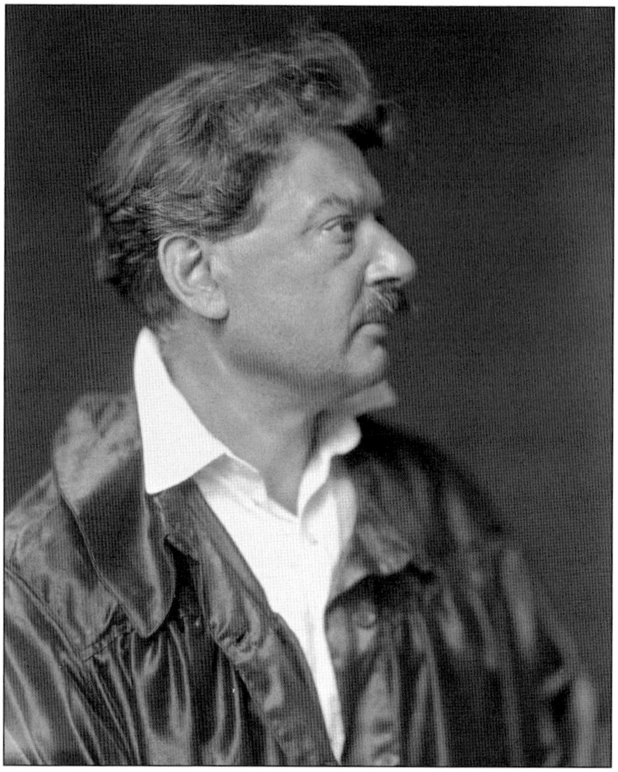

Manahan created this portrait of John H. Garo on September 7, 1925. Garo was a prominent Boston society photographer. Throughout his career, he photographed powerful and influential people, including heads of state and artists. He made a photography career glamorous. To master his trade, Garo studied artwork at museums and learned painting and printing techniques. His technique of using the concept of "Rembrandt lighting" from the world of painting in his portrait photography became known as the "Garo Way."

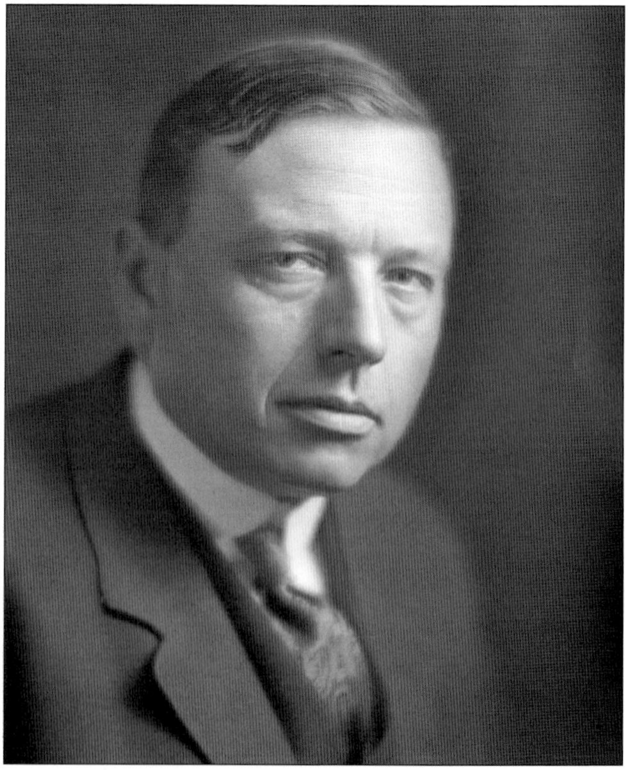

Garo was a friend and professional associate of Manahan. He was a mentor to many budding photographers including Yousuf Karsh, who apprenticed under him in Boston. Karsh is famous for his iconic portraits of Albert Einstein, Winston Churchill, Pablo Picasso, and nearly all of the US presidents of his lifetime. There is no doubt that Garo also shared his techniques with Manahan. Garo took this portrait of Manahan in his younger years in 1919.

Throughout his career, Manahan took thousands of pictures of different animals and wild game. It was not uncommon to find baby chicks, cats, or rabbits roaming around his studio. This chick found its way into a wine goblet. This image was utilized in a postcard with the title "Plymouth Rock Cocktail."

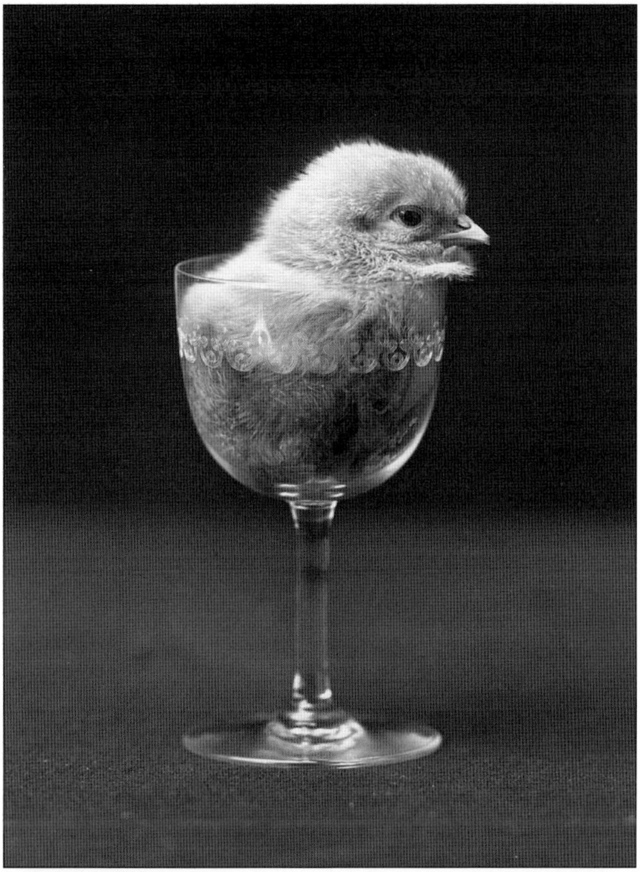

Who knew that animals could read? Just as we encourage our children to start reading at a young age, it seems that kittens do the same. One has to wonder what book has these kittens so intrigued—maybe the classic, *Of Mice and Men*.

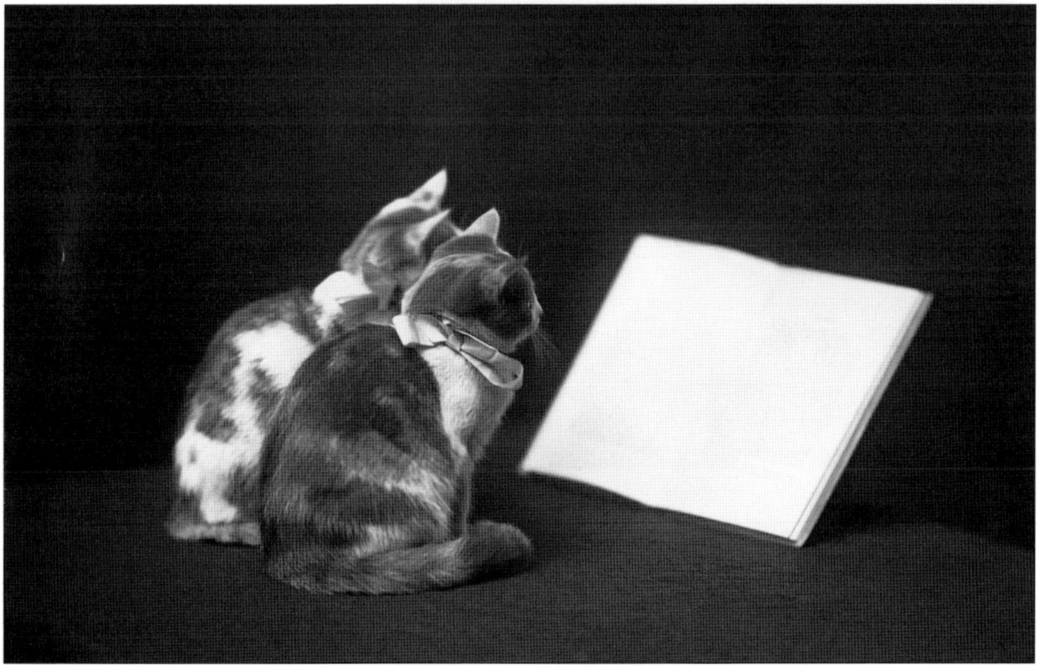

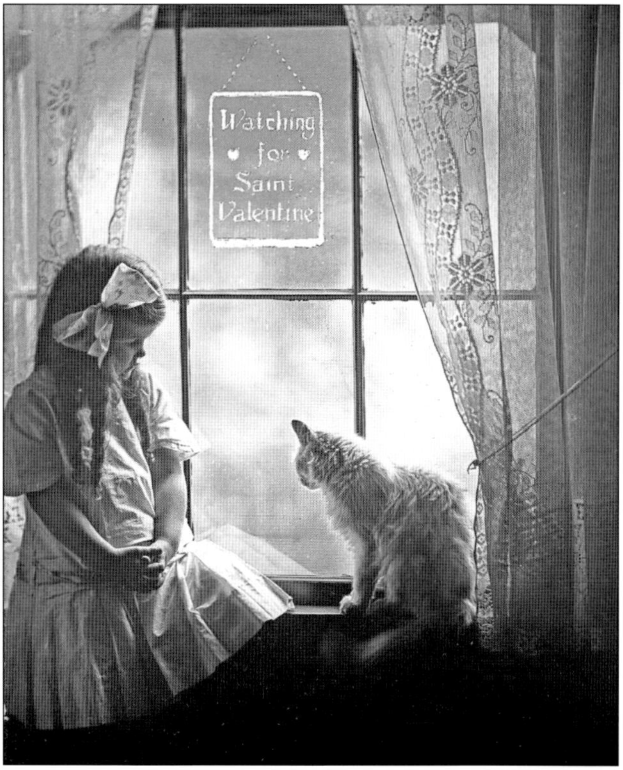

It seems that it has always been difficult to get a child to sit properly for a picture. The little girl pictured here, Marjorie Sholes, tried her best to sit for a portrait, but was too tempted by her desire to play with one of Manahan's studio cats. Even though it was not the intended shot, the true innocence of this picture probably made it the best of the session.

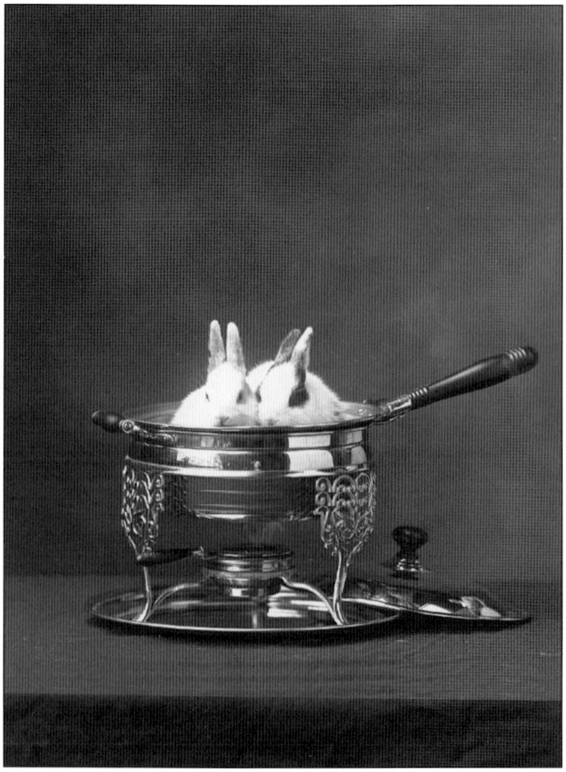

Fortunately for these rabbits, they were not on the dinner menu for the day. One has to wonder how Manahan was able to get all the animals he photographed to sit still. A true sportsman, Manahan not only photographed animals but authored several articles in *Field & Stream*, including "A Morning Sport in New Hampshire" and "A Convenient Swamp."

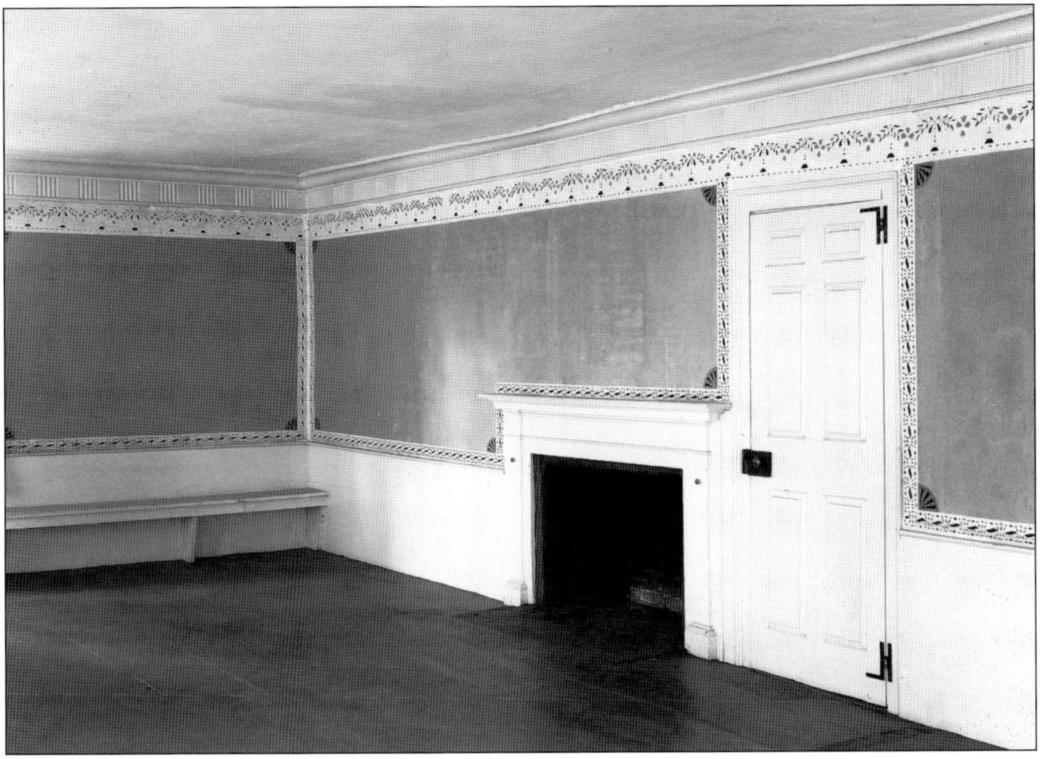

The book *Early American Stencils on Walls and Furniture*, by Janet Waring, was published in 1937. Many of Manahan's photographs of wall stencil work in homes in Hillsborough and surrounding towns were used in this book. The walls of the ballroom in the Pierce Homestead, pictured here, are a deep rose color with borders that consist of black stencil work with touches of red on a white background. It is said that Benjamin Pierce chose the stencil patterns himself.

Brothers Lemuel and Isaac Cooledge built two brick homes on Cooledge Road in Hillsborough in 1808. In the home of Isaac, to the left of the main entrance is a large parlor room with stencil work that appears to be from the kit of Moses Eaton. The walls are a rose color with a stencil pattern that contains green leaves and dark red flowers.

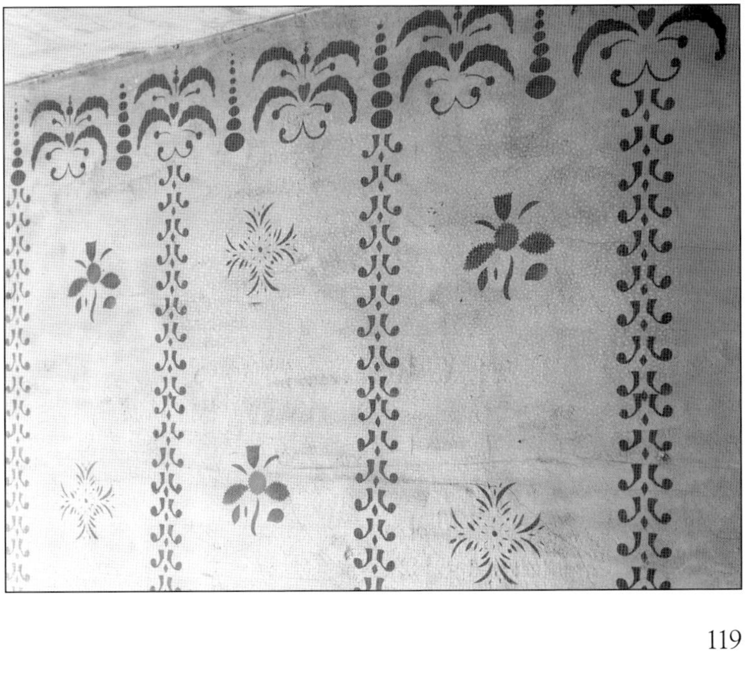

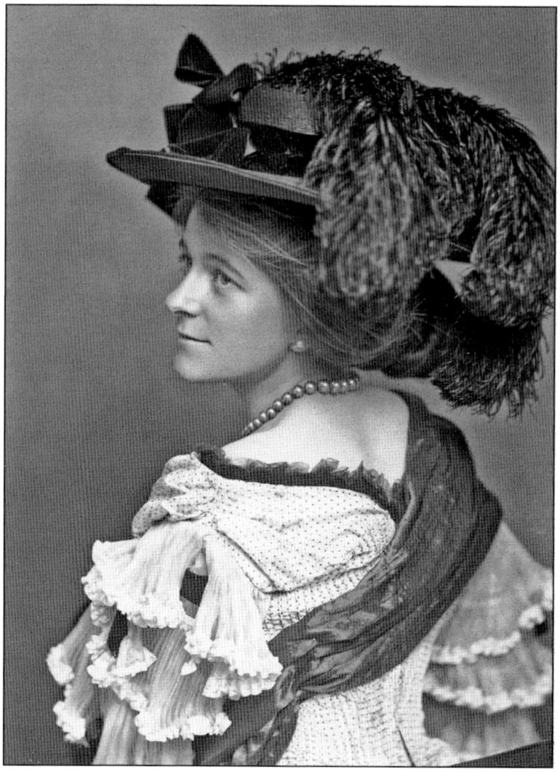

This portrait of Mary Pierce, the grandniece of Pres. Franklin Pierce, was taken in her early 20s. Her father, Kirk D. Pierce, was a lawyer who opened an office in the same building his uncle Franklin Pierce had worked in. Following the death of her mother in 1910, Mary, along with her father and sister, moved into the former home of her great-uncle Franklin Pierce.

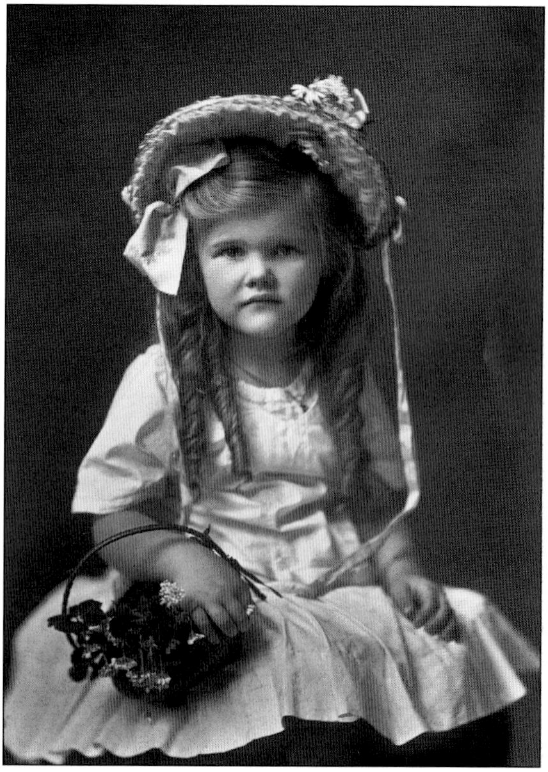

It appears the young Marjorie Sholes finally sat for her portrait during the spring of 1905, with her ornate straw hat and basket full of fresh flowers from one of the many meadows in Hillsborough. She went on to teach second grade in Franklin, New Hampshire, and lived to see her 92nd birthday.

The Hall family established its roots in Hillsborough when Enoch Hall bought the McColley farm in 1826. The farm was located in the "Sulphur Hill" section of town. Legend has it that the name came from the smell generated by the large quantity of sulfur one of the residents bought to cure "the itch." This portrait is of Agnes Hall, one of the young maidens in Hillsborough during the early 1900s.

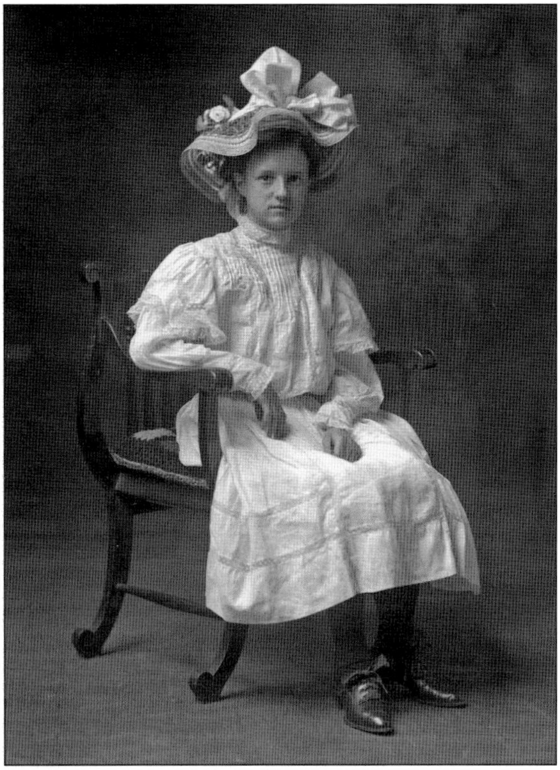

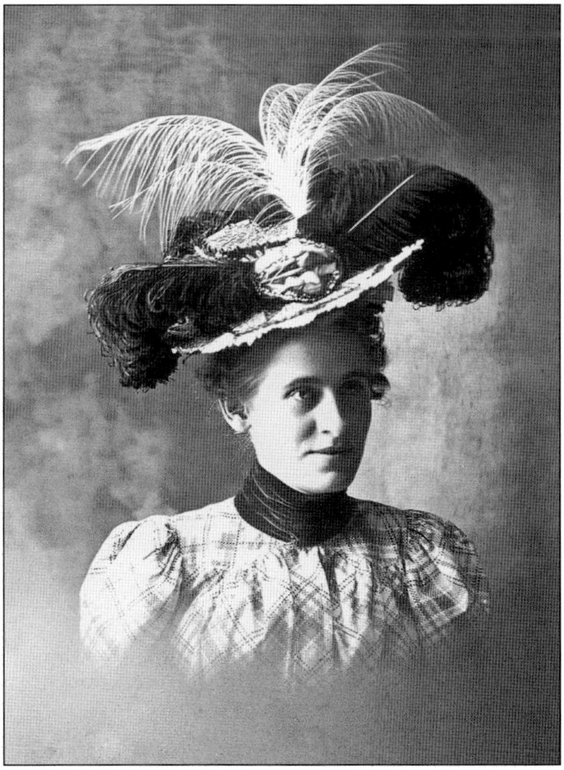

Pictured here is Grace Griffin showing off her extravagant Victorian-style feathered hat. Around 1818 was when the first descendants of the Griffin family appeared in Hillsborough. Eben Griffin, originally from Gloucester, Massachusetts, moved here with his wife, Susan, and settled on a farm in the northeast section of town.

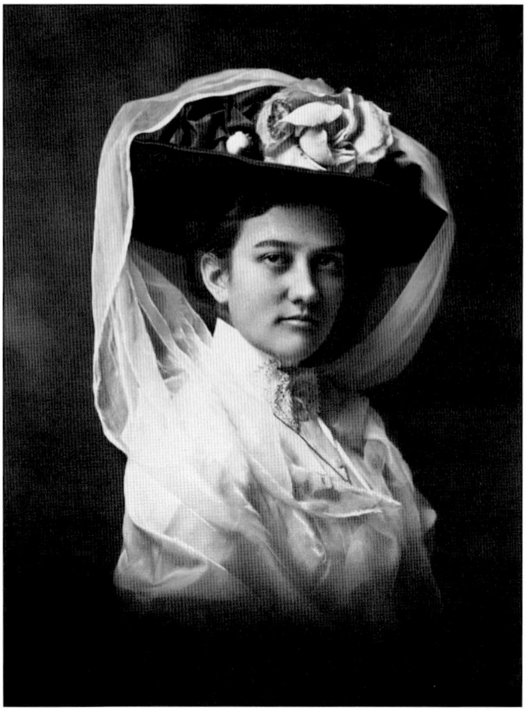

This c. 1905 photograph of Pauline Brockway was taken when she was in her teenage years. She lived on a farm in the western part of town with her parents, Fred and Alice, until she married Andrew J. Sargent in 1914. Together, Pauline and Andrew had four children: Elizabeth, Katherine, Virginia, and Polly. Pauline was the sister-in-law of the photographer of her portrait, William H. Manahan Jr.

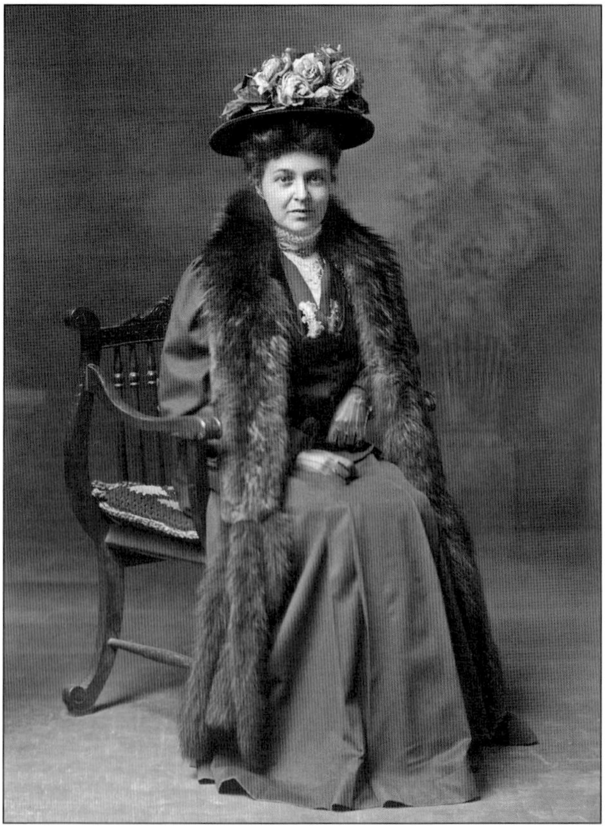

Mrs. Charles F. (Irene) Butler posed for this portrait in 1905, wearing some of her finest clothes: an ornate flower hat, long fur shawl, and ladies' dress gloves. Charles Butler did much public good for the town of Hillsborough. Once the president of the board of trade and town clerk, he was instrumental in organizing "Merchant Week" and town "Clean-up Week," as well as creating publicity for the town. He also owned a news store on the corner of School Street in the Child's Opera Block.

Spring is in the air and the tree blossoms are in full bloom—another beautiful day in the Hillsborough countryside. Most of these landscape pictures were made into postcards and sold to tourists. Enlarged versions were sometimes colored with fine pencil work in the Wallace Nutting hand-finished print tradition.

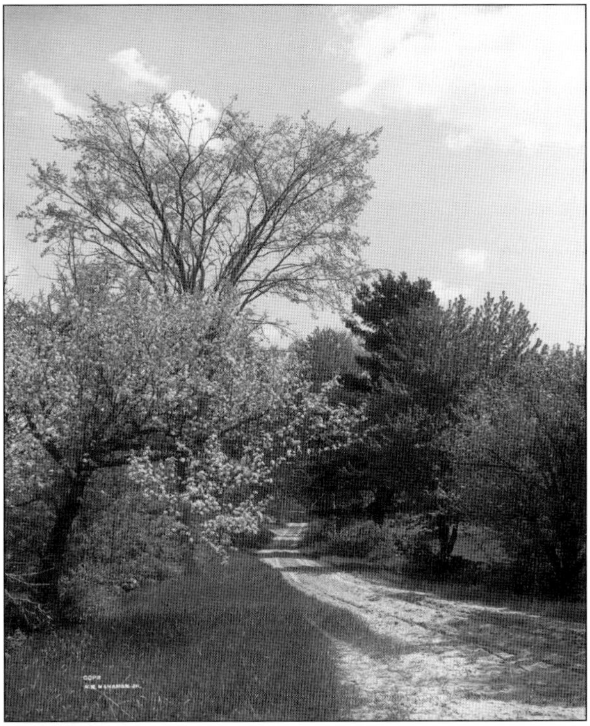

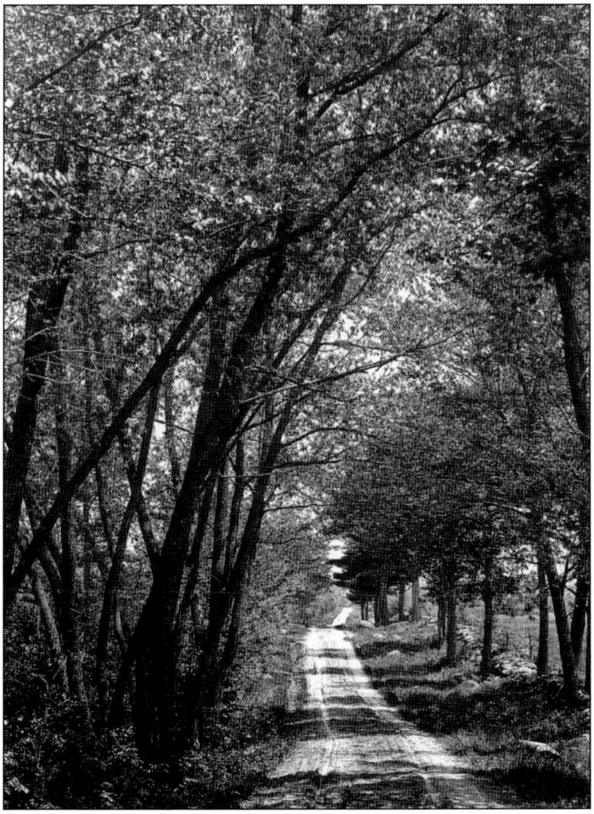

Appropriately named "Where the Willows Grow," this c. 1912 photograph was made into a postcard. Like most dirt roads in town, a canopy of foliage overhangs it, along with stone walls running along the edge. The rural image of Hillsborough, combined with convenient passenger rail service, made it attractive to tourists and summer residents.

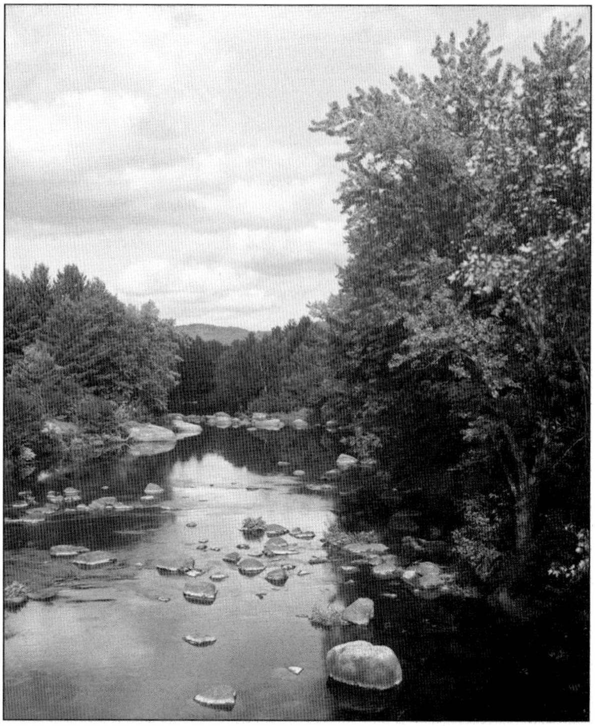

Shown is one of the many streams flowing through the town where one could take a swim to cool off from the summer heat, go fishing, or skip rocks along the banks. With the water level low, boys could attempt the challenge of crossing the stream by jumping on the exposed rocks.

New England winters could be harsh and long. Here, Manahan was able to capture one of the first snowfalls of winter along Beard Brook. Beard Brook is a major stream in the area and empties into the Contoocook River. Franklin Pierce found the brook great for trout fishing and often reminisced about his boyhood experiences there.

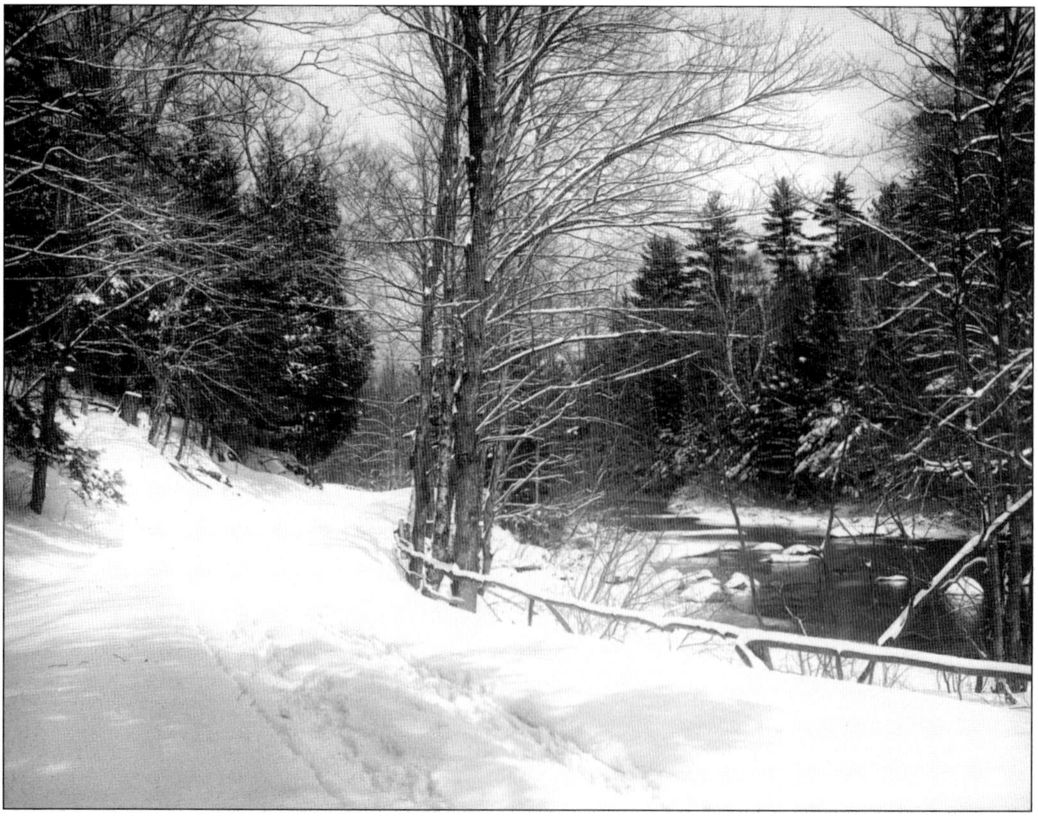

A slow-moving brook winding its way through one of the many open fields in town represents the best in rural life. It may have been a watering spot for the animals put out to pasture. Manahan took several landscape pictures of Hillsborough in 1912 and 1913, which were used to attract tourists to the area.

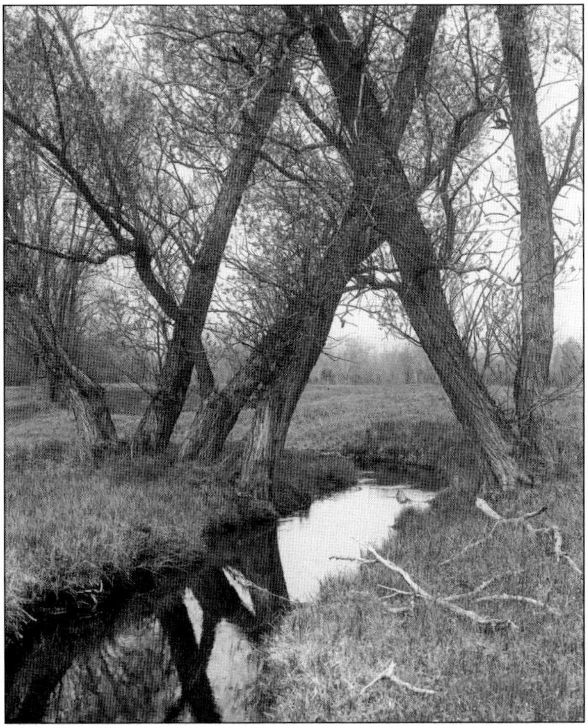

This long dirt road leads to an old farmhouse nestled at the foot of a hill. This farmhouse was one of the many rented out during the summer months to tourists seeking a break from the hustle and bustle of the big city, Boston. The major road to the right leads to Stowe Mountain, and the one on the left is a "road less travelled."

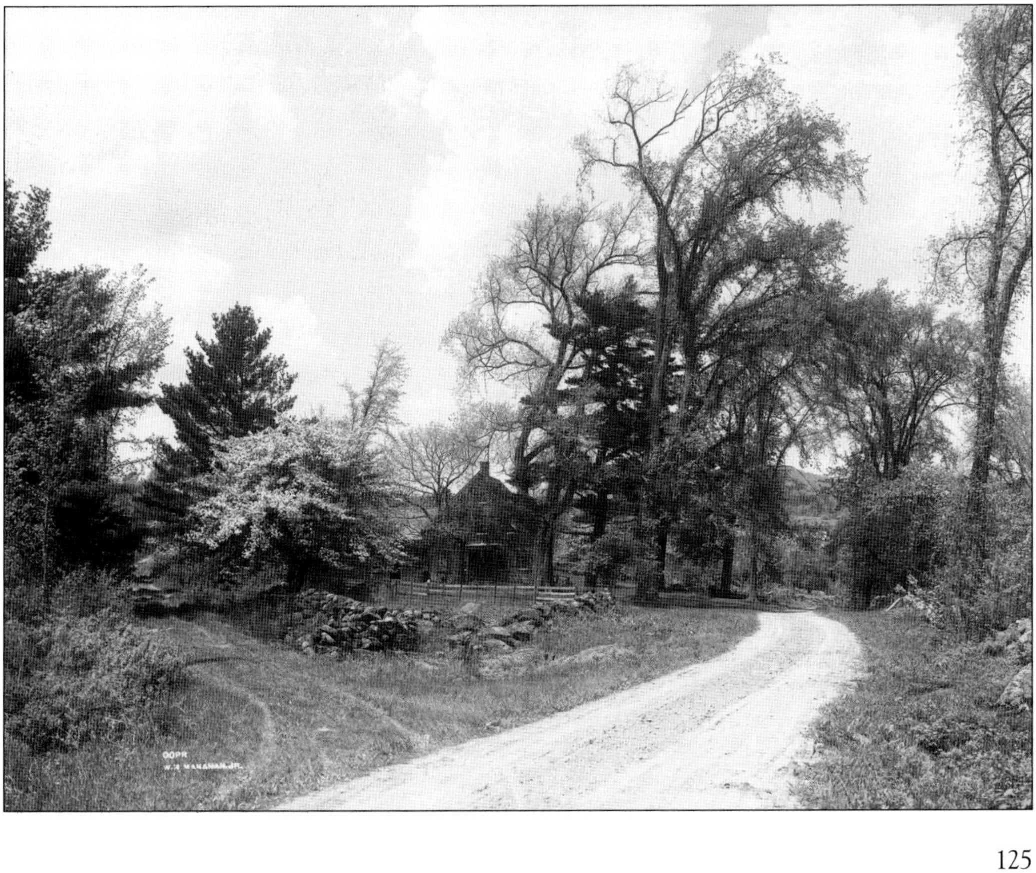

About the Manahan Collection

The Manahan Collection represents a series of photographic art from 1866 until 2002. The collection exceeds over 100,000 images of Hillsborough and the Contoocook Valley Area, including portraits, landscapes, historic sites, and depictions of everyday life. Below is listed the known photographers and a representative ad circa 1900.

1868-1871	Solon Newman
1872-1875	Charles McClary
1875-1877	Frank D. Darrah
1878-1884	George W. Lincoln
1885	J. D. Hunting
1887-1892	Charles Brockway
1899-1953	William H. Manahan Jr.
1953-1971	Cyrus Phelps
1971-2002	Donald McCulloch

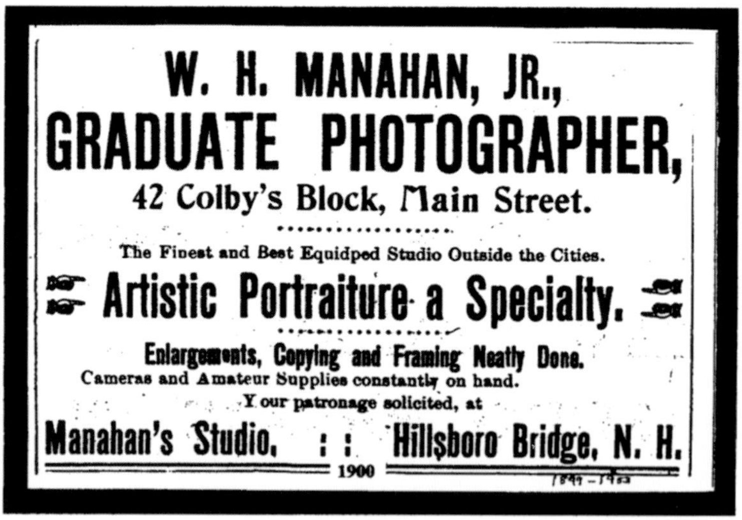

The Manahan collection uses several different technologies, including early ambrotype glass plates, dry plates, early flexible film, and 35-millimeter film. The collection has a significant inventory of railroads—both trains and stations—and covered and stone bridges, as well as New Hampshire churches and public buildings. In the tradition of William Manahan Jr. and his predecessors, each image is available for purchase as a print, postcard, or poster.

Bibliography

Baldwin, Harrison. *History of Hillsborough New Hampshire 1921–1963*. Peterborough, NH: Transcript Printing Company, 1963.

Brown, Waldo. *History of Hillsborough N.H. 1735–1921*. Manchester NH: John P. Clark Company, 1921.

Hillsboro NH, The Switzerland of New Hampshire. Hillsboro, NH: Messenger Publishing Company, 1910.

Official Program, Hillsboro Bicentennial. Hillsborough, NH: The Messenger, 1972.

The Valley of the Contoocook, Hillsborough NH. Hillsboro Messenger Press, 1911.

Van Hazinga, Cynthia. *History of Hillsborough, New Hampshire 1960–2000*. Portsmouth, NH: Peter E. Randall Publisher, 2001.